Bristol Dragway

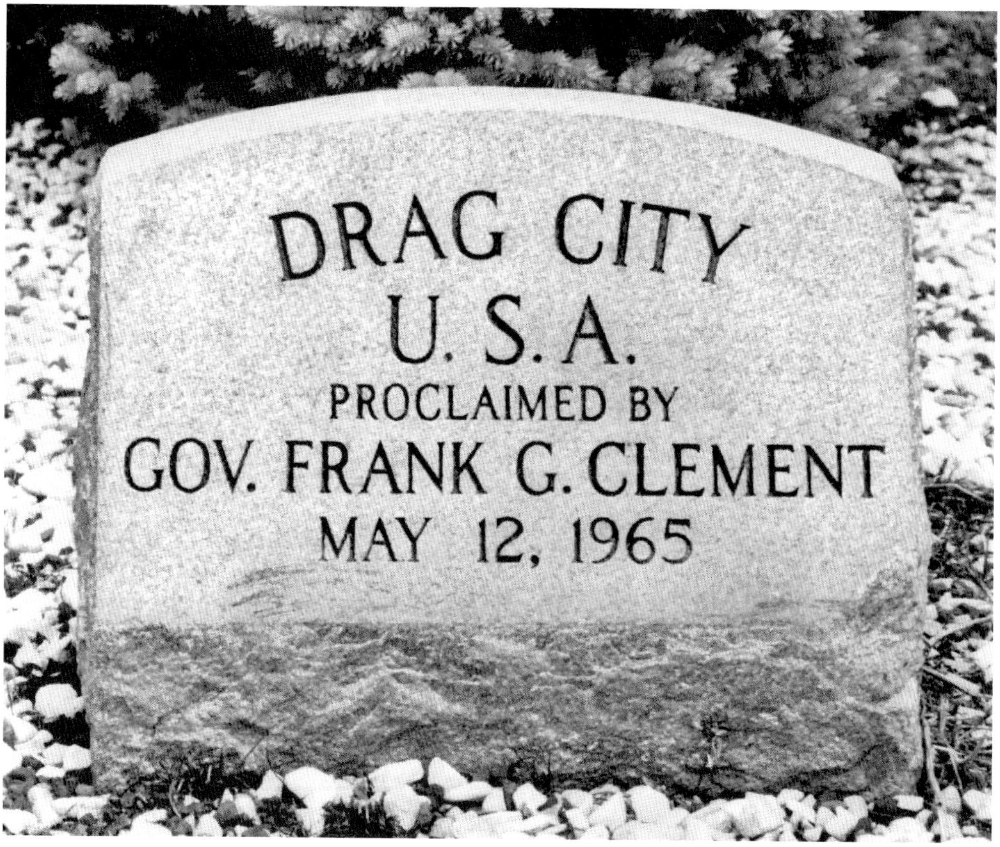

Former Tennessee governor Frank Clement proclaimed Bristol Dragway as "Drag City USA" in May 1965. The honorary title refers to the name of a nationally popular 1963 song by rock-and-roll duo Jan and Dean. The proclamation came a few weeks before the new facility opened for its first event, the National Hot Rod Association (NHRA) Spring Nationals. Track founders Larry Carrier and Carl Moore commissioned this marble stone to celebrate the occasion. After more than 40 years, the marker remains an important link to the track's storied past. (Photograph by David McGee.)

Front Cover: John Force had little success during his early trips to Bristol Dragway in the 1980s. In the past decade, Force won the 1999 Winston Showdown and the 2004 Thunder Valley Nationals. (Photograph by David McGee.)

Cover Background: The background image features the Sox and Martin team that swept multiple world championships in 1971. Driver Ronnie Sox recorded Bristol wins over four decades, from the 1960s through the 1990s. (Photograph by John Beach.)

Back Cover: Shown on the back cover is the modern Bristol Dragway. (Courtesy of Bristol Motor Speedway [BMS] archives.)

BRISTOL DRAGWAY

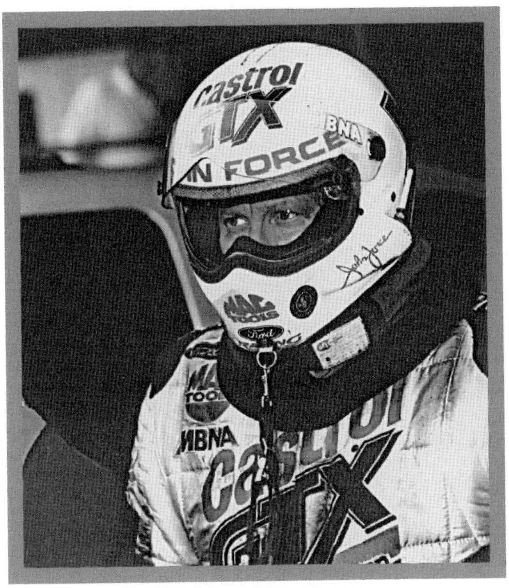

David M. McGee
with a foreword by Kenny Bernstein

ARCADIA
PUBLISHING

ISBN 978-0-7385-4444-1

Published by Arcadia Publishing
Charleston, South Carolina

Printed in the United States of America

Library of Congress Catalog Card Number: 2007920804

For all general information contact Arcadia Publishing at:
Telephone 843-853-2070
Fax 843-853-0044
E-mail sales@arcadiapublishing.com
For customer service and orders:
Toll-Free 1-888-313-2665

Visit us on the Internet at www.arcadiapublishing.com

For my mom, Phyllis McGee, for love and support of her son's fascination with racing and for John Beach, who generously loaned great images that made this project complete.

CONTENTS

Foreword by Kenny Bernstein 6

Introduction 7

1. Through the Decades 9

2. Top Fuel 31

3. Funny Cars 43

4. Pro Stock 61

5. Pro Modified and Top Sportsman 79

6. A Place to Race Everything 91

7. Monster Machines 107

All-Time Top Fuel Winners 122

All-Time Funny Car Winners 123

All-Time Pro Stock Winners 124

All-Time Pro Modified Winners 125

Acknowledgments 126

About the Author 127

FOREWORD BY KENNY BERNSTEIN

Some of the best racing fans in the country come to Bristol, and whether it's NASCAR or drag racing, they're going to get a spectacular show.

I began participating as an owner/driver in drag racing in the early 1970s and as a NASCAR team owner for about 10 years in the mid-1980s to the mid-1990s.

My memories of Bristol begin back on the drag strip, when I was campaigning on a more part-time basis. Bristol was one of the jewels that you wanted to go to. It had an aura about it. The drag strip was cut between two mountains, and when the powerful cackle of the nitro-fueled Top Fuel and Funny Cars reverberated and bounced off the mountains, it sounded like thunder because it was so loud. Hence the name "Thunder Valley."

In the early days, the stock car track was smaller than it is today. At that particular time, drag racing was as important as stock car racing was at that venue.

It would often fog in and rain at this track. I remember running the "Night of Fire" there. One night we were waiting until after midnight for track officials to get one last qualifying session in the books.

Larry Carrier, track owner at the time, came down and talked to the drivers. "We're going to run these things," said Carrier. By now it was about two in the morning and the fog was so thick you couldn't see your hand in front of you. Carrier had also told us we'd be able to see as we drove, but I don't think anyone was buying into that. But if one driver was willing to take the risk, then we were all in.

I'll never forget we lined up and ran right through the fog just as Carrier predicted. And believe it or not, I could actually see pretty well. You could just see enough of the racetrack to keep going forward. That's a memory that will always stick with me.

We did pretty well at Bristol through the years. We went to the final round five times, four in Funny Car and once in Top Fuel.

When I retired from the cockpit in 2002, Jeff Byrd, one of my best friends, who is also president and general manager of Bristol Dragway, presented me with my own chair in the starting line grandstand, now named the Kenny Bernstein Grandstand. It's nice to know I'll always have a front row seat for all the drag strip action!

Bristol is a beautiful setting. It's been a real part of racing history for a long time and part of our history, too.

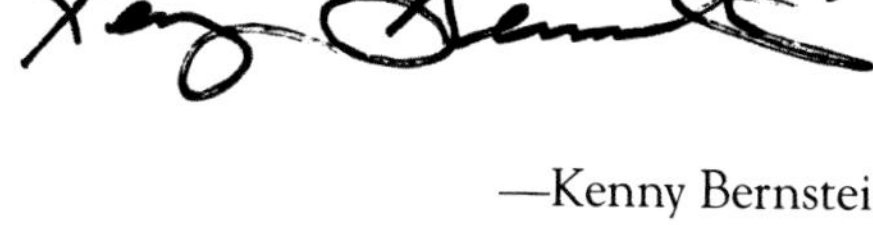

—Kenny Bernstein

INTRODUCTION

For more than four decades, Bristol Dragway has been hallowed ground for all who worship the exotic, fire-breathing machines of drag racing and the daredevils who drive them.

Like the wildly popular adjacent NASCAR oval, "Thunder Valley" is widely known as one of the world's finest places to experience drag racing's unique brand of 300-mile-per-hour excitement.

But Bristol Motor Speedway and Dragway share more than just East Tennessee real estate. The two legendary facilities are joined by common owners, common history, and a common legacy of greatness. Both now represent the pinnacle of their respective sports.

Established in 1965, four years after the oval track opened, Bristol Dragway was quickly recognized as the premier facility in all of drag racing. At a time when many of the nation's drag strips were converted airports with temporary bleacher seating, Bristol was a purpose-built track carved into a valley just east of the speedway.

"We plan to have the finest drag racing plant in the world," dragway cofounder Larry Carrier said in a December 1964 article in *National Dragster* magazine. "Race fans have shown that they want and expect the best when they come to Bristol and that's what they will receive."

Just over five months later, those words rang true when Carrier, partner Carl Moore, and their staff hosted the track's grand-opening event—the 1965 Spring Nationals. The race was sanctioned and conducted by the California-based National Hot Rod Association.

The Spring Nationals was only the third major race ever on NHRA's national calendar and the first in the Southeast. Only NHRA's premier event, the U.S. Nationals in Indianapolis, preceded Bristol as a stop east of the Mississippi River.

What hundreds of racers and thousands of fans from across the nation found in June 1965 was a sparkling facility with expansive parking and massive concrete grandstands carved into the mountain along the wide, smooth racing surface. Its most distinctive landmark, a four-story control tower for officials, the media, and invited guests, was a decade ahead of its time.

From all sides, the response was overwhelmingly positive, and that first event was deemed an immediate success. The seats were filled, speed records were established, and a new chapter of the rapidly expanding sport was written.

But Bristol provided more than just great action, amenities, and unmatched scenery. It also provided a sensory experience unmatched in drag racing. For unlike 200-mile-per-hour contests on flat land, the mountains that cradle the Bristol track provide an echo chamber that makes the sounds of unlimited racing engines reverberate from the hillsides.

On the heels of that initial success, NHRA returned in 1966 and 1967, before Carrier and Moore sought a better financial arrangement with the rival American Hot Rod Association (AHRA).

Carrier and Moore's new deal included a second national event for Bristol in the AHRA's Grand American series. While the Spring Nationals remained locked in early June, the second race was run in late summer 1969 and 1970.

How big was drag racing back then? During that era, crowds at Bristol's major drag-racing events rivaled and sometimes exceeded attendance at the oval track.

With that kind of momentum, Carrier and Moore dropped another bombshell in late 1970. The pair announced plans to take their track and start a third, rival sanctioning group. Dubbed the International Hot Rod Association (IHRA), the Bristol-based organization quickly assembled a small group of loyal track operators and announced a five-event schedule that featured two races at the flagship track.

It wasn't easy. Carrier and Moore persevered through lean years and rained-out races as they struggled to earn respect against the more established groups. But through it all, the Bristol events remained wildly popular and financially solid.

Carrier, who also operated the NASCAR oval track at that time, used his connections to bring R. J. Reynolds and its Winston brand into drag racing. Their corporate support stabilized IHRA and significantly raised the group's profile.

In 1983, the partners sold control of the Bristol facilities and IHRA to California businessman Warner Hodgdon. But when his tenure was cut short by financial problems in other businesses in 1985, a bankruptcy court awarded Carrier control of both Bristol facilities.

The following year, Carrier opted to sell the dragway to Kentucky businessman Jim Ruth and focus his energies on the speedway.

Ruth, a longtime racer, worked tirelessly to improve and expand the physical plant while keeping Bristol at racing's forefront. But IHRA faced tumultuous times, and Ruth wound up as majority owner of the sanctioning group in early 1989.

Bristol's race-event profits were often needed to prop up the organization, which was struggling to re-establish itself. When Ruth died suddenly in December 1990, at the age of 50, his sons, Rick and Duane, made certain that Thunder Valley kept operating.

But with IHRA struggling to attract some of the star power of previous years, the historic facility was at a crossroads.

Speculation about the dragway's future loomed large in 1996, after the Ruth brothers sold the property to Bruton Smith and Speedway Motorsports, Inc. Smith had already added the Bristol oval to his growing stable of NASCAR tracks, and a multi-million-dollar renovation plan was beginning.

For a time, it appeared the dragway might disappear and the property would be used to support the needs of the NASCAR operation. Speculation was rampant since, at that time, Smith had no ties to the straight-line sport. But Bristol's new general manager did.

Jeff Byrd spent more than 20 years working in Winston's racing programs and understood the importance and legacy of Thunder Valley. The new administration quickly established a vision to redevelop the track into one of the sport's premier facilities.

The keys to that plan featured the return of NHRA and former corporate partner Winston. Bristol would present a unique all-star race that pitted the Top Fuel dragsters versus Funny Cars with a $200,000 top prize.

Nearly two years and $18 million later, the second generation Bristol Dragway opened to rave reviews in 1999.

In 2001, Bristol turned another corner when NHRA replaced the all-star show with one of its national events featuring full fields of NHRA's professional and sportsman categories.

Despite battling some less-than-perfect weather conditions, another part of the Bristol legacy, the Thunder Valley Nationals has become the fastest growing event on NHRA's 23-race schedule.

In the years since the renovation, the track has added new seats, hospitality suites, and parking to accommodate a growing demand for tickets.

Which brings the Bristol story full circle because, much like 1965, Thunder Valley is again the envy of the sport.

1

Through the Decades

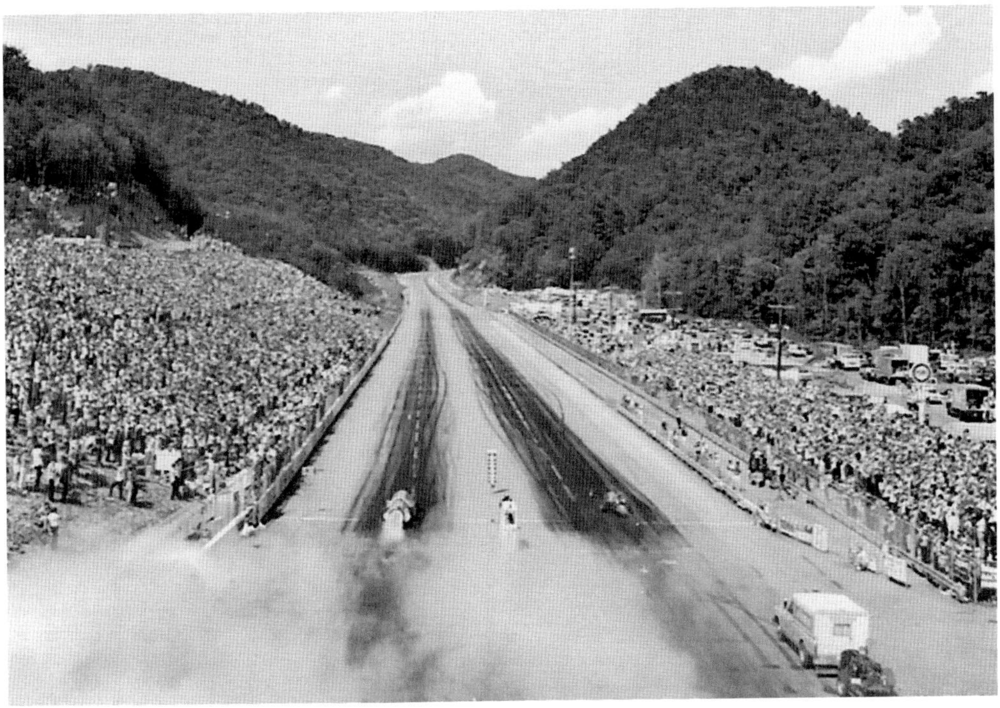

For more than four decades, race fans from across the U.S. and several foreign countries have jammed in to Thunder Valley to experience the sights, sounds, and smells of professional drag racing. From radical nitromethane-burning dragsters to the birth and evolution of Funny Cars and the evolution of mountain motor Pro Stocks and Top Sportsman into Pro Modified, Bristol fans have been witness to drag-racing history. And as in this shot from the 1969 Spring Nationals, there have been any number of jet-powered and other exhibition vehicles to provide nearly non-stop thrills. (Courtesy of BMS archives.)

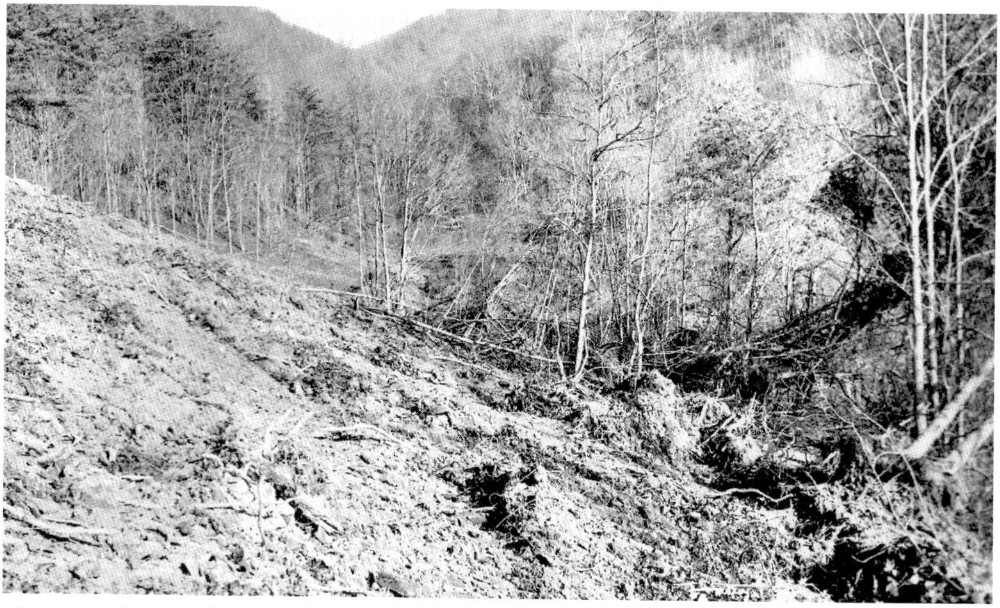

The natural box valley that would become Bristol Dragway was much narrower than it is today. Crews began working in 1964 to clear away trees and carve out the racing facility. Long the home of horsepower, local legend has it that early settlers and Confederate soldiers once used the valley to corral horses. Construction of the dragway took nearly a year. (Courtesy of BMS archives.)

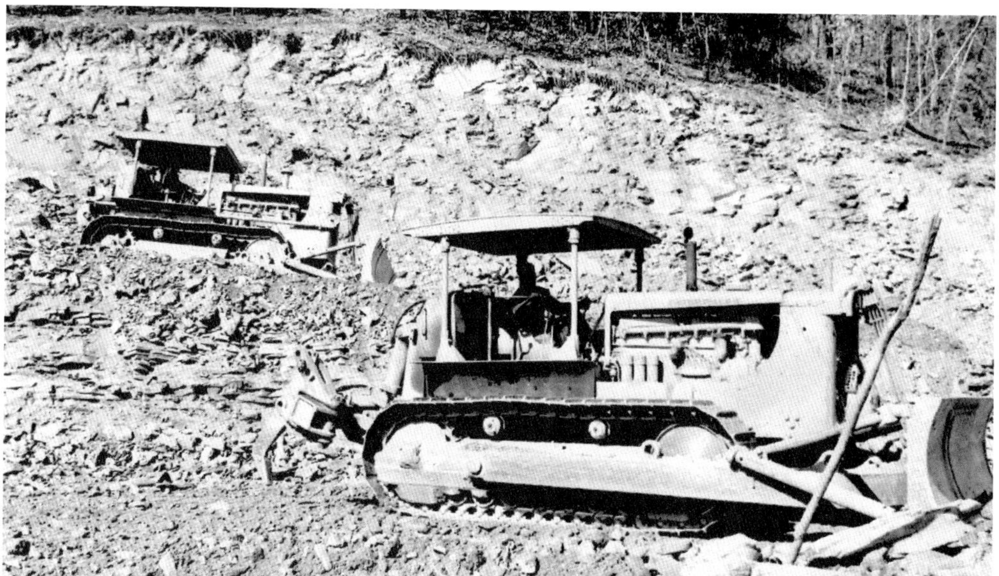

Workers using heavy-duty bulldozers moved thousands of cubic yards of East Tennessee dirt to prepare the foundation for the massive dragway complex. While many drag strips of that era were set up on former airport runways or industrial sites, property owners Larry Carrier and Carl Moore chose to build their track the hard way, on land adjacent to Bristol Motor Speedway. (Courtesy of BMS archives.)

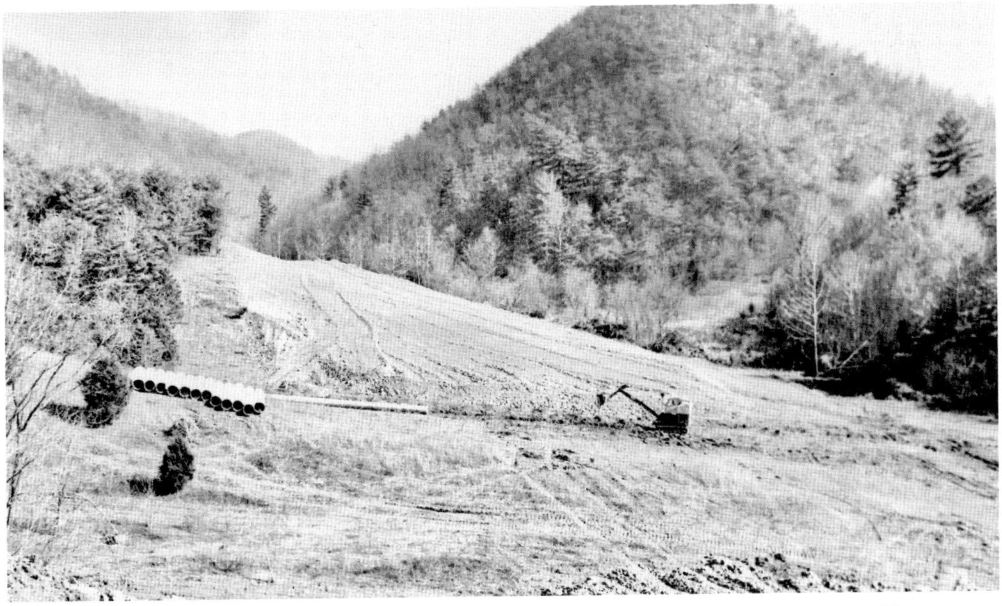

Carving a racetrack into a valley means accommodating the runoff from rainstorms. Here a crew installs drainage tile as the facility begins taking shape. Rain and runoff problems haunted Bristol races for decades. Inclement weather has forced many major events to be delayed or rescheduled. In earlier times, water often seeped through the surface during races and created safety concerns. (Courtesy of BMS archives.)

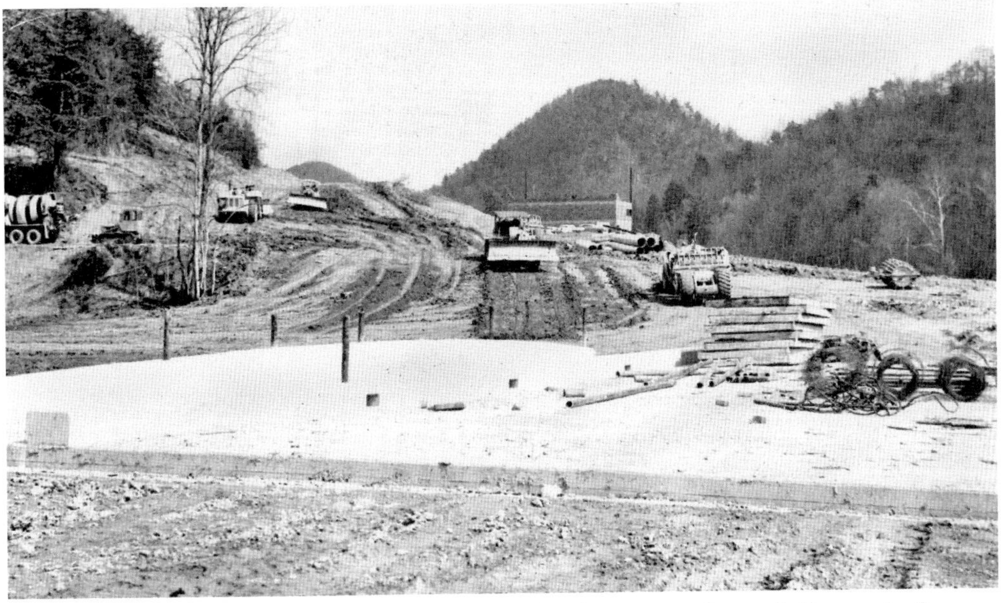

To connect the new dragway to the parking lots of the adjacent speedway, a bridge was built across Back Creek, which flows through the property. In the background, bulldozers continue carving out access to the hillside grandstands and staging lanes, where hundreds of racecars would soon assemble. (Courtesy of BMS archives.)

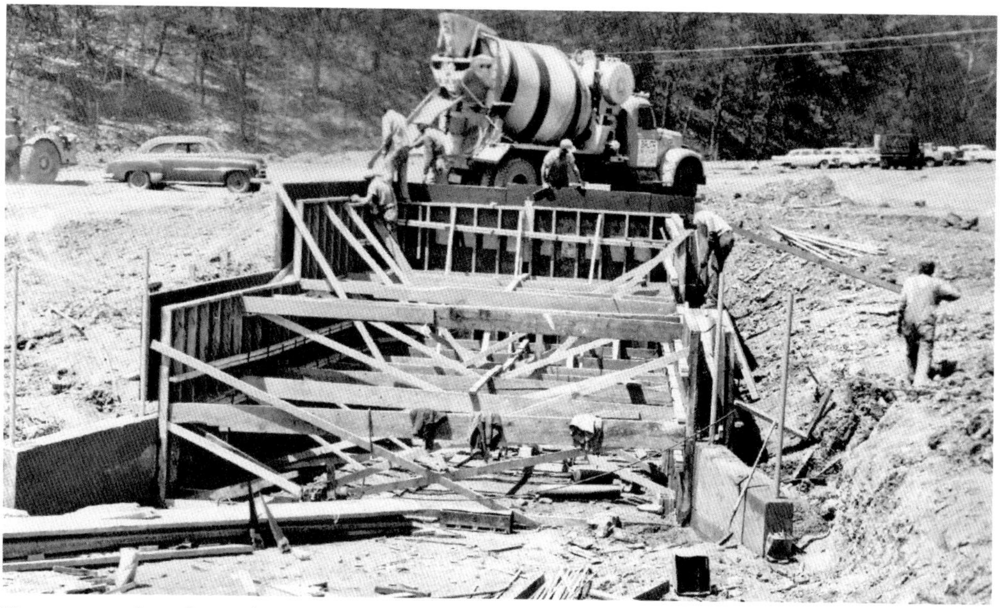

To separate fans from the race machines pulling into the staging lanes, crews built a tunnel beneath that area. Fencing was later used to direct fans into the pit area, where they could look at the cars and talk to drivers. More than four decades later, fan access to the stars of the sport remains one of drag racing's greatest appeals. (Courtesy of BMS archives.)

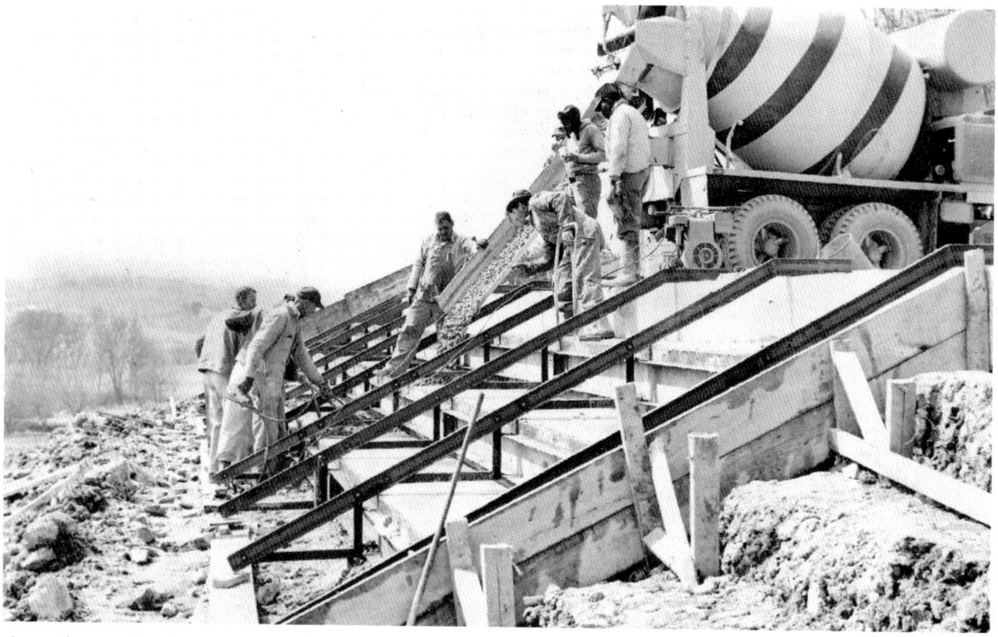

A work crew begins pouring the massive concrete grandstands that were part of Thunder Valley's landscape for more than 30 years. Track founders Larry Carrier and Carl Moore used the terraced hillside as the foundation for seating that held thousands of race fans. The concrete stands were removed in 1998. (Courtesy of BMS archives.)

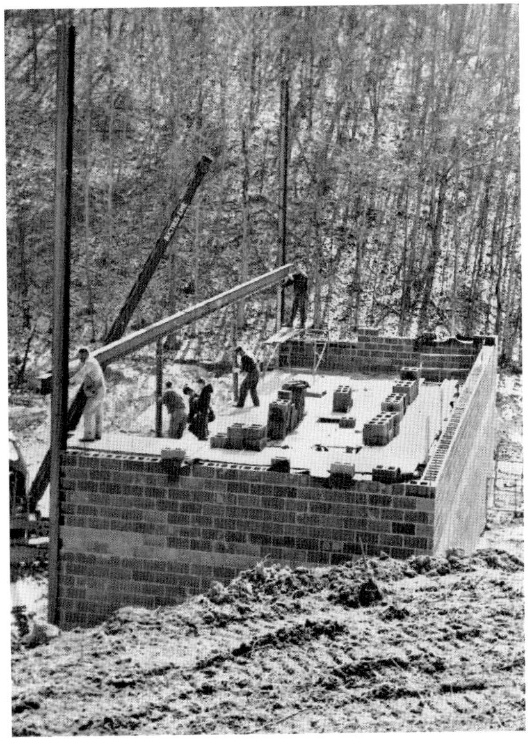

As grading work continued, construction also began on the landmark Bristol tower. The four-story building was positioned at an angle behind the racing surface. In addition to race control facilities for the officials, the concrete block building contained a work area for newspaper, radio, and television reporters, a medical care center, and upstairs viewing accommodations for invited guests. Local radio station WJCW carried live, daily broadcasts of the first major event. Major-league drag racing was just beginning to get national recognition, and the tower's design was years ahead of its time. (Courtesy of BMS archives.)

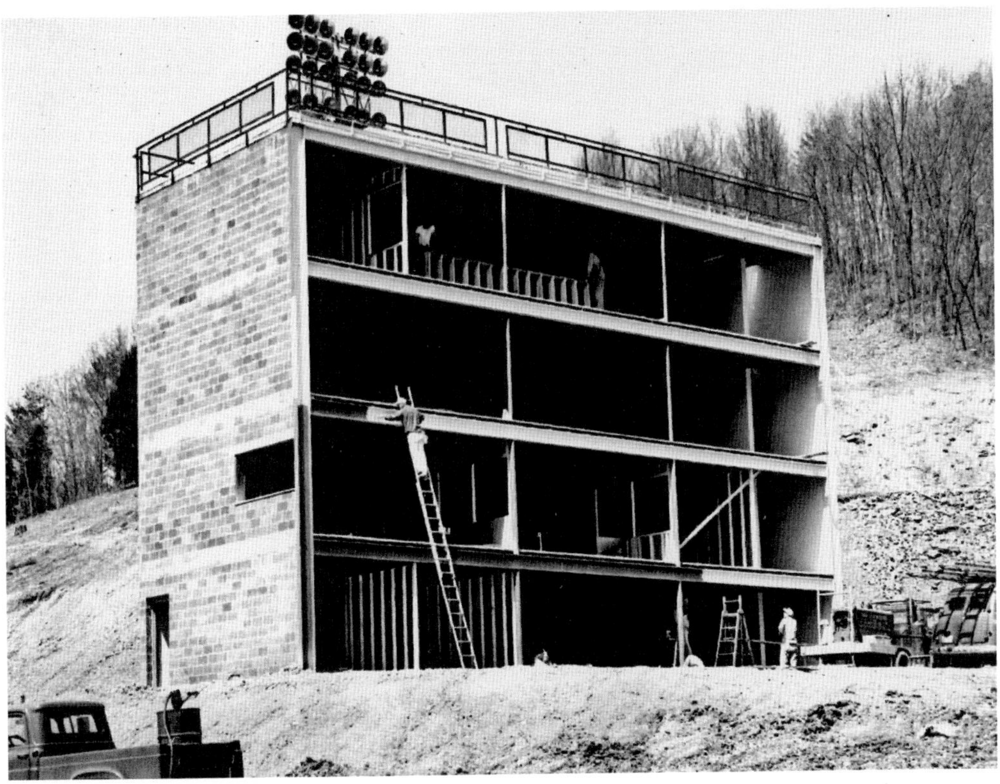

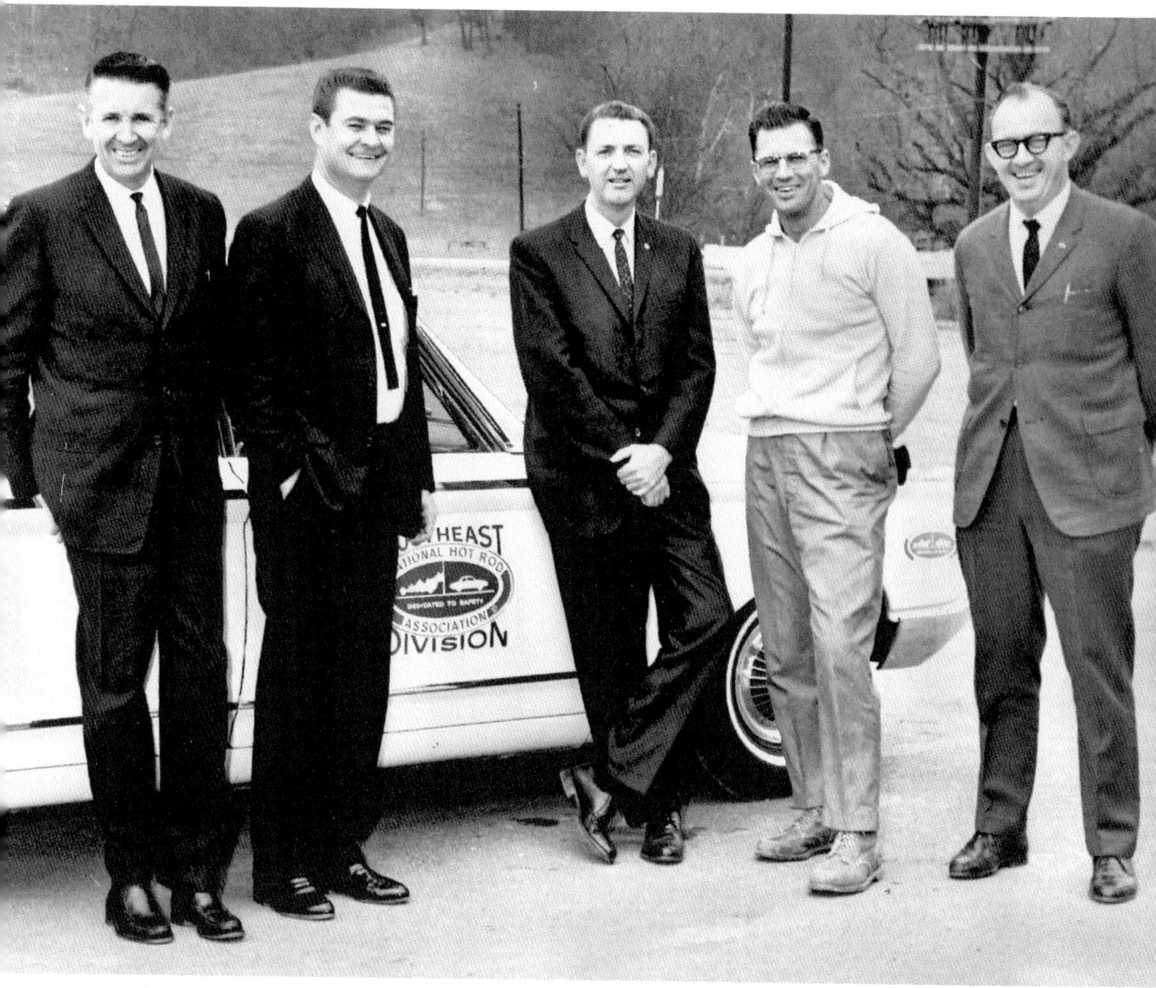

In the months before the Bristol track was completed, officials announced that the California-based National Hot Rod Association (NHRA) would sanction and conduct its marquee event, the Spring Nationals. The Bristol race became only the third event on the group's national event schedule, joining the Winter Nationals in Pomona, California, and the U.S. Nationals in Indianapolis. Marking the occasion were, from left to right, NHRA founder and former president Wally Parks, Southeast director and chief starter Buster Couch, dragway owners Carl Moore and Larry Carrier, and dragway general manager Hal Hamrick. (Courtesy of BMS archives.)

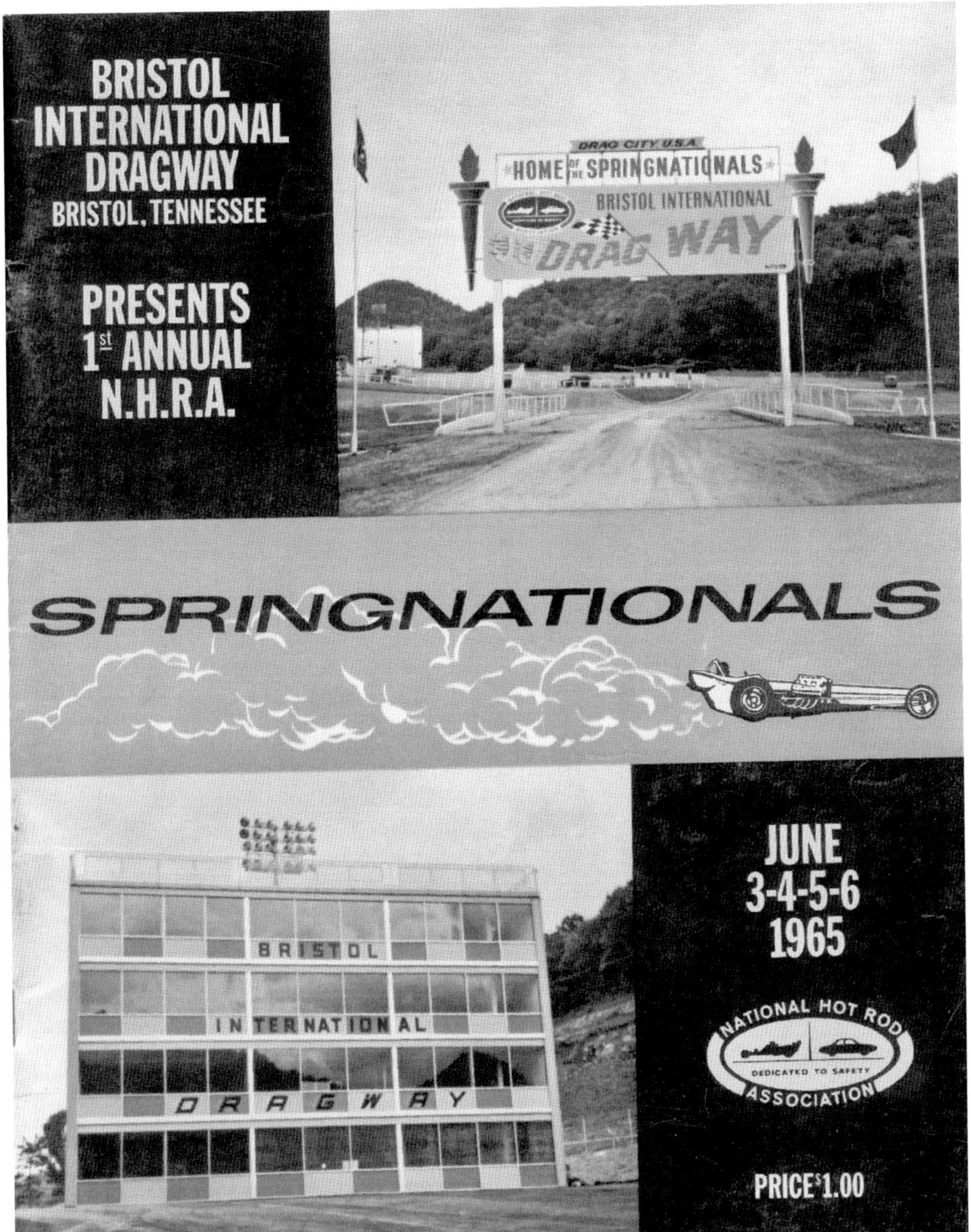

The souvenir program cover for the 1965 Spring Nationals included photographs of the still-incomplete Bristol facility. Inside General Manager Hal Hamrick wrote about "moving mountains" and how many felt a project of that scope was "impossible" to build in less than a year. When the cover photographs were taken, the track was still unpaved. Co-owner Carl Moore delights in telling how paving contractors Jack and Toto Barker got into a fight the night before the Spring Nationals, as they rushed to finish paving the facility. The work was completed by the time the gates opened the next day. (Courtesy of the author's collection.)

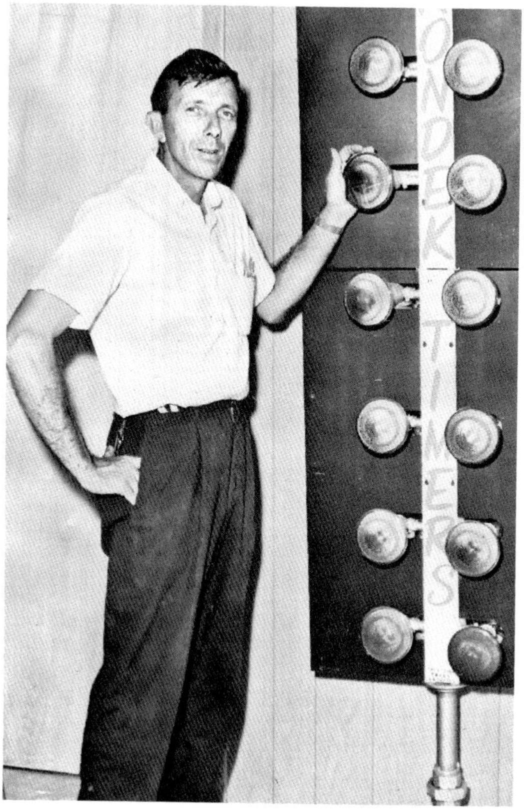

Fred Markwalter was a key figure in the success of Bristol's races for more than 30 years. One of the speedway and dragway's first fulltime employees, Markwalter handled a myriad of jobs, including keeping the electronic starting and timing system operating. Here he poses with Bristol's first "Christmas tree," a device used to signal drivers when to go. (Courtesy of BMS archives.)

A trio of race officials works in the control tower to oversee the crucial timing operation. Just like in 1965, both lanes today are timed individually. Clocks on each side register elapsed times in seconds and fractions of seconds. Just below that, a separate set of clocks registers speed in miles per hour. In some classes, head starts are given to slower cars by programming information into the center console. (Courtesy of BMS archives.)

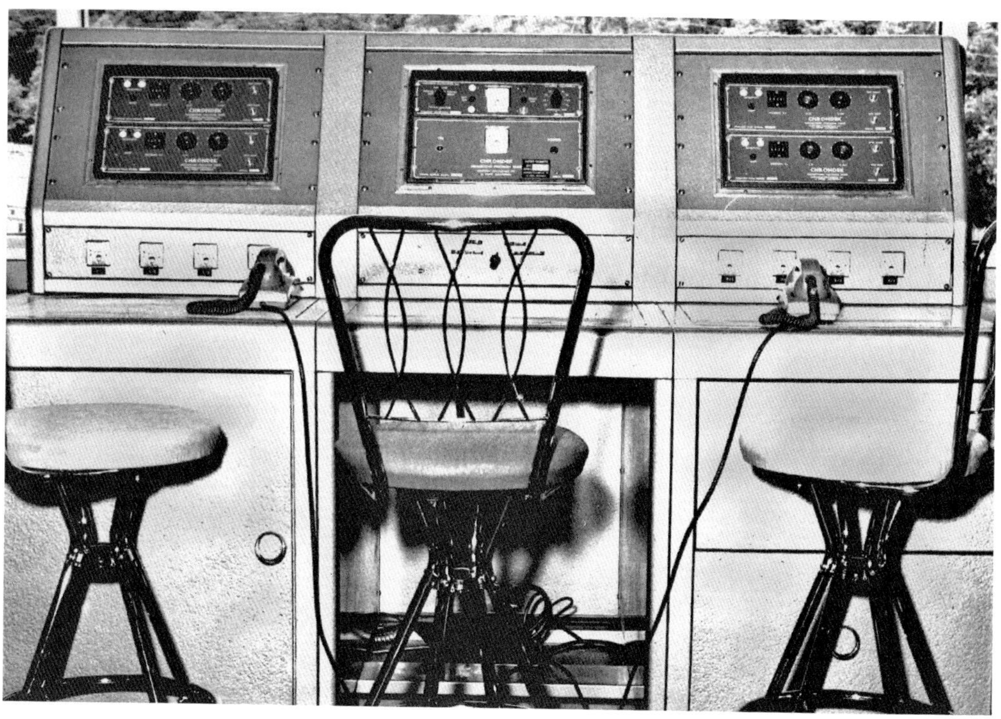

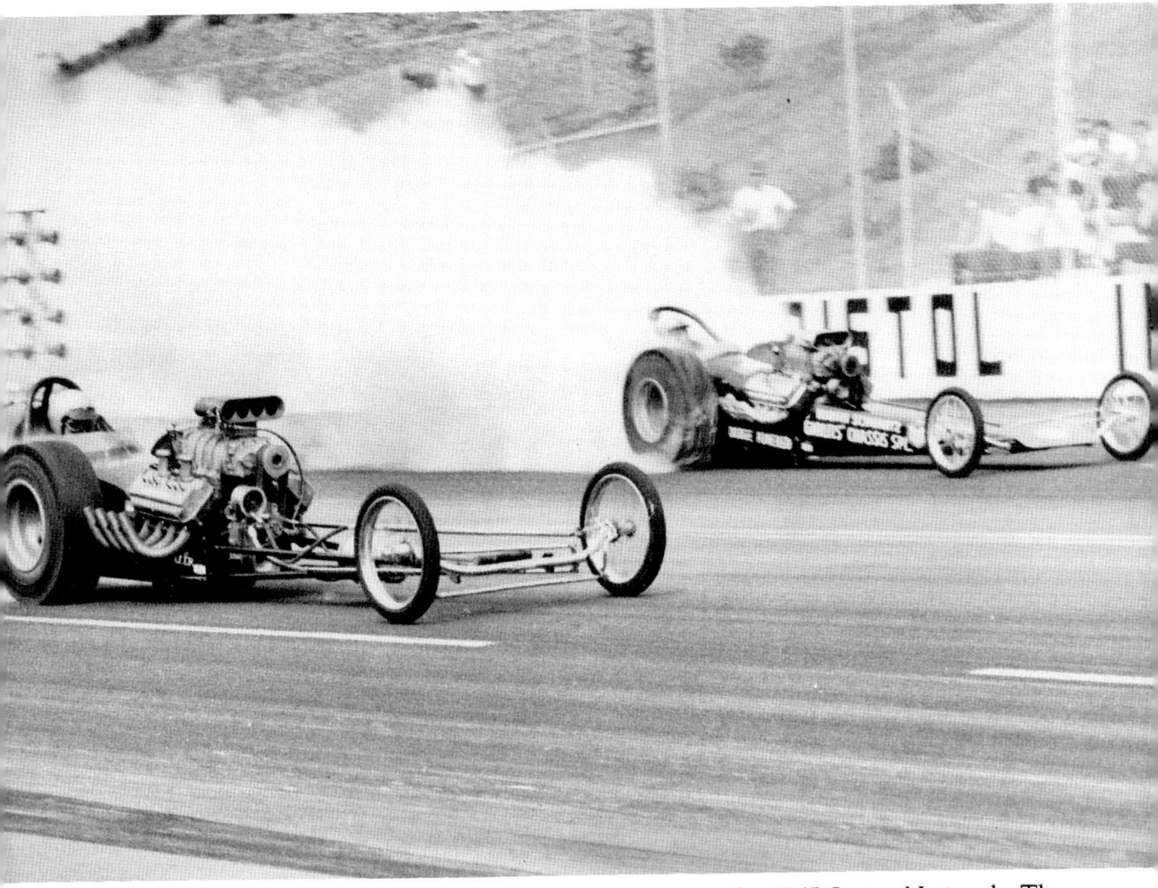

After the months of work, Bristol's grand opening event was the 1965 Spring Nationals. The event attracted hundreds of racers from across America, including Hawaiian-born Danny Ongais (near lane) and Florida's Marvin Schwartz. Ongais piloted his "Mangler" Top Fuel dragster, while Schwartz drove the Garlits Chassis Special of legendary drag racer Don Garlits. Ongais won the 1969 Bristol Spring Nationals in another category before racing open-wheel cars in the Indianapolis 500. Both drivers qualified for the 16-car final elimination field with seven-second runs at about 190 miles per hour but failed to reach the championship round. (Courtesy of BMS archives.)

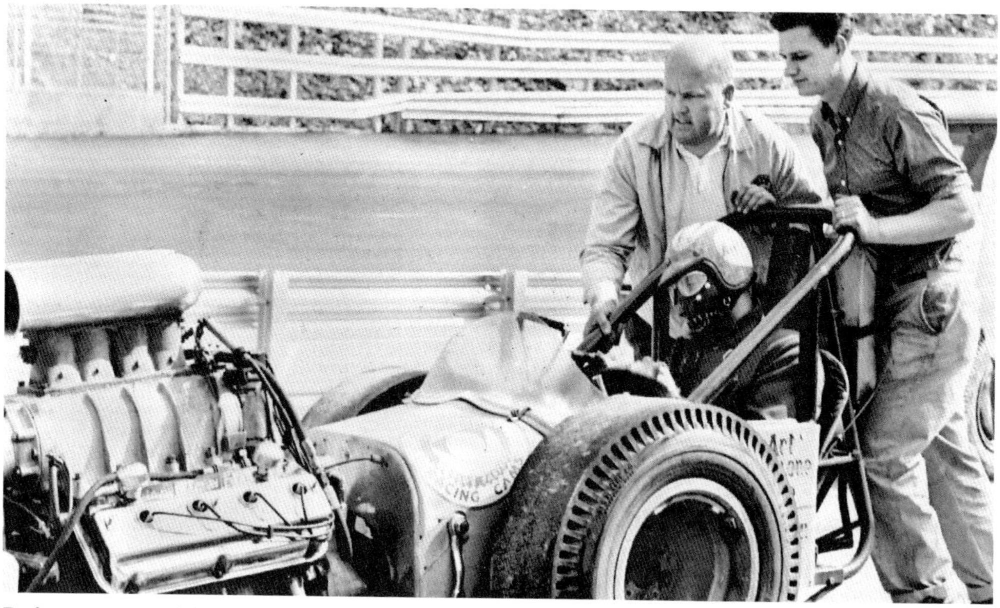

Before racers could compete, their cars had to go through a rigorous safety inspection. Here crew members push their dragster through the inspection line on pit road at the adjacent Bristol Motor Speedway. In the 1960s, the sport featured both Top Fuel and Top Gas dragsters. The machines looked similar but were separated by the fuel they burned, exotic nitromethane or gasoline. (Courtesy of BMS archives.)

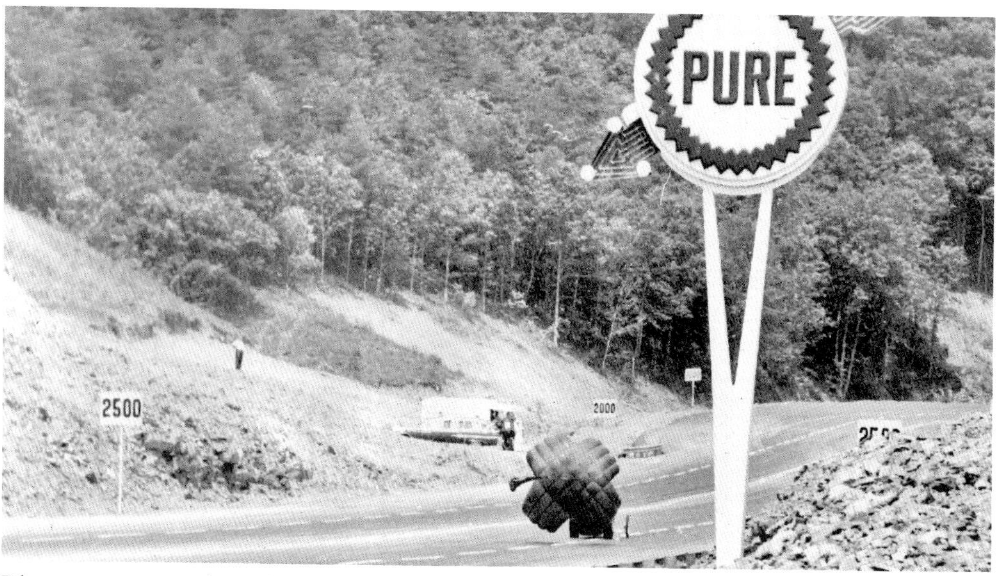

Then as now, parachutes help drivers slow the cars. The signs along the shutdown area inform drivers how much stopping distance remained. The Pure Oil sign is connected to the timing system and signals which lane won the race. Just beyond the sign, the track begins to curve right. A straight shutdown area was planned, but the course was shifted due to a large rock formation. (Courtesy of BMS archives.)

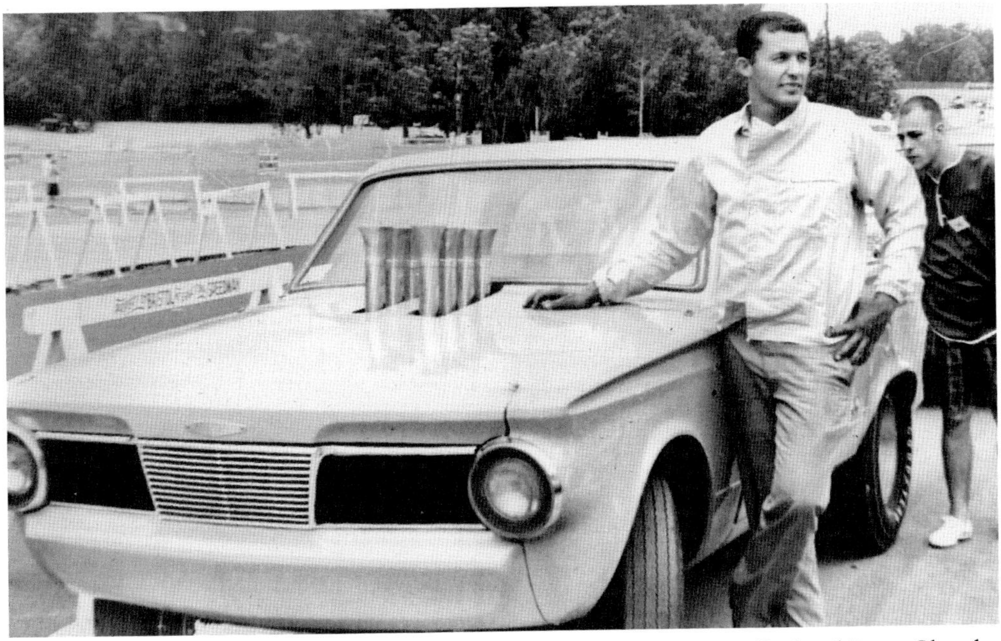

One of the stars at the 1965 Spring Nationals was NASCAR champion Richard Petty. Chrysler had temporarily pulled its teams out of stock car racing and sent Petty and others drag racing. At Bristol, Petty won the B/Altered class in this fuel-injected, Hemi-powered Barracuda dubbed "43 Jr." The 10-second, 135-mile-per-hour machine lost in the second round of Competition Eliminator. (Courtesy of BMS archives.)

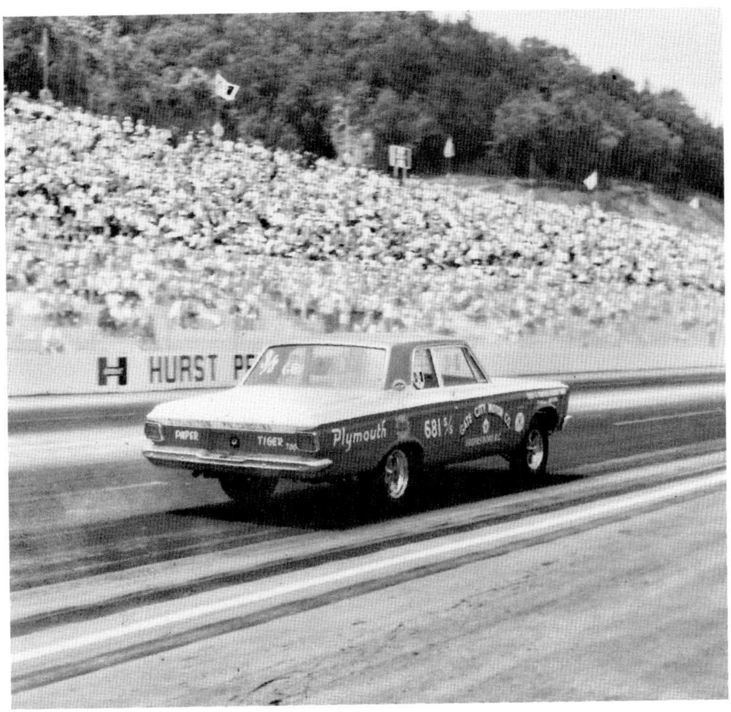

A real fan favorite in 1965 was the North Carolina–based team of Ronnie Sox and Buddy Martin. Sox drove the "Paper Tiger" Plymouth in the Super Stock class. One of the most prolific winners in track history, Sox fell short in 1965. He would return, however, to claim Bristol wins in the 1960s, 1970s, 1980s, and 1990s. (Courtesy of BMS archives.)

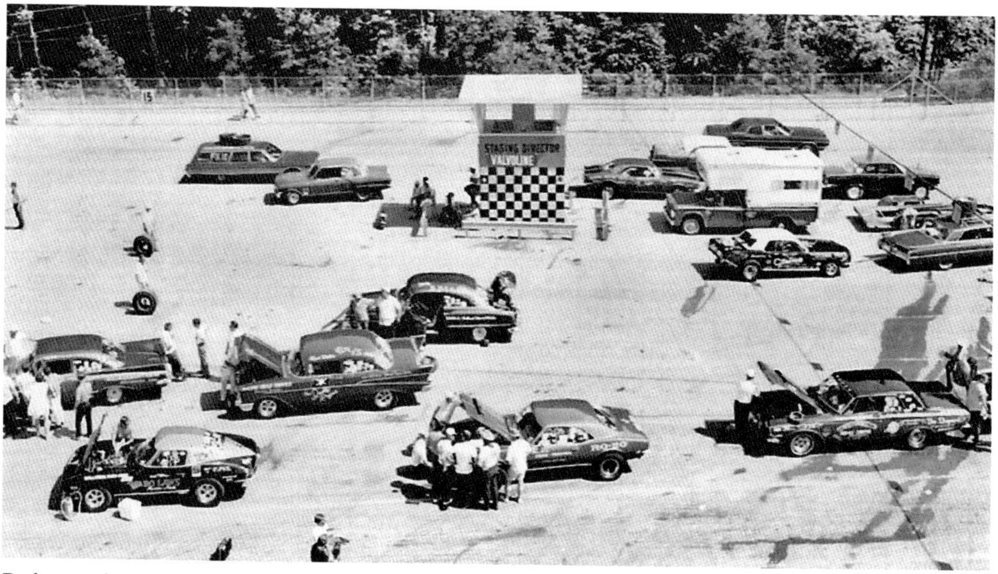

Before each run, drivers assemble in the Bristol staging lanes, where they are paired for eliminations. Several different types of race vehicles are represented in these photographs from the mid-1960s (top) and 1971 (bottom). The top photograph shows the staging tower, where pairings were decided. It was later removed, and all functions were shifted into the control room of the main tower. Bristol's staging lanes were spacious enough to hold everything from nitromethane-burning Funny Cars to Pro Stock to a wide variety of sportsman-class cars at the same time. Drag racing offers numerous options for racers to compete, depending on their skills and finances. (Courtesy of BMS archives.)

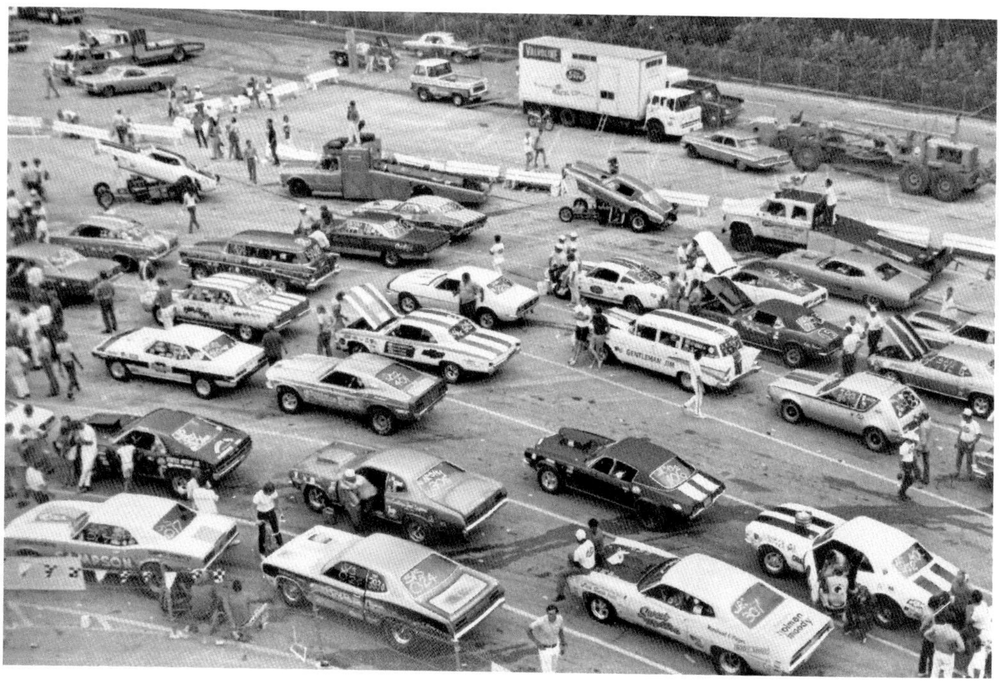

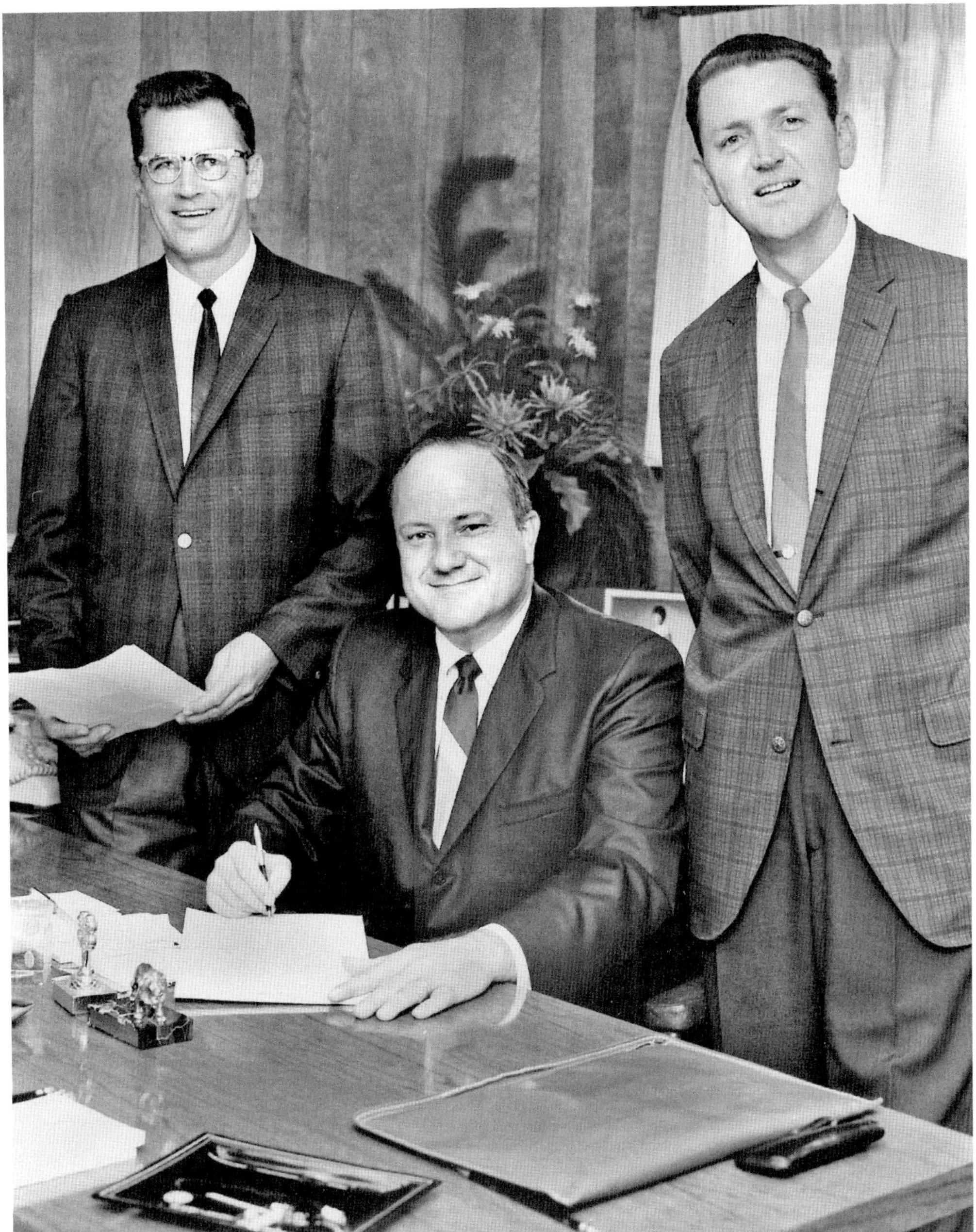

The first NHRA era ended after three seasons when Larry Carrier (left) and Carl Moore (right) switched Bristol's sanction to the American Hot Rod Association (AHRA). Here AHRA president Jim Tice signs the agreement. Carrier became an AHRA vice-president and helped add a second national event to Bristol's annual schedule. The AHRA arrangement lasted three seasons before Carrier and Moore bolted to start a new sanctioning group, the Bristol-based International Hot Rod Association (IHRA). From 1971 through 1997, the fortunes of the track and the sanctioning body were closely intertwined. (Courtesy of the Carl Moore collection.)

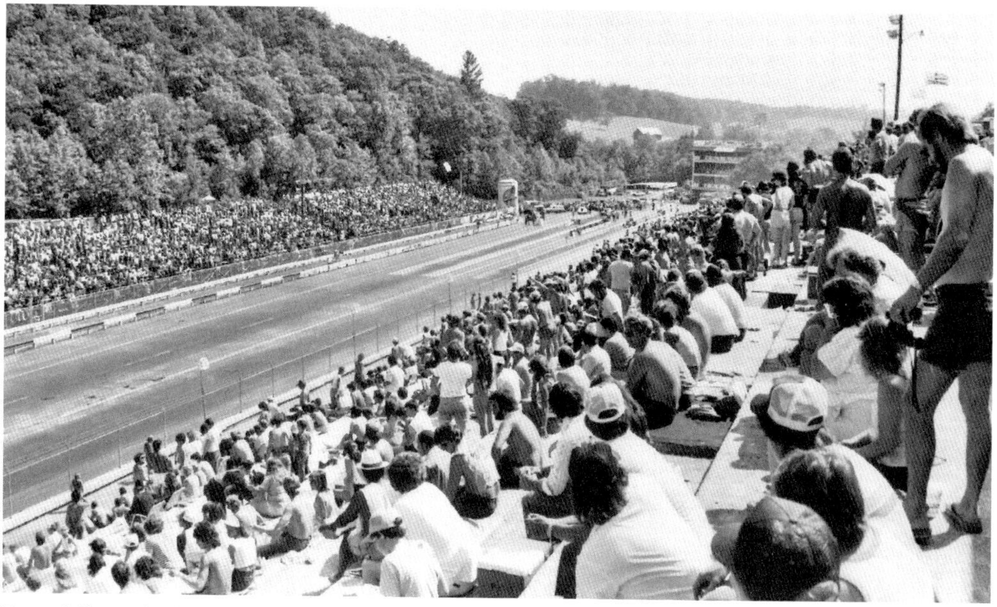

Bristol flourished through much of the 1970s and 1980s, with star-studded events, record-setting professional payouts, and close racing. During that time, IHRA and the Bristol track enjoyed the corporate support of R. J. Reynolds Tobacco and later Stroh's beer. The Spring Nationals was also included as part of IHRA's national television coverage. (Photograph by John Beach.)

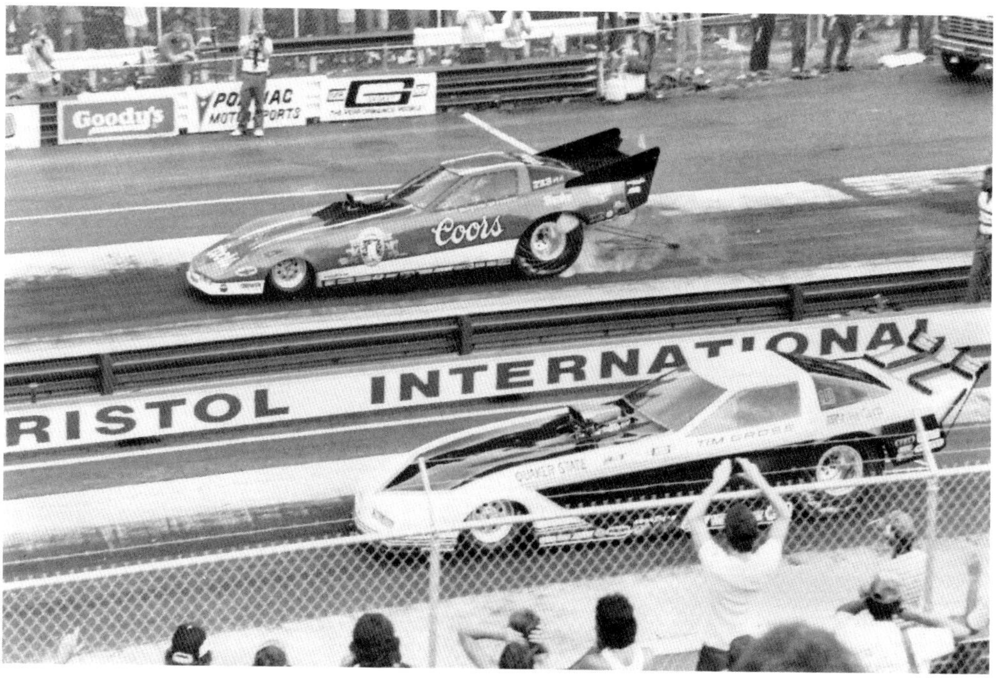

Another of the appeals of Bristol is just how close fans can get to the action. While their seats are only a short distance from the track, some diehard fans will press up next to the fence to get even closer. (Photograph by Mike O'Dell.)

Kentuckian Jim Ruth bought Thunder Valley in 1986 and owned the track until he died suddenly in late 1990. Ruth ran a number of businesses and drag raced a Pro Stock Pontiac as a hobby. His sons, Rick and Duane, took over and guided the facility until selling to new speedway owner Bruton Smith in 1996. (Courtesy of the author's collection.)

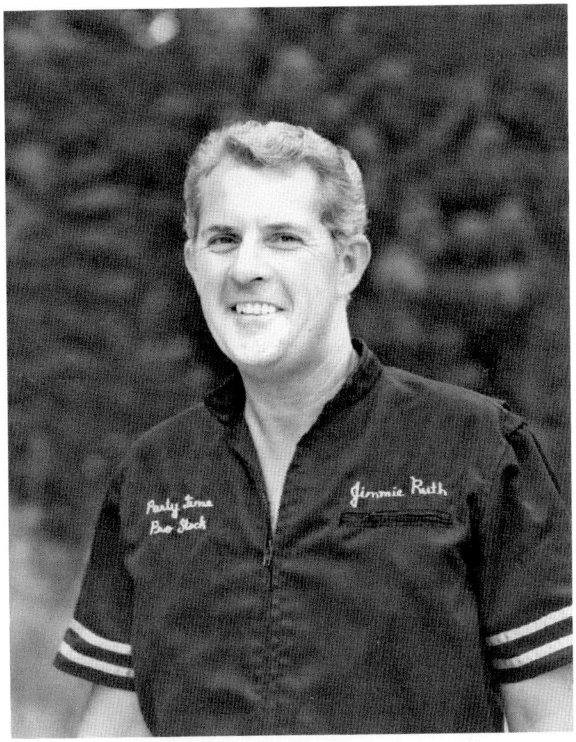

During a 1998 news conference, Bruton Smith (right) outlines his efforts to totally redevelop Bristol Dragway to former NHRA president Dallas Gardner (center) and former NHRA and BMS official Denny Darnell. During that event, Gardner announced NHRA's plans to again bring events to Bristol. (Photograph by David McGee.)

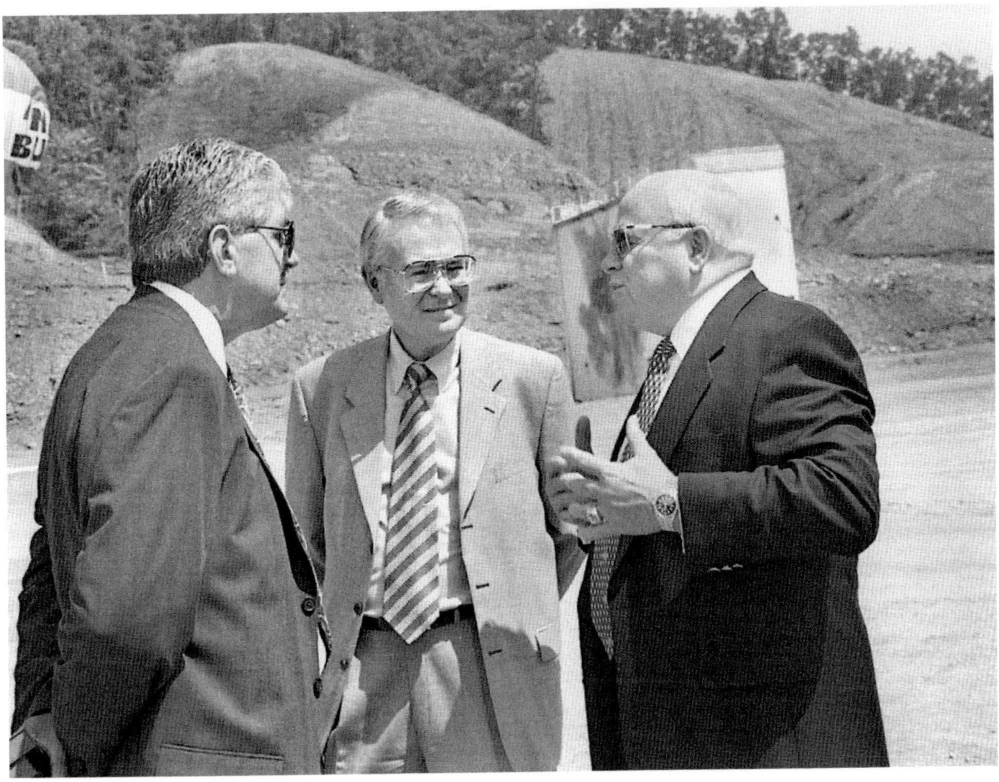

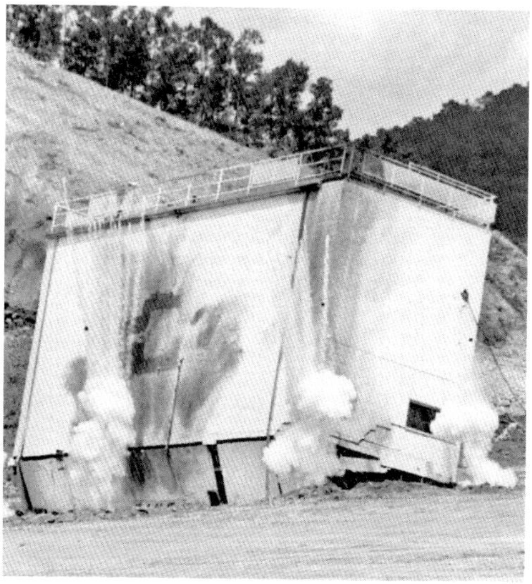

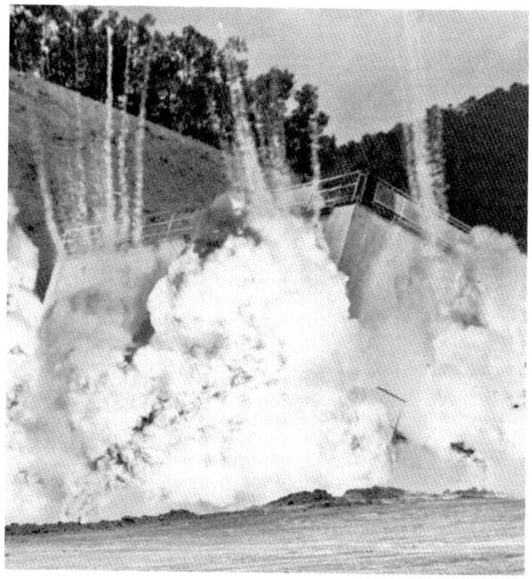

The most dramatic moment of the 1998 dragway expansion announcement was the fiery destruction of the original Bristol tower. (Photographs by David McGee.)

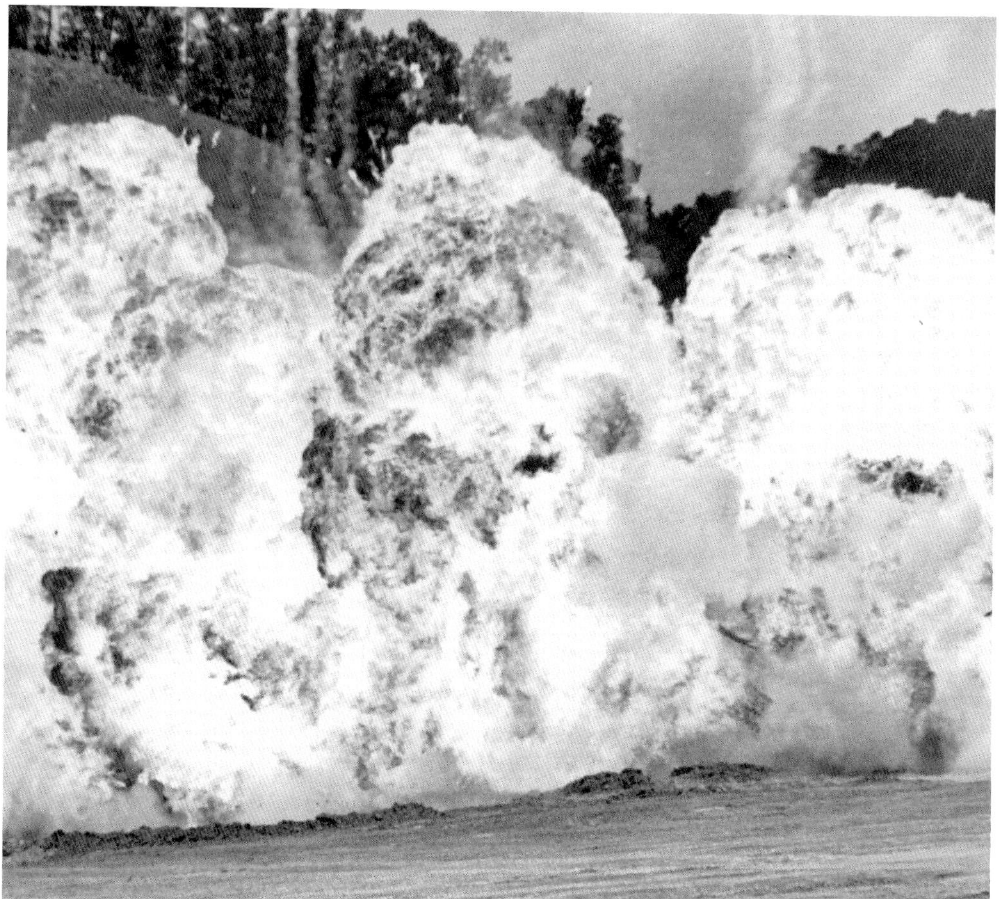

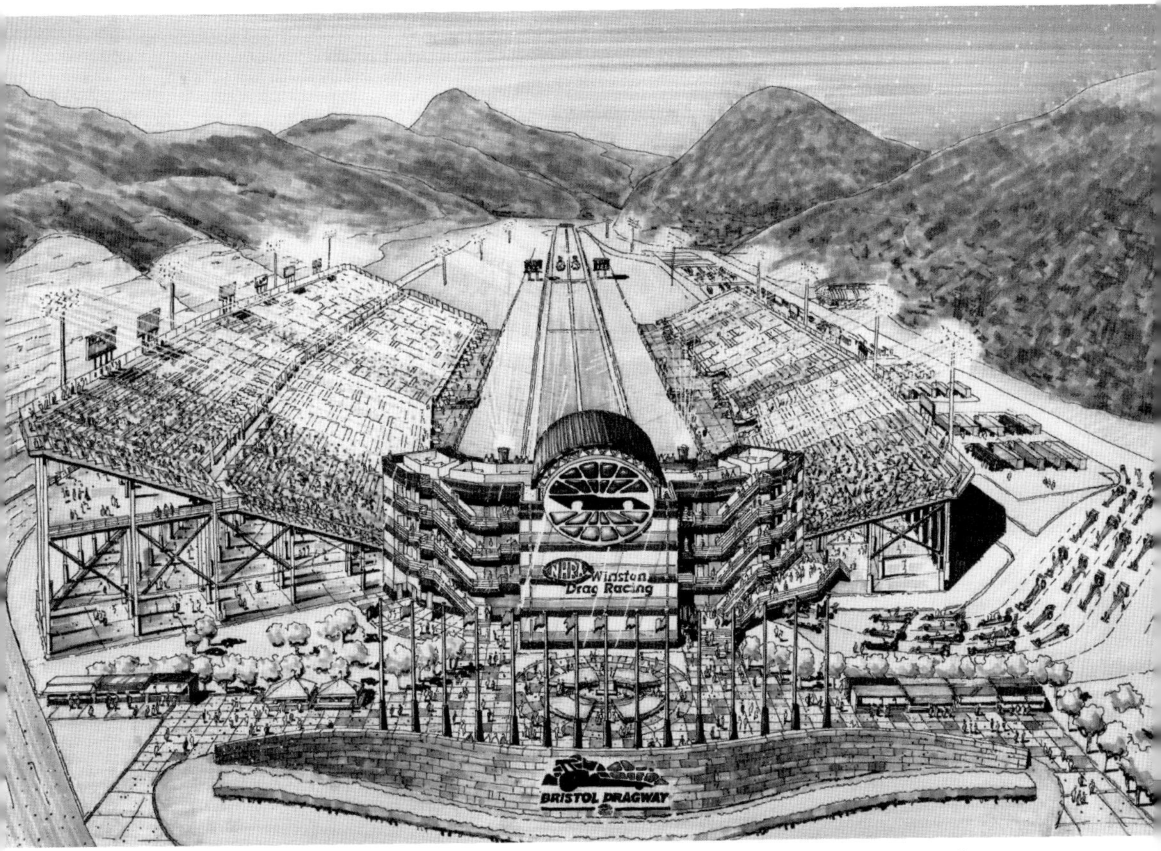

This is a copy of the initial artist's rendering for Bristol Dragway's dramatic transformation. Much like the sketch, the massive control tower, racetrack, left-side grandstands, staging lanes, and pits exist today. Most of the right-side grandstands were not built, to allow more pit space. The conceptual foreground wall, courtyard, and walkway gave way to vehicle parking. (Courtesy of the author's collection.)

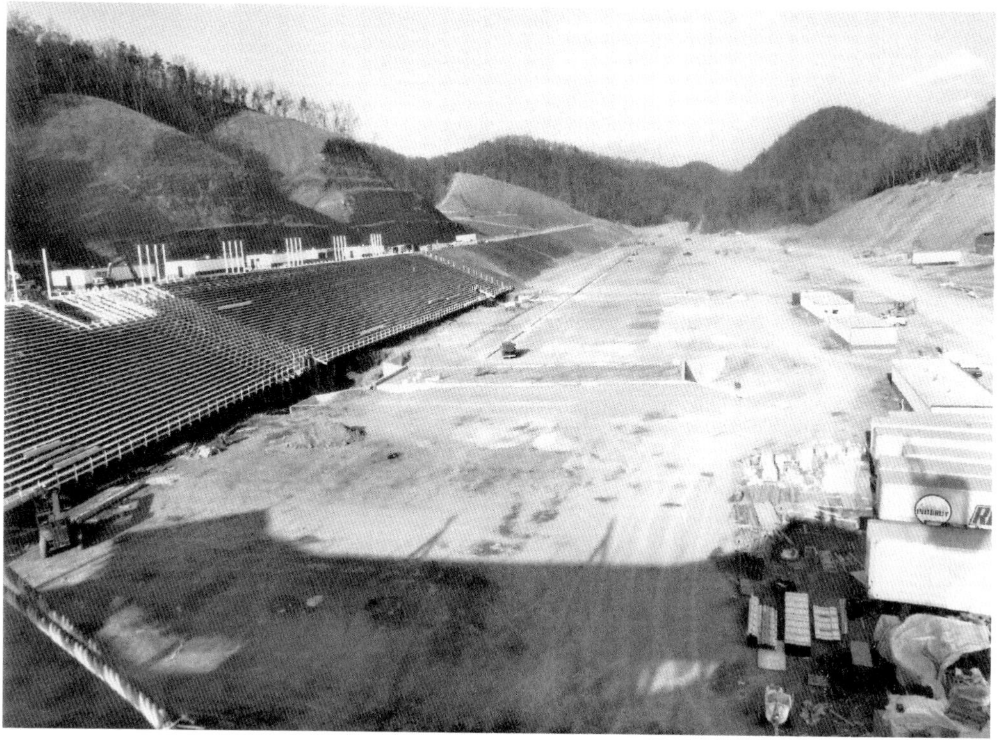

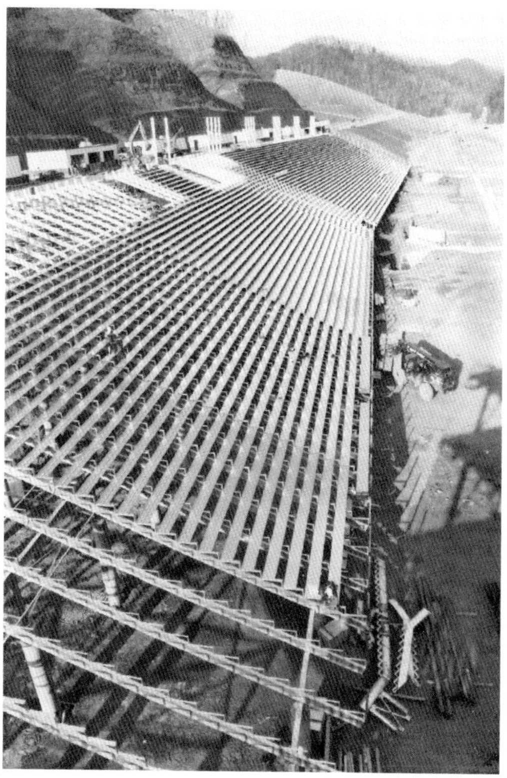

After crews spent months moving tons of dirt, effectively filling Thunder Valley in by about 20 feet, work began on laying out the new racing surface and erecting thousands of new aluminum grandstand seats. The end result produced the same look as the track's former mountainside filled with race fans but offered better access, amenities, and more comfortable seating. Construction of the two pedestrian tunnels beneath the racetrack is also visible, and this time, the shutdown area is straight, without a right-hand dogleg. The shadow in the foreground was cast by the framework for the massive new control tower. (Photographs by David McGee.)

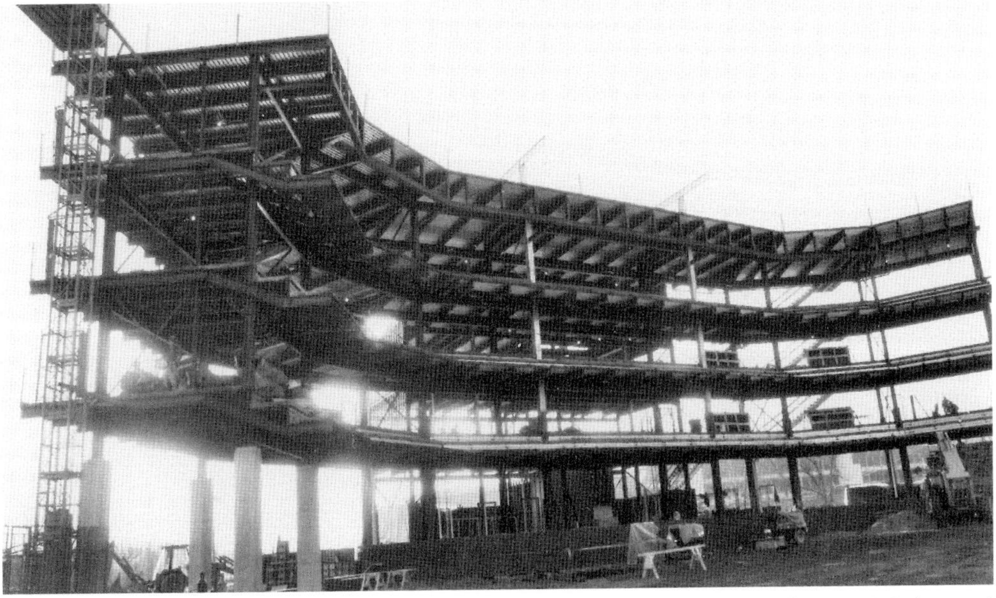

The track's second-generation, four-story control tower began taking shape in late 1998. It featured a race control center, conference room, and offices on the ground floor, suites for working members of the media on the second floor, and suites for corporate sponsors and VIPs throughout. There is also a covered rooftop viewing area. (Photograph by David McGee.)

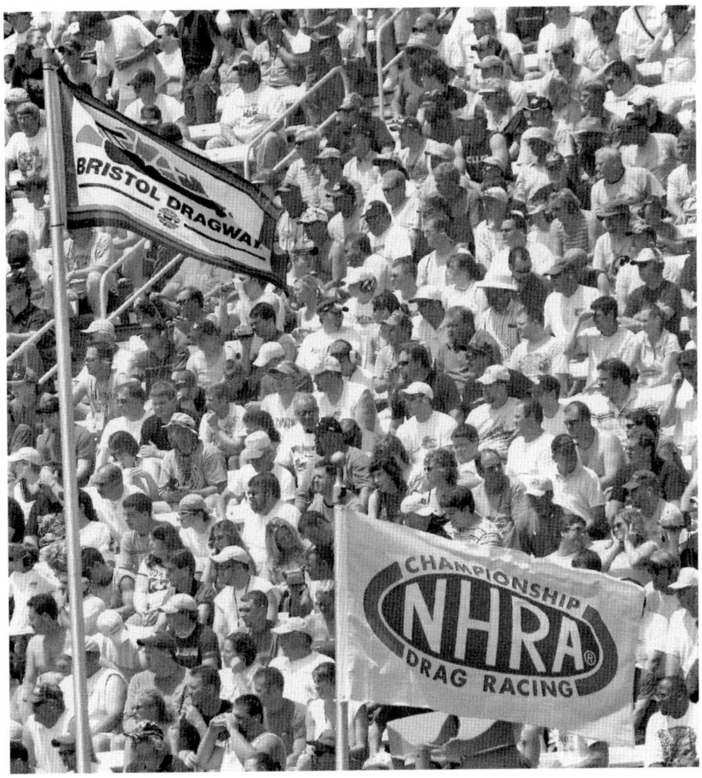

When the 1999 season arrived, the NHRA flag was flying alongside a Bristol Dragway flag for the first time since 1967. The track has hosted NHRA all-star races, Powerade Series national events, Southeast Division sportsman events, the O'Reilly Eastern Conference Jr. Dragster events, and a weekly bracket racing series. (Photograph by David McGee.)

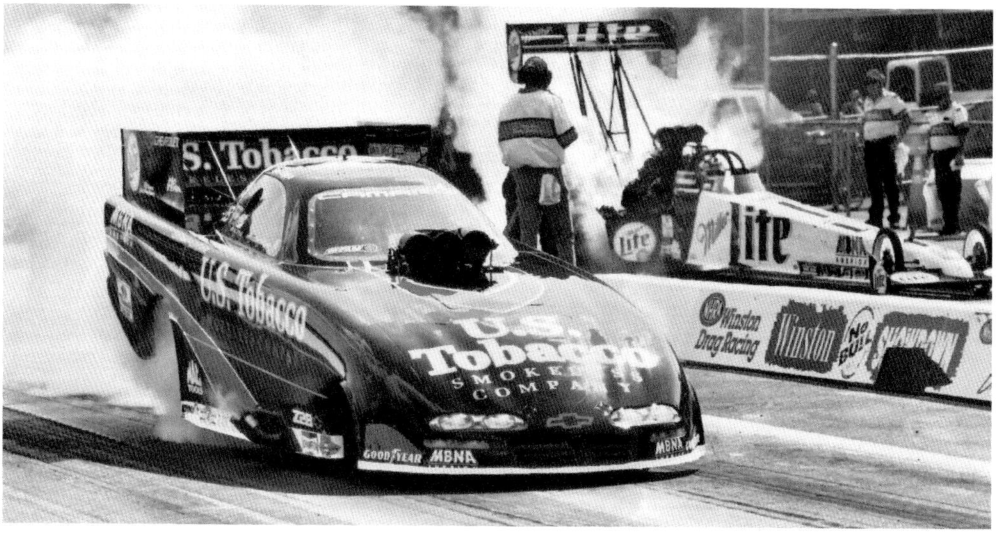

In July 1999, the new Bristol track hosted the Winston Showdown all-star race, which pitted Top Fuel dragsters versus Funny Cars for $200,000. Since the dragsters are slightly quicker, the Funny Car drivers were given a slight head-start advantage. Here Ron Capps (near lane) performs a tire-heating burnout in his Funny Car alongside teammate Larry Dixon's dragster. (Courtesy of BMS archives.)

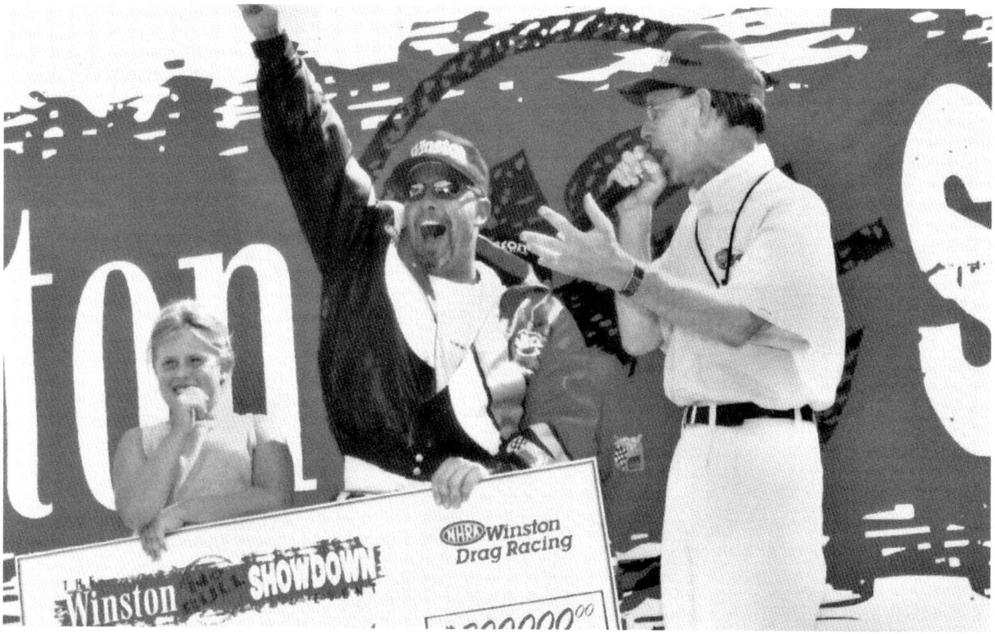

Californian Cory McClenathan (center) reacts to receiving the $200,000 prize for winning the last Winston Showdown in 2000. Also pictured are his daughter, Courtney, and NHRA announcer Bob Frey. "Cory Mac" called the victory the greatest of his career. The dragster driver defeated the Funny Car of Ron Capps in the final round, 4.852 seconds at 291.32 miles per hour to a losing 5.168, 275.28. (Photograph by David McGee.)

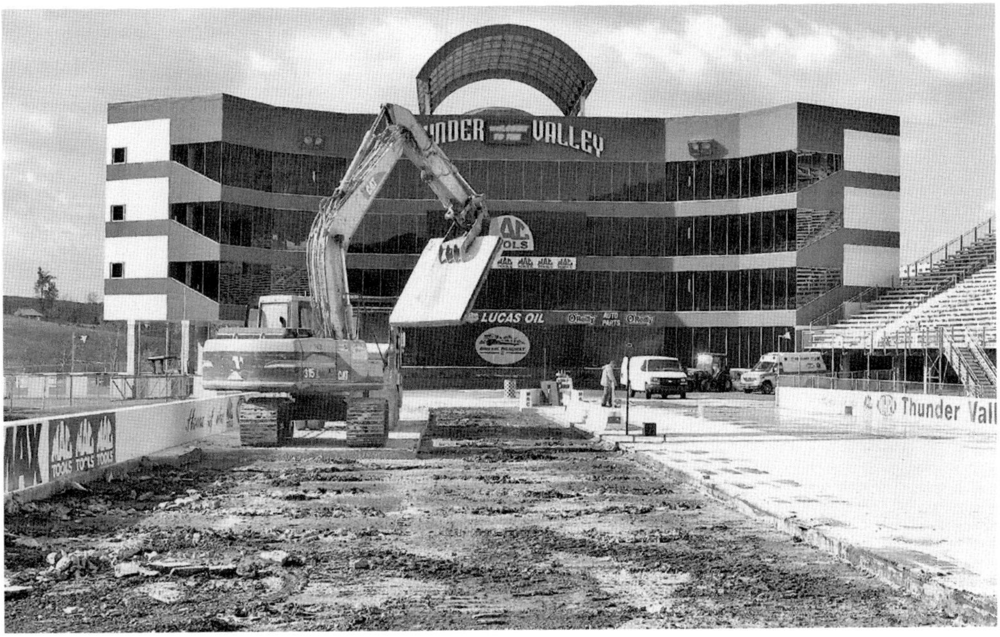

After the 2003 season was completed, track management replaced the concrete surface from the starting line to the track's midway point. The change was made to improve traction and smooth out the most critical section of the track. After the 2006 season, the remainder of the track was repaved to create an even better surface. (Courtesy of *Bristol Herald Courier*; photograph by Earl Neikirk.)

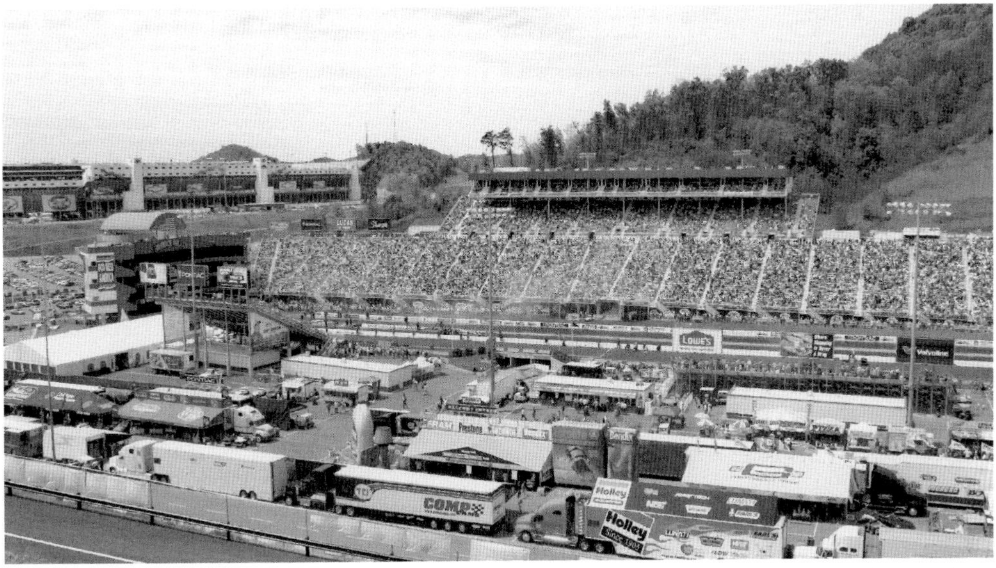

The track's skyline changed again for the 2005 season, when a series of suites and new chair-back grandstand seats were added above the existing grandstands. The unique expansion was a testament to interest and support for the Thunder Valley Nationals after only four seasons. (Photograph by David McGee.)

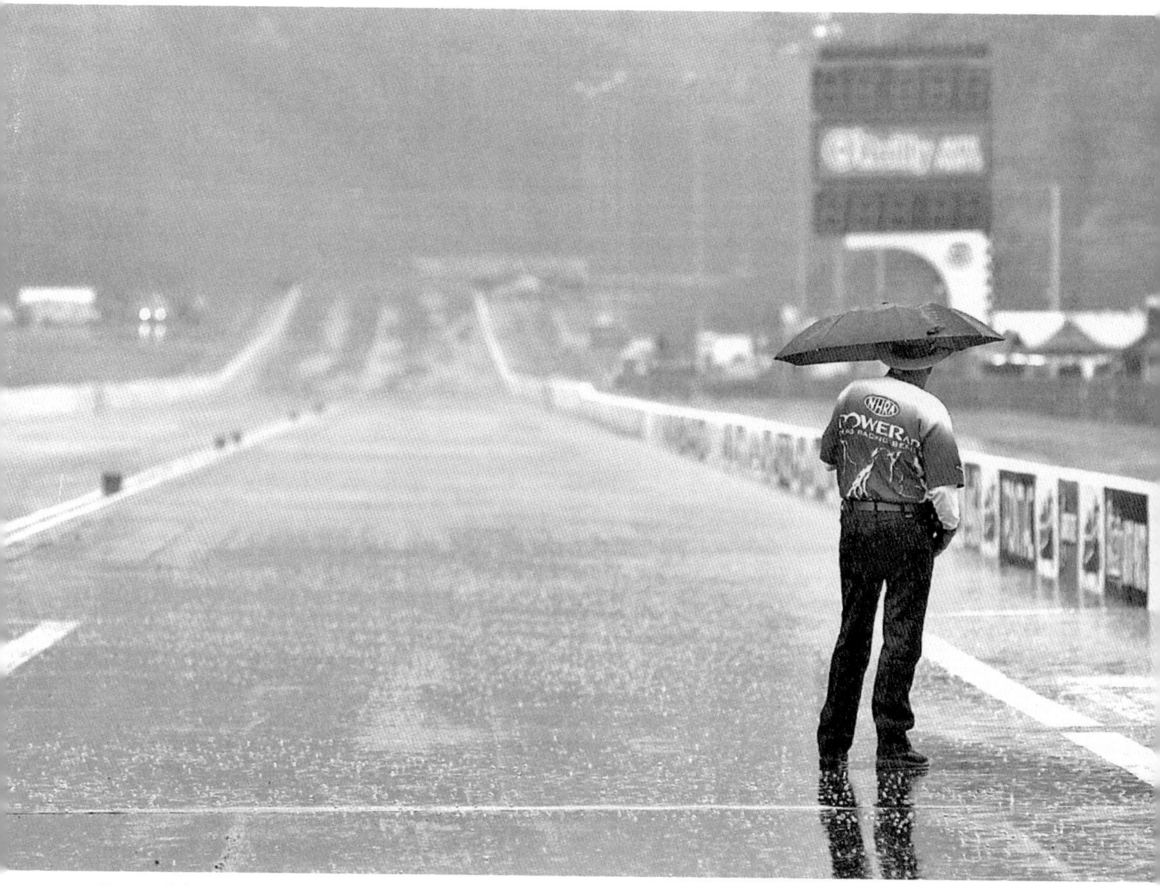

Rain delayed the first day of Bristol's first race in 1965 and has been an unwelcome visitor at numerous events since then. No matter who owned the track or what organization provided the sanction, Thunder Valley events have often been plagued by precipitation. Here an NHRA official surveys a wet Thunder Valley during a recent event. (Courtesy of *Bristol Herald Courier*; photograph by Earl Neikirk.)

2

Top Fuel

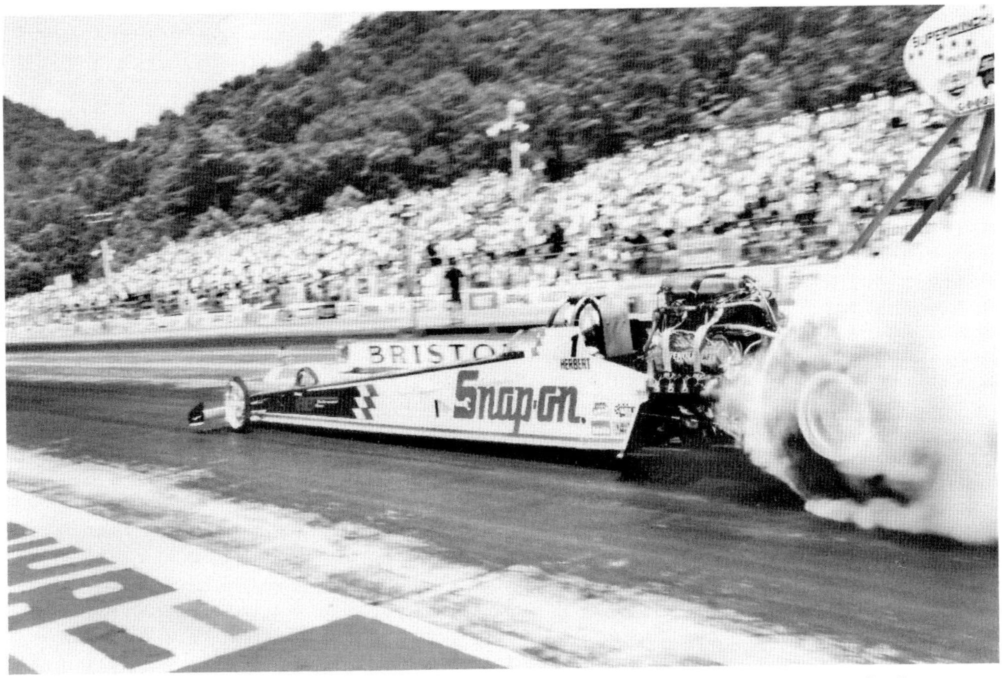

Top Fuel dragsters, the "kings of the sport," are the quickest and fastest-accelerating vehicles in auto racing. Modern cars can cover the measured 1,320-foot distance in 4.4 seconds at more than 330 miles per hour. The machines have evolved mightily since their performance at Bristol's opening event. In 1965, drivers sat precariously behind the engine and spun the rear tires throughout the quarter-mile to achieve 200-mile-per-hour runs. Modern cars used clutch technology and a massive rear wing to maximize traction to the rear tires. Since his first Bristol start in 1992, Doug Herbert has been the track's king of Top Fuel. He scored six wins in six straight years in the 1990s and was runner-up at the 2003 Thunder Valley Nationals. He was also the first Top Fuel racer to clock 4-second and 300-mile-per-hour runs at Thunder Valley. Top Fuelers have run at Bristol every year except 1984 through 1986, when IHRA temporarily dropped the class. (Photograph by David McGee.)

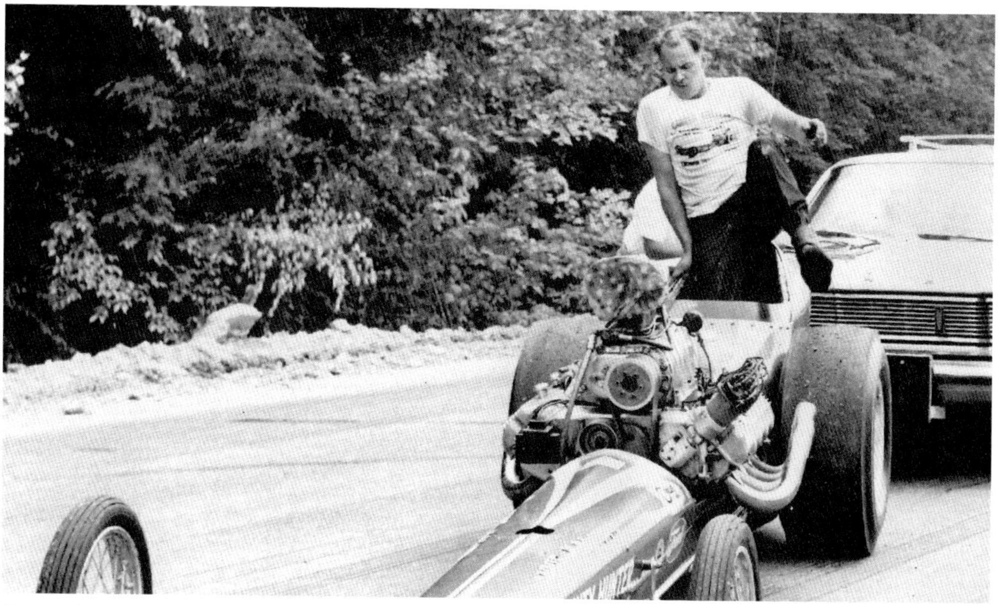

Conrad "Connie" Kalitta exits his Ford-powered Top Fuel dragster during Bristol's inaugural NHRA national event. Kalitta stunned the capacity 1965 crowd with successive elimination runs of 207, 208, and 209 miles per hour. All three runs exceeded Kalitta's existing 206-mile-per-hour national speed record. The Michigan driver's "Bounty Hunter" machine ran 7.82 at 205.94 in the finals but lost to Maynard Rupp's 7.59-second run at 203.16 miles per hour. (Courtesy of BMS archives.)

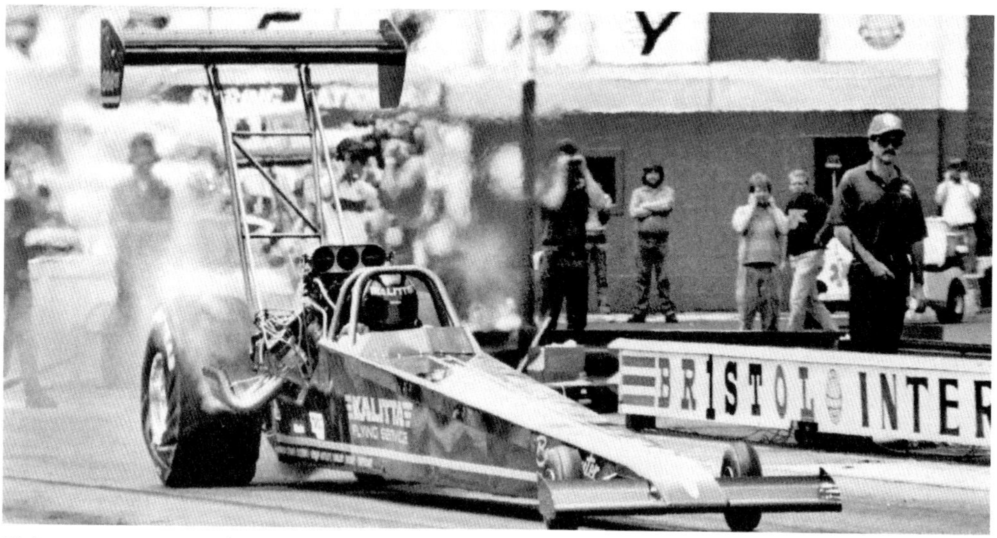

Kalitta was again a player in the Top Fuel class at 1989's 25th-anniversary Spring Nationals. His rear-engine, 300-inch-wheelbase dragster qualified for what was, at that time, the quickest eight-car field in Bristol history. He registered a 5.337-second run at 271.05 miles per hour in the first round of eliminations but lost to eventual winner Jim Head's 5.337 at 261.90 miles per hour. (Photograph by David McGee.)

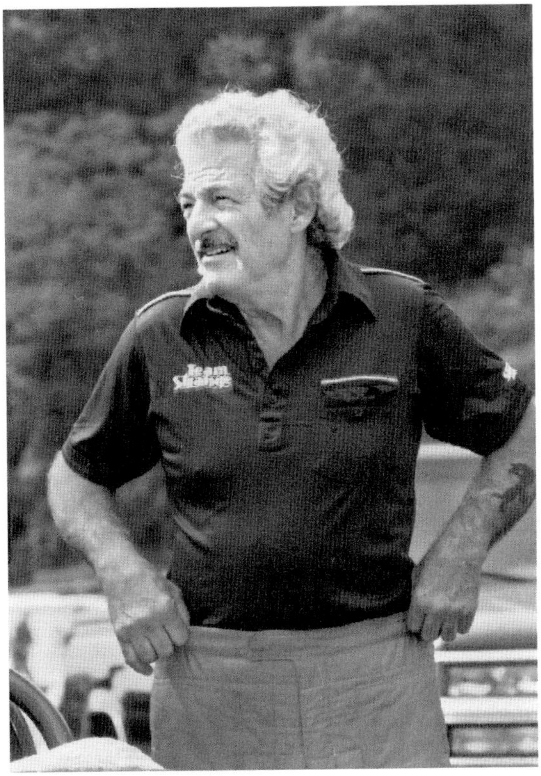

Chris "The Greek" Karamesines recorded Bristol's first 200-mile-per-hour run during the 1965 Spring Nationals. His blast of 202.70 miles per hour gave the first indication of just what kind of performances the Bristol track would yield. He won Top Fuel at the 1968 Spring Nationals, the track's first AHRA-sanctioned event. He returned to driving in the 1990s and qualified for Bristol's 1996 Fall Nationals. (Photograph by David McGee.)

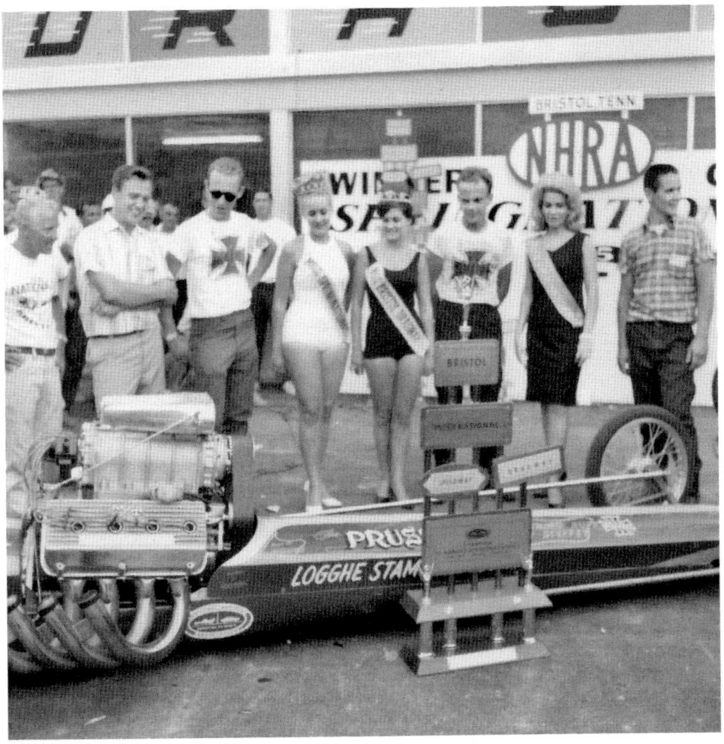

The Michigan team of Logghe, Steffey, and Rupp won the first Spring Nationals Top Fuel trophy with their "Prussian" dragster. The blue machine featured a tubular chassis by Logghe Stamping Company, one of the top car builders of the era. It was powered by a supercharged, 392-cubic-inch Chrysler Hemi engine. (Courtesy of BMS archives.)

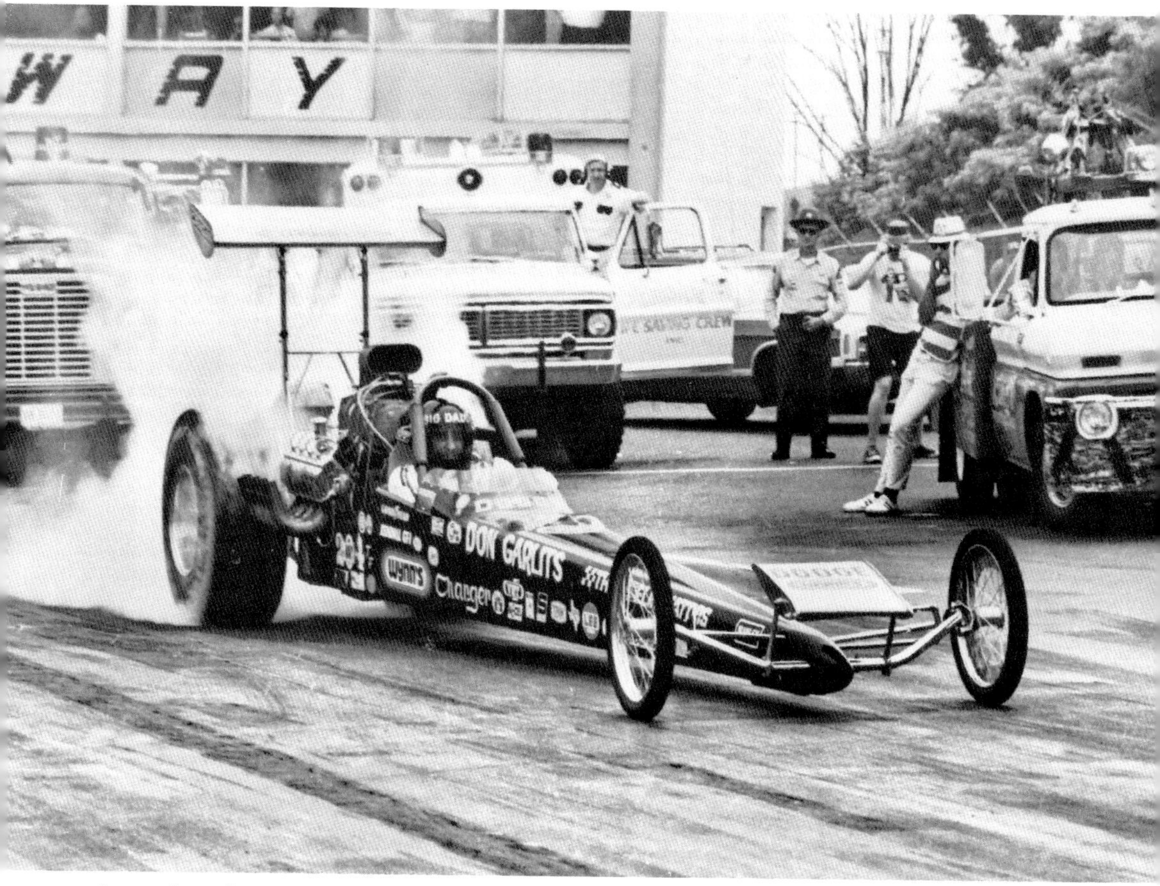

Legendary drag racer "Big Daddy" Don Garlits enjoyed his share of success at Bristol. Here Garlits performs a burnout in his "Wynn's Charger" during the 1972 Spring Nationals. That event marked his first of four Bristol victories. After being seriously injured by a 1970 clutch explosion in his old front-engine car, Garlits revolutionized the sport in 1971 by relocating the engine behind the driver. Garlits drove a front-engine car only once after that accident, at the 1970 Bristol Spring Nationals. He made a couple of runs, setting low ET and top speed at 6.80 seconds, 224 miles per hour, before turning the controls back over to driver Connie Swingle. (Photograph by John Beach.)

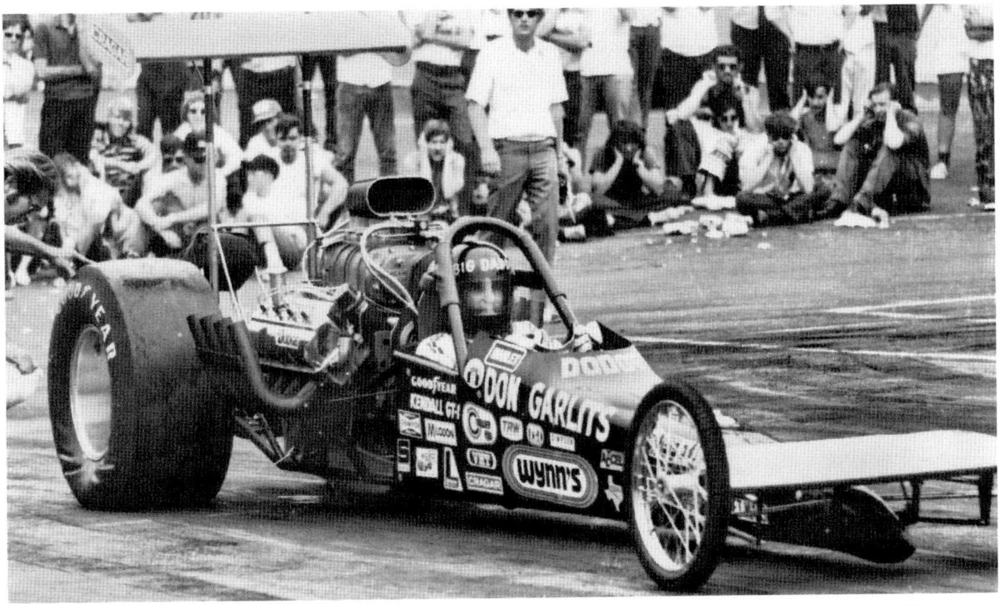

The innovative Garlits also tried out a shorter, 175-inch-wheelbase car during the 1972 Spring Nationals. Nicknamed "Shorty," the car continually lost traction and saw only limited duty after that. This unique footnote of drag-racing history has been restored and is part of the collection on display at the Garlits Museum of Drag Racing in Florida. (Photograph by John Beach.)

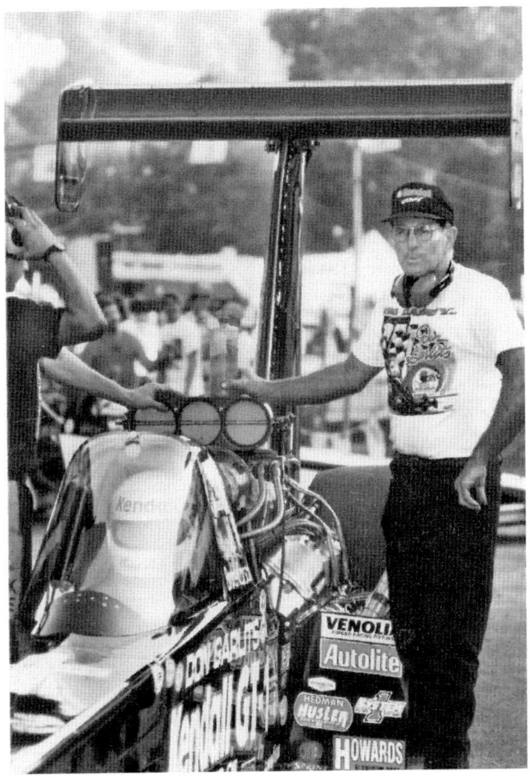

As a car owner, Don Garlits (standing) and driver Bruce Larson earned one Bristol win in two final-round appearances. Larson beat Richard Langson for the 1992 Fall Nationals victory. The car featured a revolutionary single, center support for the rear wing (shown here). Garlits claimed the design improved safety by reducing the likelihood of the wing being ripped off in an accident. (Photograph by David McGee.)

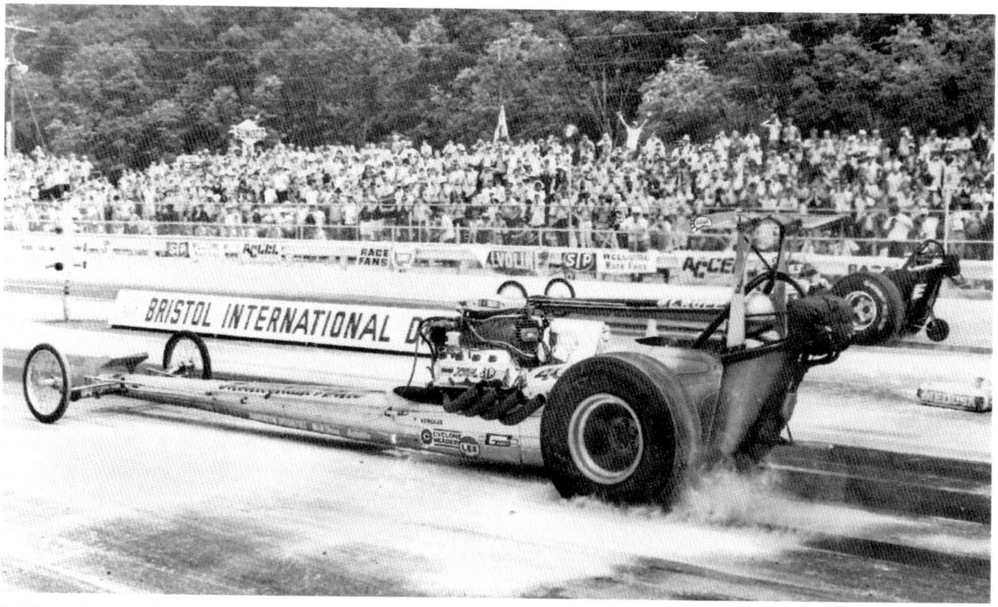

Mike Martini (near lane) piloted Gene Mooneyham's front-engine Top Fuel dragster to the 1971 Bristol win, the track's first under IHRA sanction. The white dust beneath the car is concrete. Due to problems with a new top layer of asphalt, track crews used concrete to temporarily patch the surface. All drag-strip starting lines are now made of concrete. (Photograph by John Beach.)

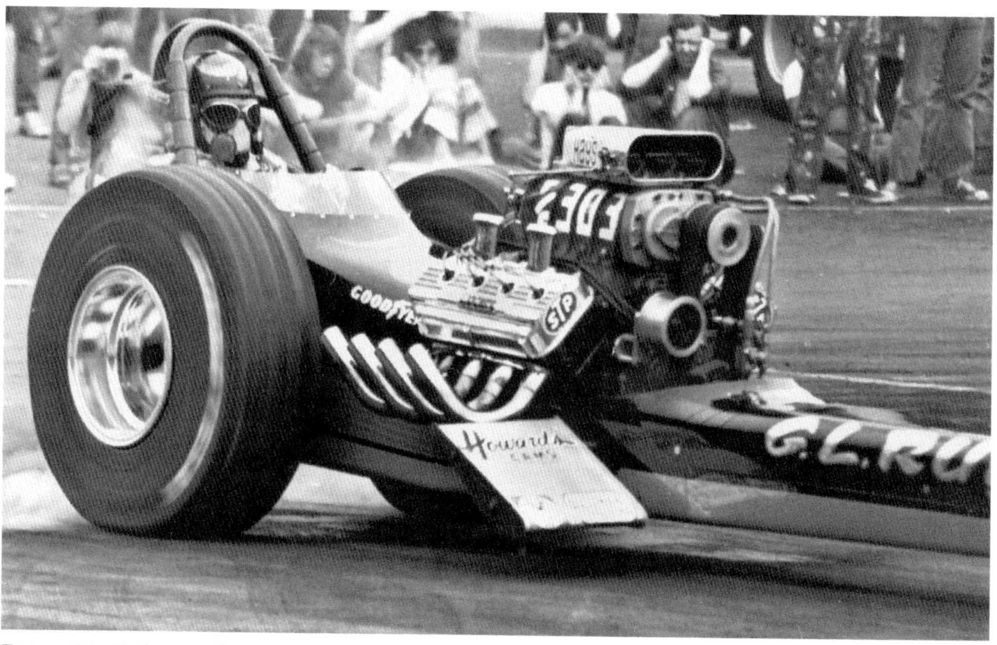

Driver Pat Dakin and partner G. L. Rupp finished runners-up to Don Garlits at the 1972 Spring Nationals and won that year's All-American Nationals. By beating Marvin Graham in the finals, the Ohio team became the last front-engine dragster to win Top Fuel at Bristol. Dakin later finished runner-up at the 1989 Spring Nationals. (Photograph by John Beach.)

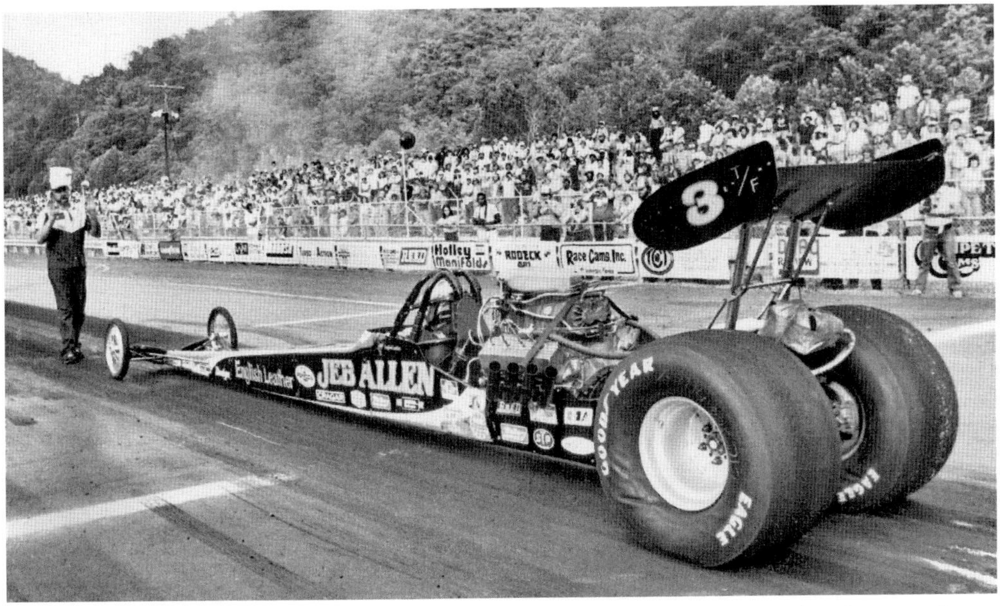

Crew chief Lance Larsen (left) guides driver Jeb Allen back into his tire tracks after completing the burnout. Allen won the 1980 IHRA Top Fuel world championship and the 1981 NHRA title. He scored two career wins in four final-round showings at Bristol. He defeated Richard Tharp in the 1981 Spring Nationals final, avenging a 1980 Bristol loss to the Candies and Hughes–owned team. (Photograph by David McGee.)

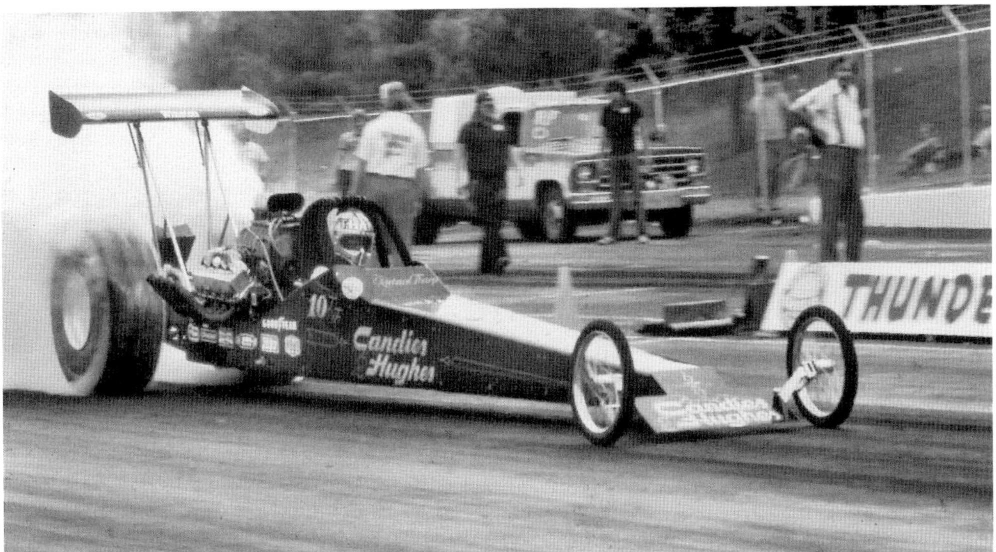

Richard Tharp drove the Paul Candies and Leonard Hughes–owned Top Fuel dragster to three straight Bristol finals in 1980 and 1981. The car broke in the 1980 Spring Nationals final, but the team rebounded three months later to win the Summer Nationals. The enigmatic Tharp, who lived by the motto, "A saint I ain't, a star I are," reached five Bristol final rounds. (Photograph by David McGee.)

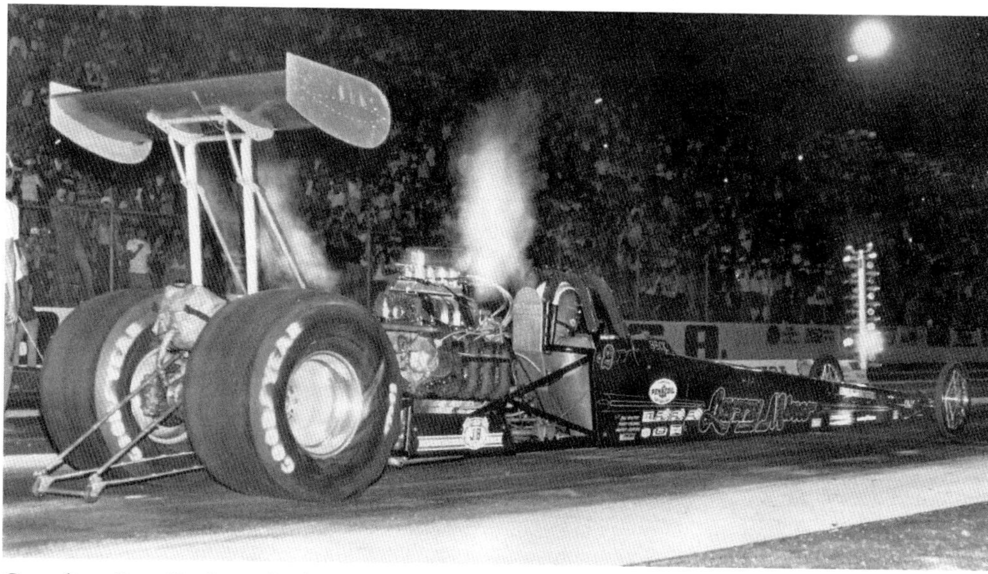

Canadian Gary Beck reached Bristol final rounds in three straight years and won the 1981 and 1983 Spring Nationals aboard Larry Minor's car. The team later won the 1983 NHRA world championship. He finished runner-up to Don Garlits in his first Bristol appearance at the 1975 Spring Nationals. (Photograph by David McGee.)

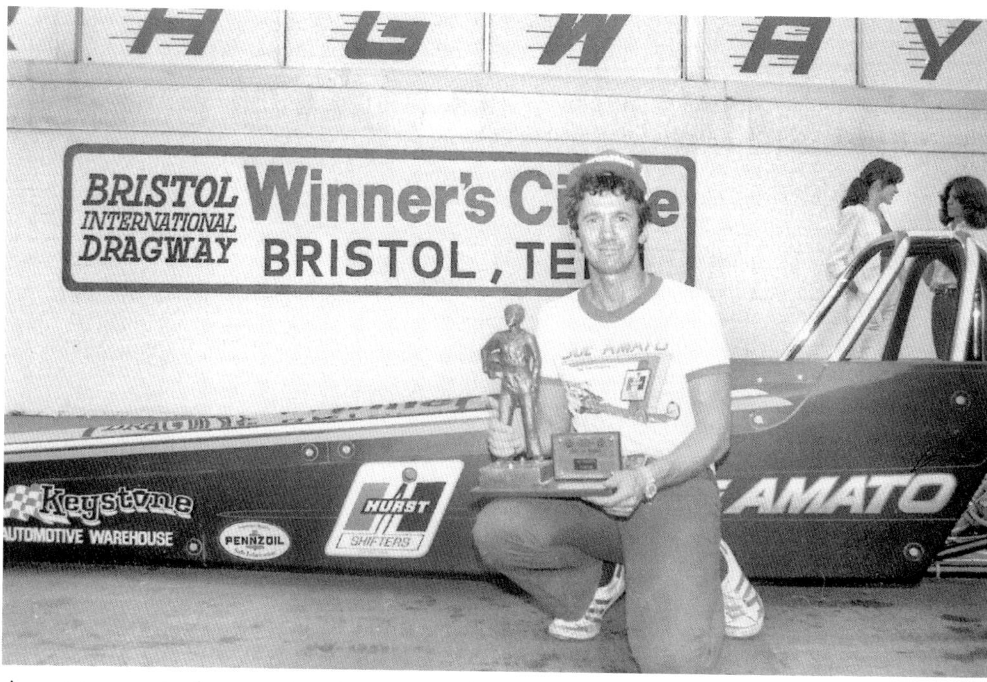

As a rising star in the sport, Joe Amato won the 1983 Fall Nationals, the last time Top Fuel cars would run at Bristol under IHRA auspices until 1987. Amato won his second NHRA championship in 1988, the same year he captured Bristol's Spring Nationals. That race featured what many consider to be the best IHRA Top Fuel field ever assembled. (Photograph by David McGee.)

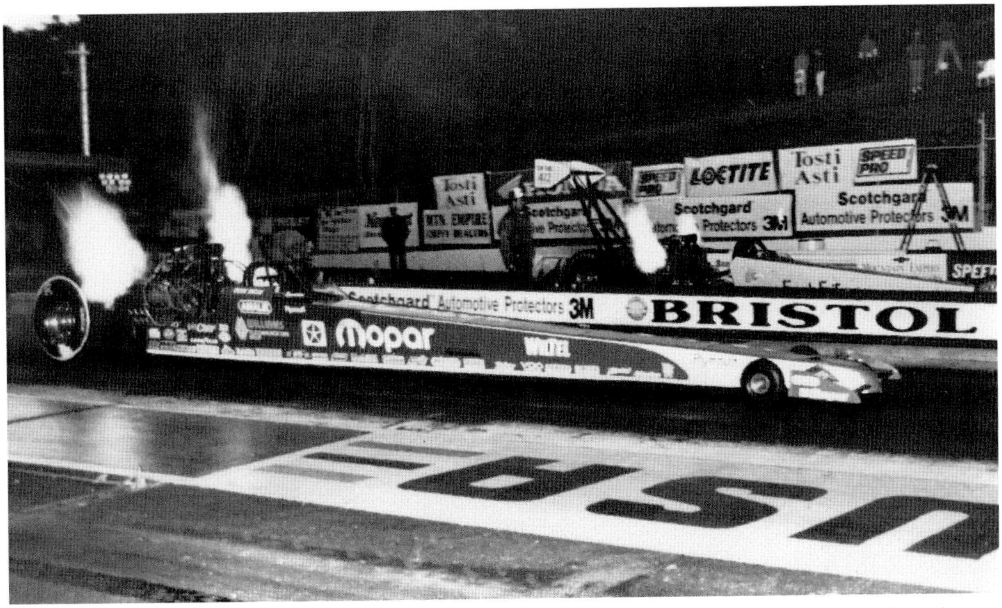

Gene Snow (near lane) launches his Mopar Top Fuel dragster off the Bristol starting line during the 1991 Spring Nationals. The legendary Texas racer earned one of his three Bristol Top Fuel wins that season to go along with two in Funny Car. Snow won world championships in three sanctioning bodies. (Photograph by David McGee.)

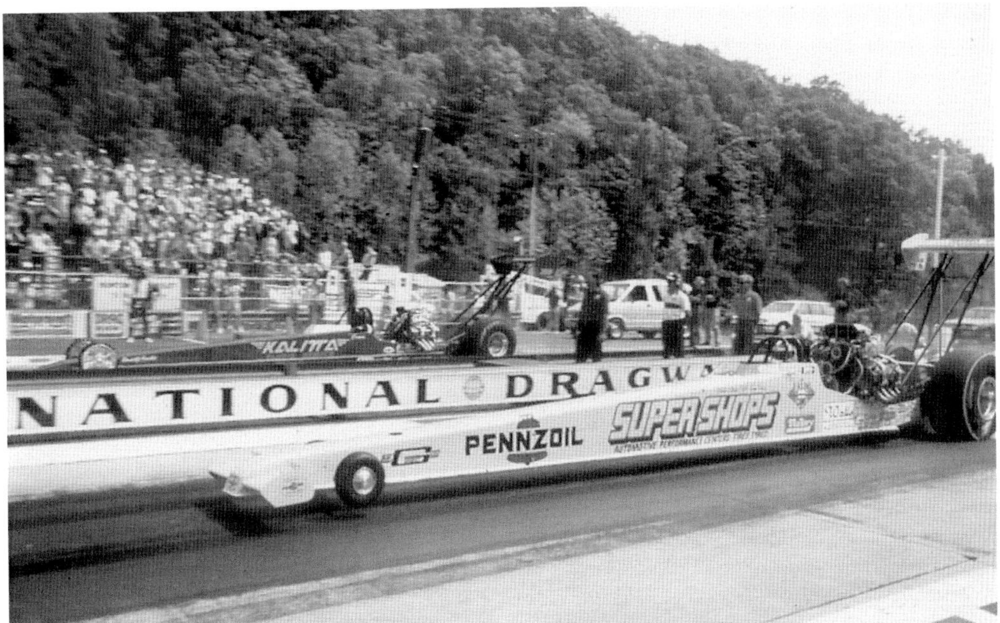

Eddie Hill (near lane) had a perfect race at the 1988 Fall Nationals. The Texas speedster qualified first in the Top Fuel field, defeated Gene Snow in the final round, and established the track elapsed time record of 5.110 seconds. It was part of a memorable season for Hill, who became the first Top Fuel driver to run in the 4-second range. (Photograph by David McGee.)

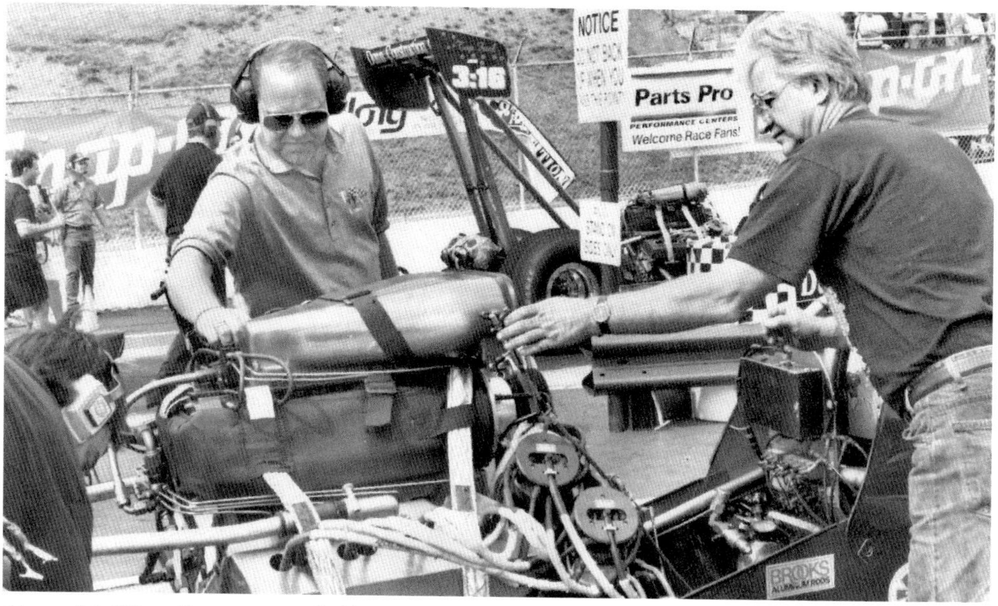

Crew chief Ron Swearingen (left) makes a last-second adjustment as car owner Frank Faifer looks on. The team and driver Richard Langson won the 1993 Fall Nationals and IHRA world championship in the same final-round race. The St. Louis–based team returned the following year and won the Spring Nationals with driver Jim Bailey. (Photograph by David McGee.)

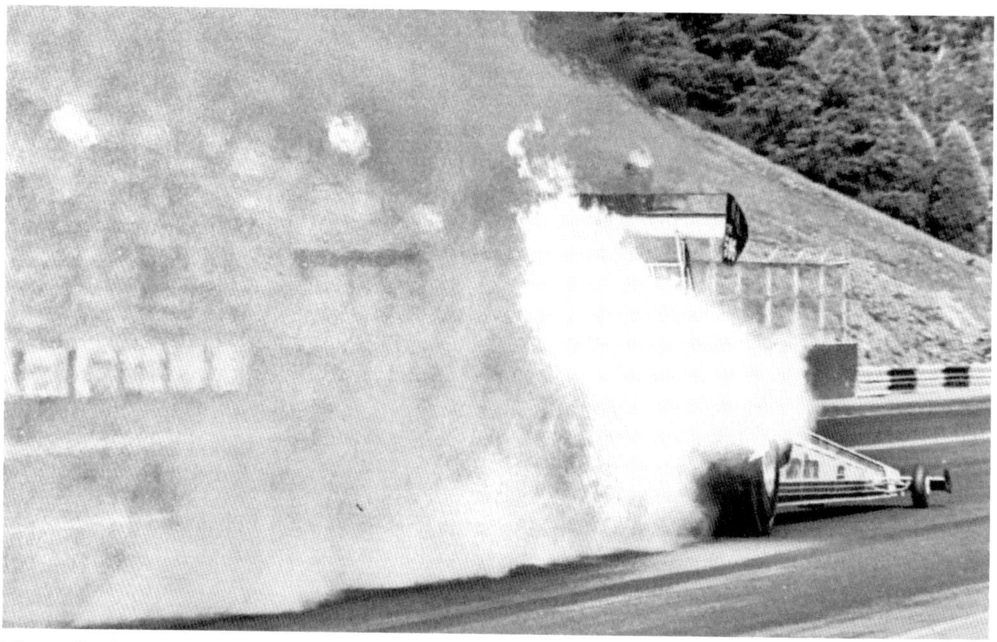

The volatile nitromethane and methanol fuel mixture burned by Top Fuel dragsters and Funny Cars can often have disastrous results. Here Kansas racer Randy Meyer suffers an engine explosion and resulting fireball. Despite significant damage, professional teams typically replace or repair complete engines in less than 90 minutes. (Photograph by David McGee.)

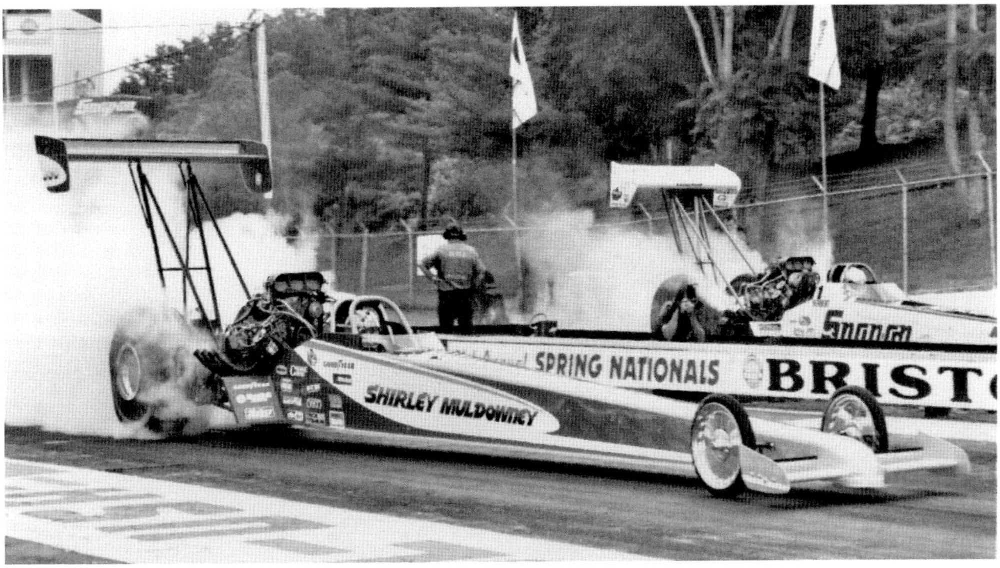

Three-time world champion Shirley Muldowney (near lane) burns out alongside Doug Herbert prior to the 1995 Spring Nationals final. Rain began failing as the pair was preparing to race, so officials moved the contest to Monday afternoon. Both machines struggled to maintain traction before Herbert got the lucky win. Herbert also beat Muldowney in the 1996 Fall Nationals final round. (Photograph by David McGee.)

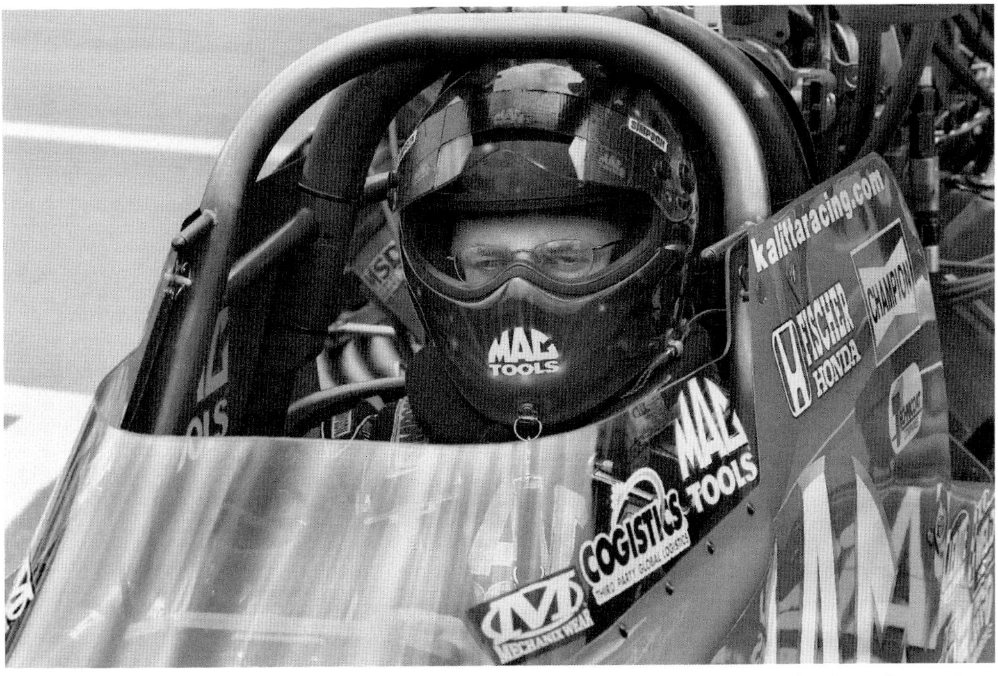

Doug Kalitta has continued to etch his family's name into the Bristol record books. The nephew of racing pioneer Connie Kalitta, Doug won Top Fuel at the 2001, 2005, and 2006 Thunder Valley Nationals in the Mac Tools dragster. (Photograph by David McGee.)

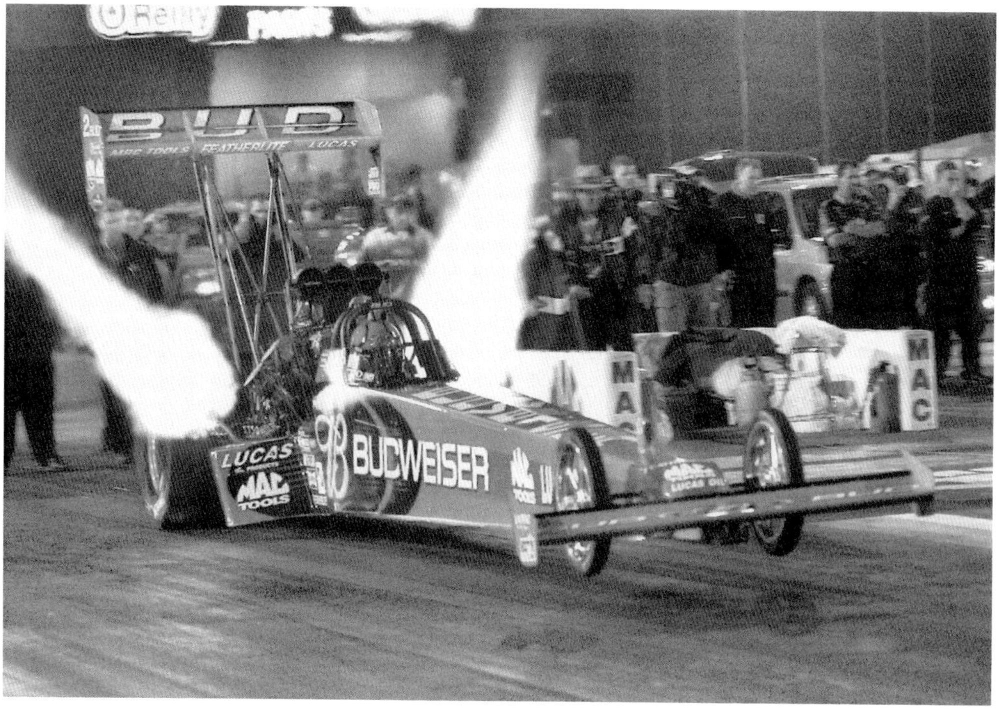

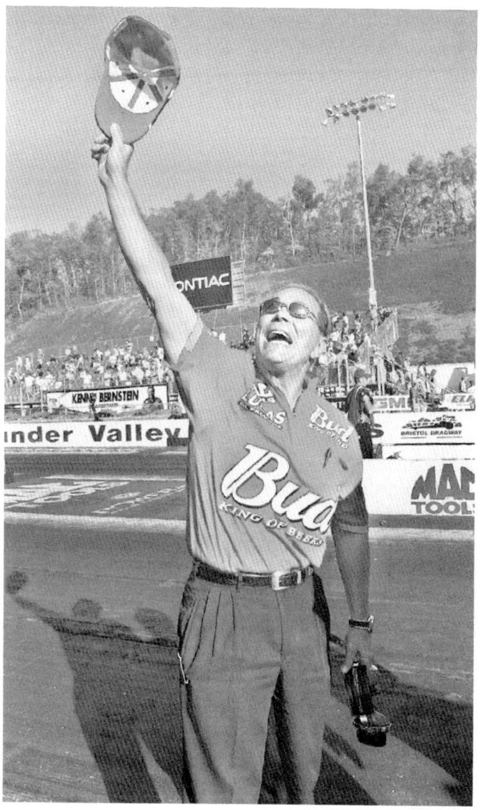

Brandon Bernstein (above) swept Top Fuel in his first visit to Bristol, beating Doug Herbert in the 2003 Mac Tools Thunder Valley Nationals finals. The win was the third in a rookie season cut short by a serious back injury suffered in a racing crash in New Jersey. His famous father, Kenny (left), celebrates after Brandon turns on the win light. Multi-time world champion Kenny Bernstein was winless at Bristol in five final-round appearances. (Photographs by David McGee.)

3

Funny Cars

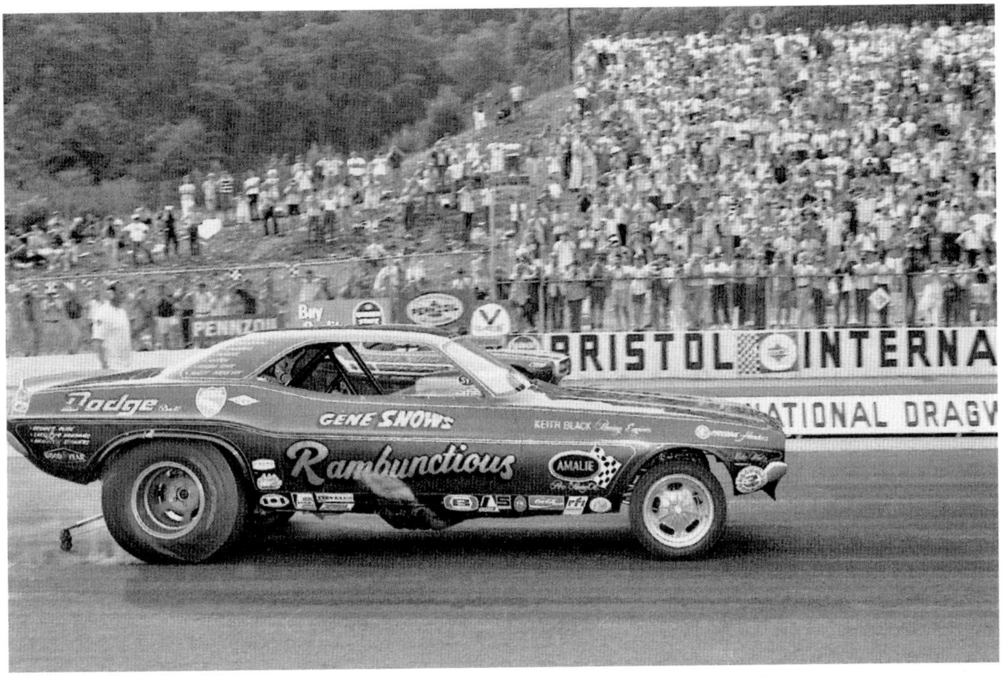

Call them floppers, plastic fantastics, or fuel coupes, Funny Cars have been drag racing's wild child division since the late 1960s. The class evolved from match-race super stockers, featuring tubular chassis and supercharged and injected nitromethane-burning engines beneath flip-top bodies that resemble popular street cars. Texan Gene Snow became the first Funny Car driver to win both Bristol races in a single season, wheeling his "Rambunctious" Dodge Challenger to the 1970 AHRA Spring Nationals and AHRA All-American titles. Those wins helped Snow capture the AHRA series championship in addition to winning the NHRA title. Early Funny Cars ran in the seven-second range at 180 to 190 miles per hour, but modern fuel floppers nearly match their Top Fuel brothers with performances in the 4.6-second range at 320 miles per hour. (Photograph by John Beach.)

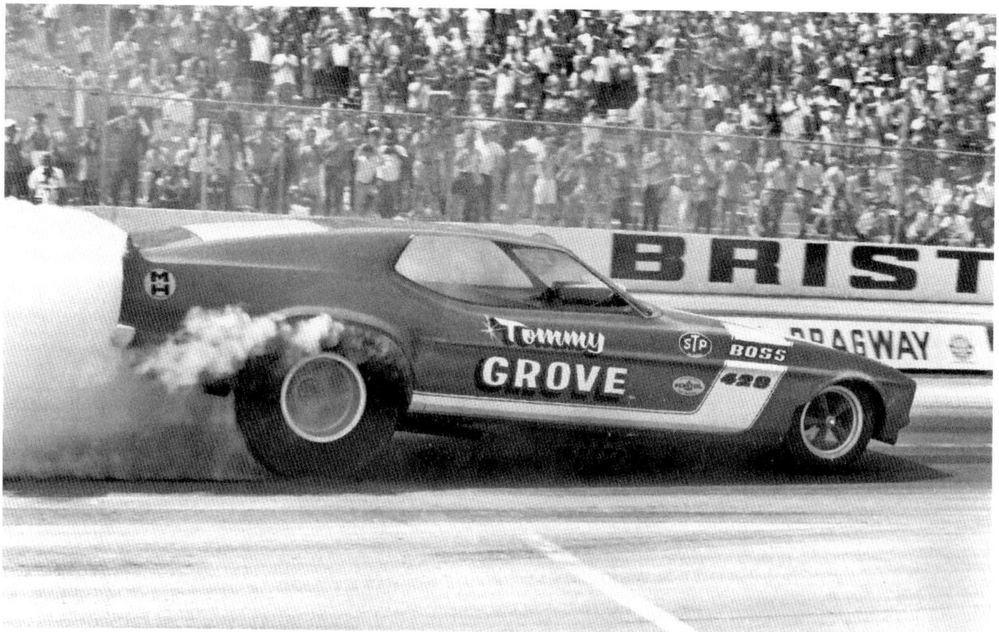

Bristol winner Tommy Grove remained loyal to Ford when he raced this Ford-powered Mustang Funny Car in 1971. Grove won NHRA's first-ever Funny Car title in 1967 in a seemingly outdated "Ford Charger" Mustang. It was the same car Grove used to win the Spring Nationals Competition Eliminator title in 1966. (Photograph by John Beach.)

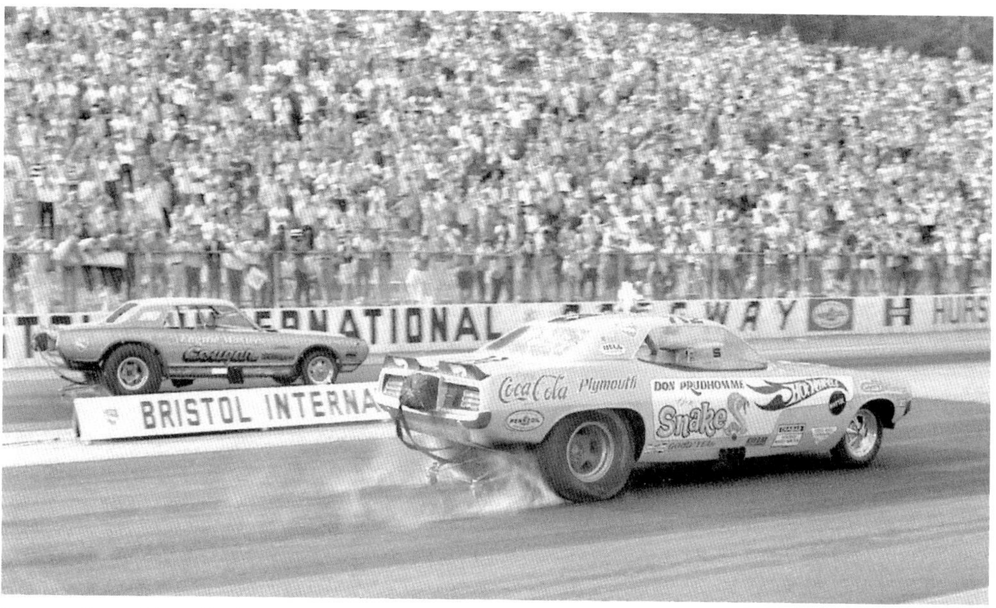

Former Bristol Top Fuel champion Don Prudhomme made the jump to Funny Car in 1970 with his "Hot Wheels" Plymouth Barracuda. The California native reached the finals of Bristol's last AHRA race, the 1970 All-American world championships. Here Prudhomme races against Kenny Bernstein in Ray Alley's Engine Masters Cougar. (Photograph by John Beach.)

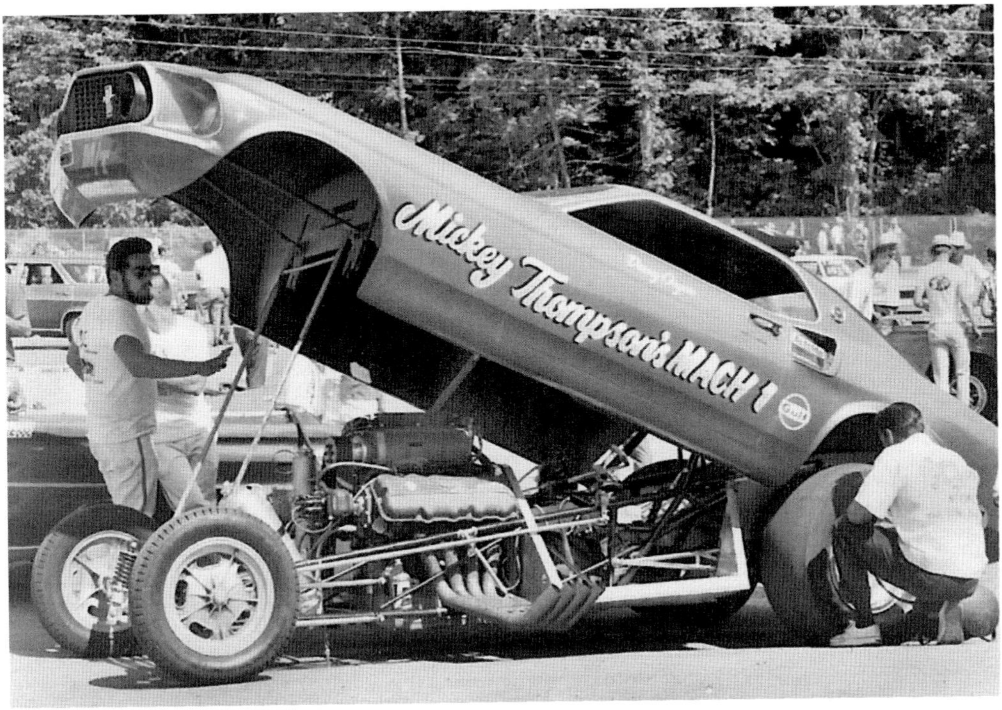

The crew of Mickey Thompson's feared "blue" Ford-powered Mustang Mach 1 makes final preparations while waiting in the Bristol staging lanes. Danny Ongais drove the car, which featured the first dragster-style chassis in the class, to the 1969 AHRA Spring Nationals title. Note how stock the body of the 7-second, 190-mile-per-hour machine appears with its door handle, badges, and grill. (Courtesy of the author's collection.)

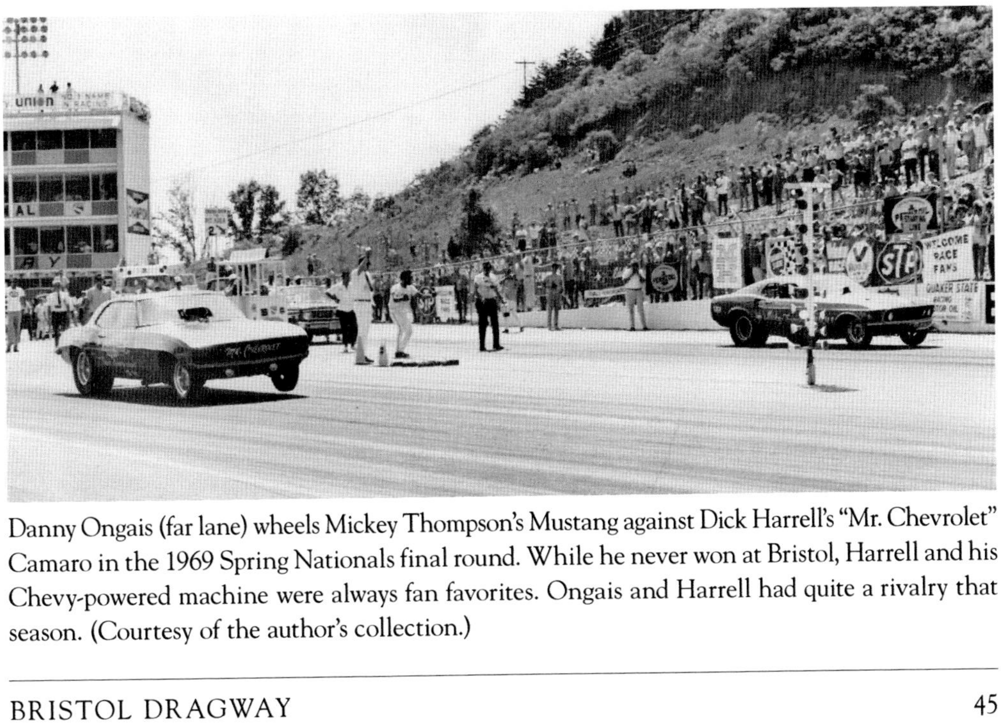

Danny Ongais (far lane) wheels Mickey Thompson's Mustang against Dick Harrell's "Mr. Chevrolet" Camaro in the 1969 Spring Nationals final round. While he never won at Bristol, Harrell and his Chevy-powered machine were always fan favorites. Ongais and Harrell had quite a rivalry that season. (Courtesy of the author's collection.)

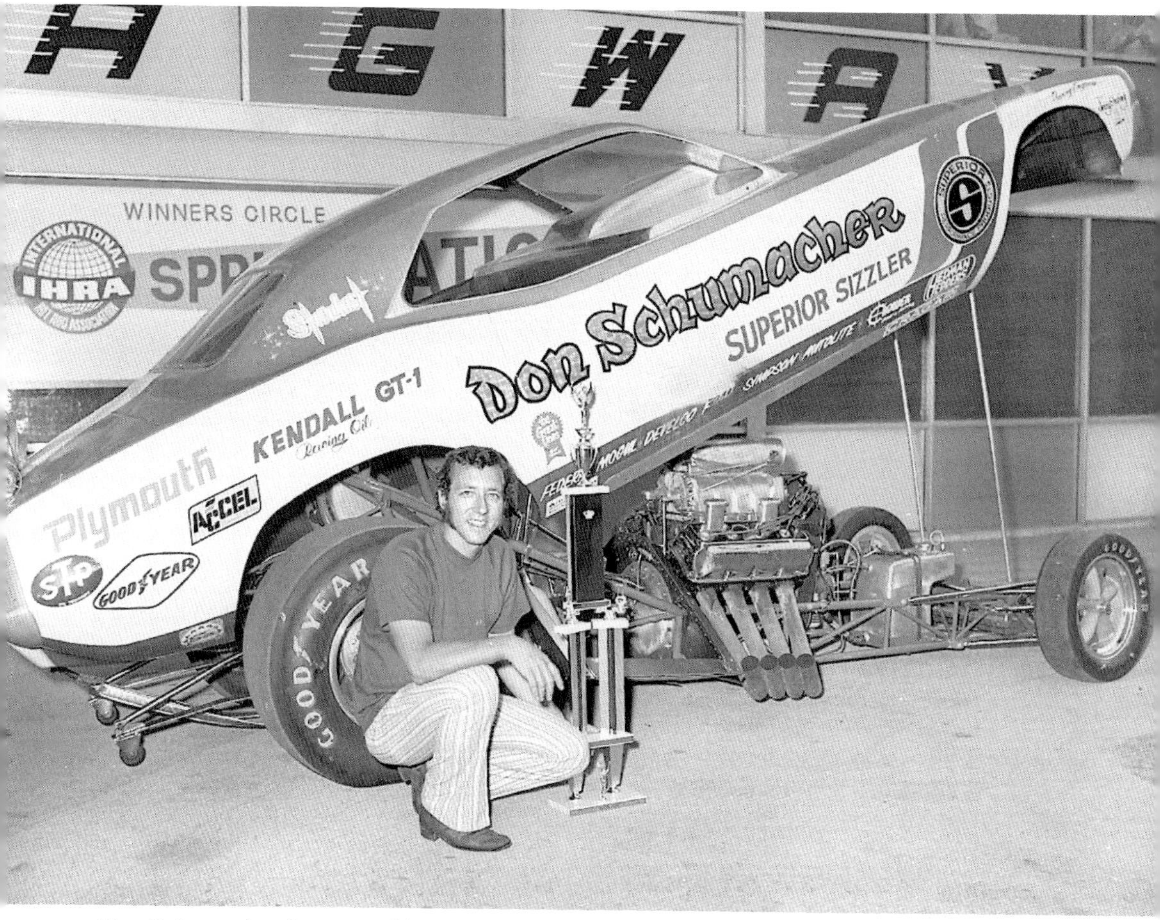

Don Schumacher first carved his name into the Bristol record books by winning the 1971 Spring Nationals in the track's first IHRA race. The Illinois native and his Plymouth Barracuda–bodied machines also swept both Bristol races in 1972. More than 30 years later, Schumacher's son, Tony, captured the Top Fuel title at the 2004 O'Reilly Thunder Valley Nationals. (Photograph by John Beach.)

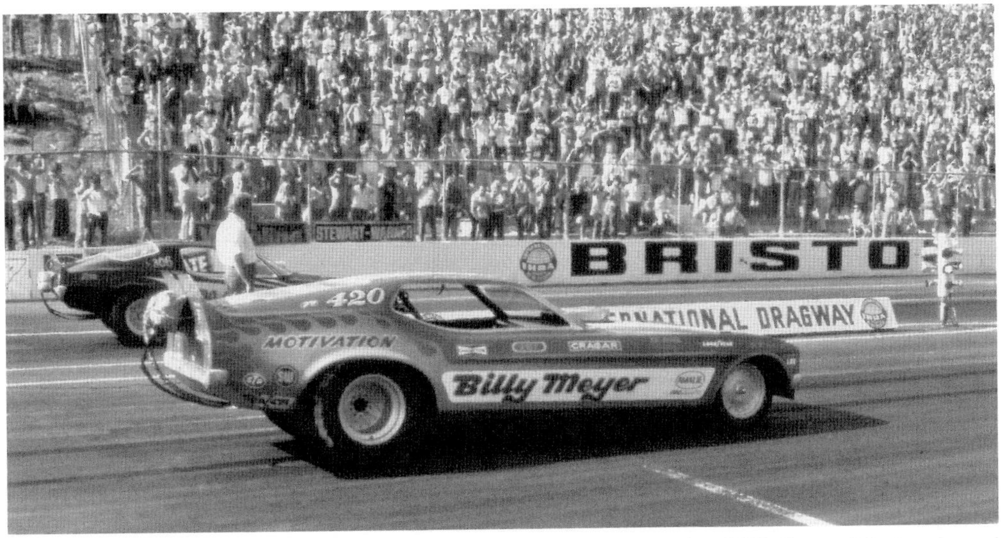

Texas teenager Billy Meyer made his first Bristol appearance at the 1972 Spring Nationals and went on to become a four-time Spring Nationals champion. Meyer won the 1974 Spring Nationals at age 18, making him the youngest professional winner in drag racing history. He later bought IHRA from Larry Carrier in late 1987 and temporarily moved the group's operations to Texas. (Photograph by John Beach.)

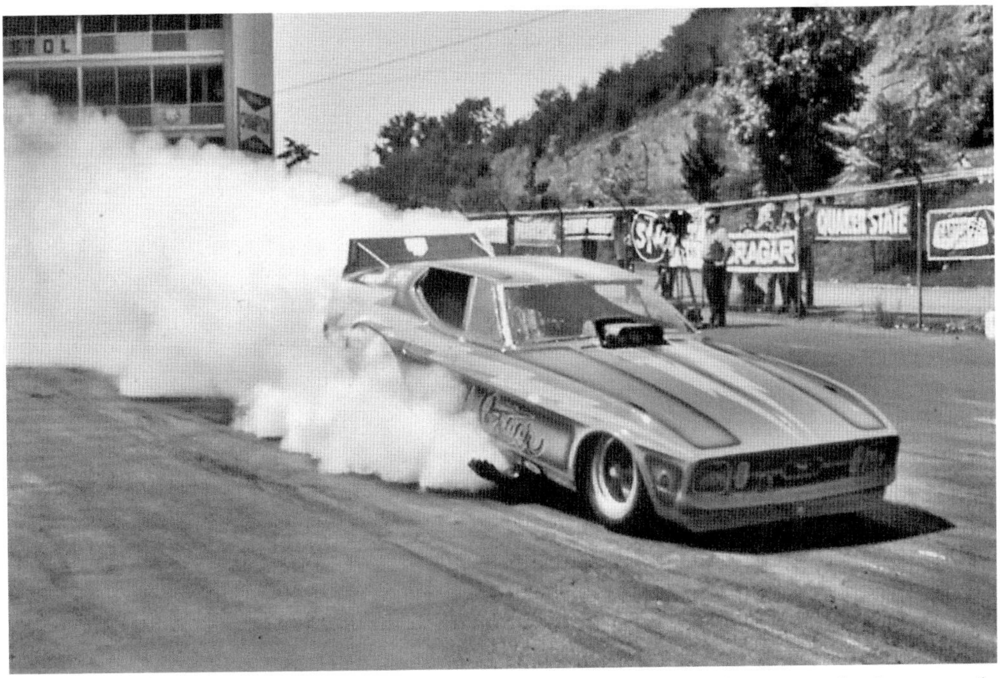

Shirl Greer, 1974 NHRA world champion, enjoyed some success while racing at his home track. Greer, from nearby Kingsport, Tennessee, competed at Bristol's first race in 1965 and won the 1974 and 1975 All-American Nationals. Here he performs a pre-race burnout with his "Chain Lightning" Mustang. (Photograph by John Beach.)

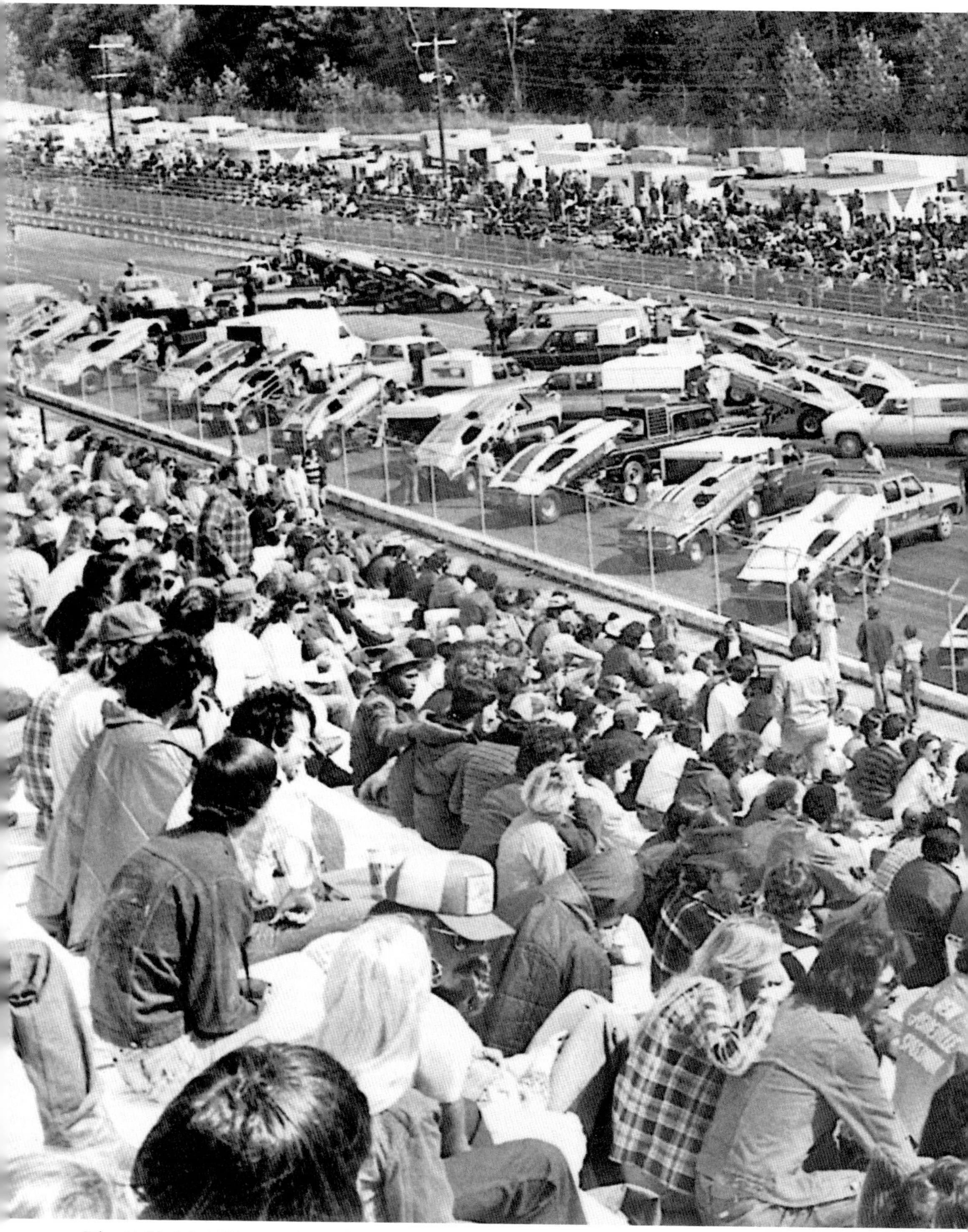

The 1977 IHRA Funny Car and Sports Nationals was the scene of the track's only "California fire up." All 32 Funny Cars on the Bristol Dragway property, including 16 nitro cars, were pulled onto

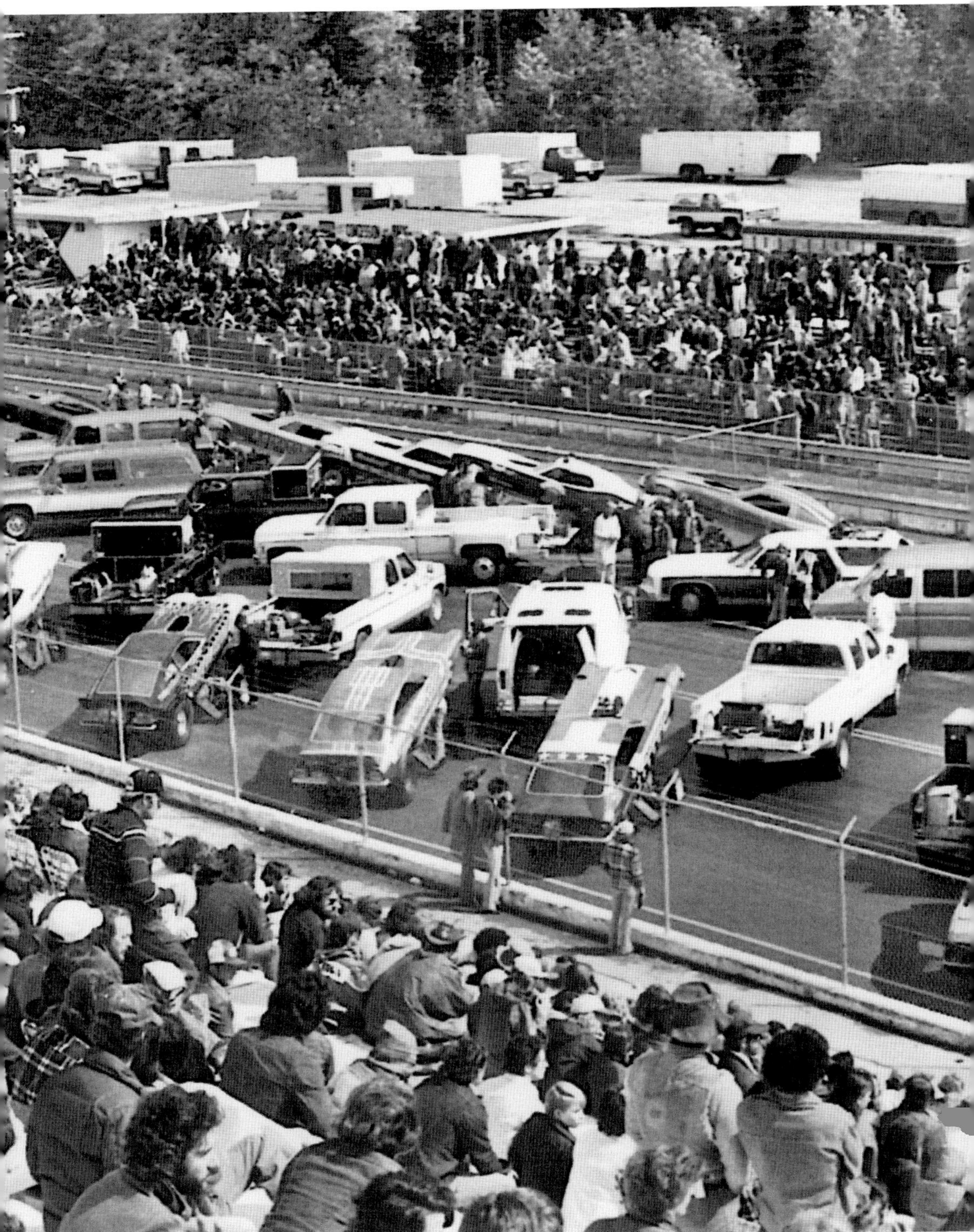

the track and started simultaneously. (Courtesy of BMS archives; photograph by Dave Bishop.)

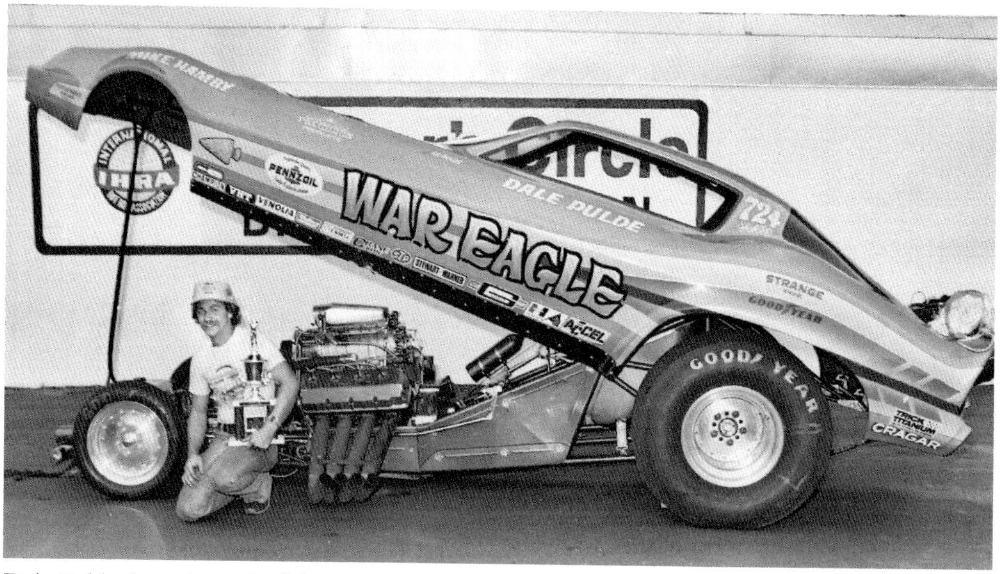

Dale Pulde drove his colorful "War Eagle" Pontiac to the 1977 Spring Nationals title. The win was the team's third of the 1977 IHRA season and helped pave the way toward their first of three championships. Pulde and partner Mike Hamby captured four more Bristol wins over the following nine seasons. (Photograph by John Beach.)

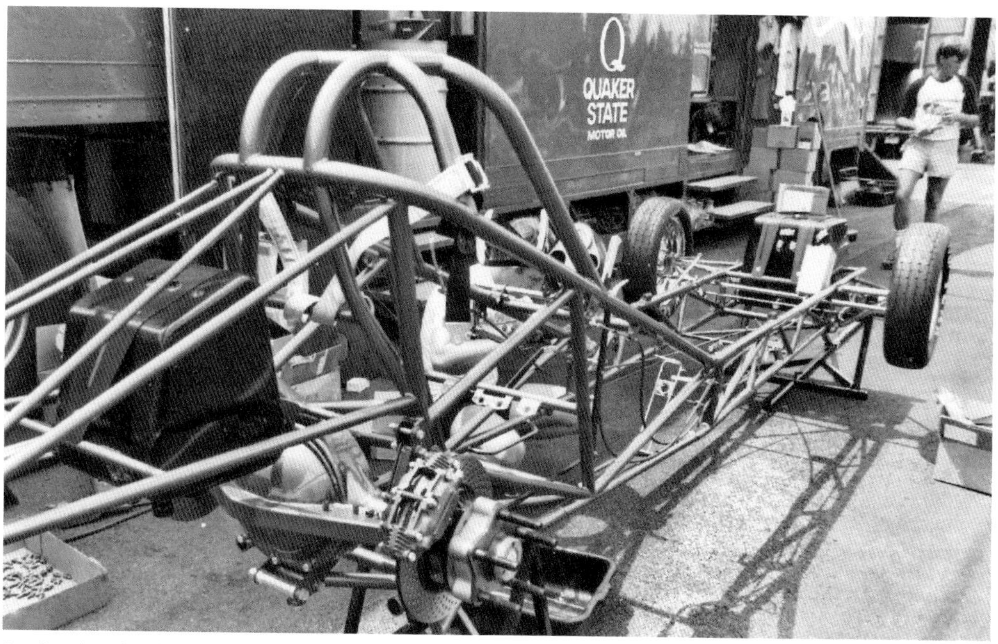

In the days leading up to the 1985 Spring Nationals, the Pulde and Hamby team assembled their new Buick Funny Car in the Bristol pits. While it first resembled a giant model car kit, the team qualified atop the track's first all-five-second Funny Car field and then won the event on Sunday. They returned in September to sweep the Fall Nationals and their third IHRA title. (Photograph by David McGee.)

Raymond Beadle and the legendary "Blue Max" Funny Car were always fan favorites at Bristol. The Texas native, sitting here in the machine's cockpit (right), scored Bristol wins in the 1981 Summer and 1982 Spring Nationals. His Plymouth-bodied entry (pictured below) carried the number 1, representative of winning the NHRA Funny Car championship. Beadle also recorded the track's first 5-second Funny Car run, a 5.98, at the 1981 Spring Nationals. (Photographs by David McGee.)

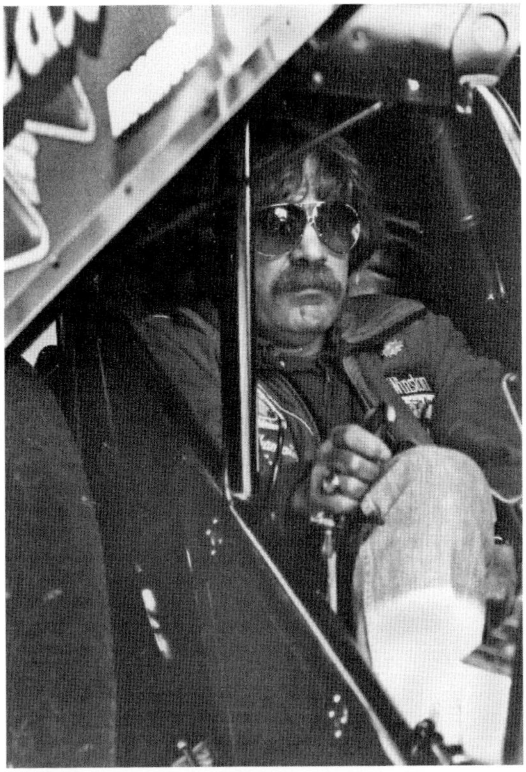

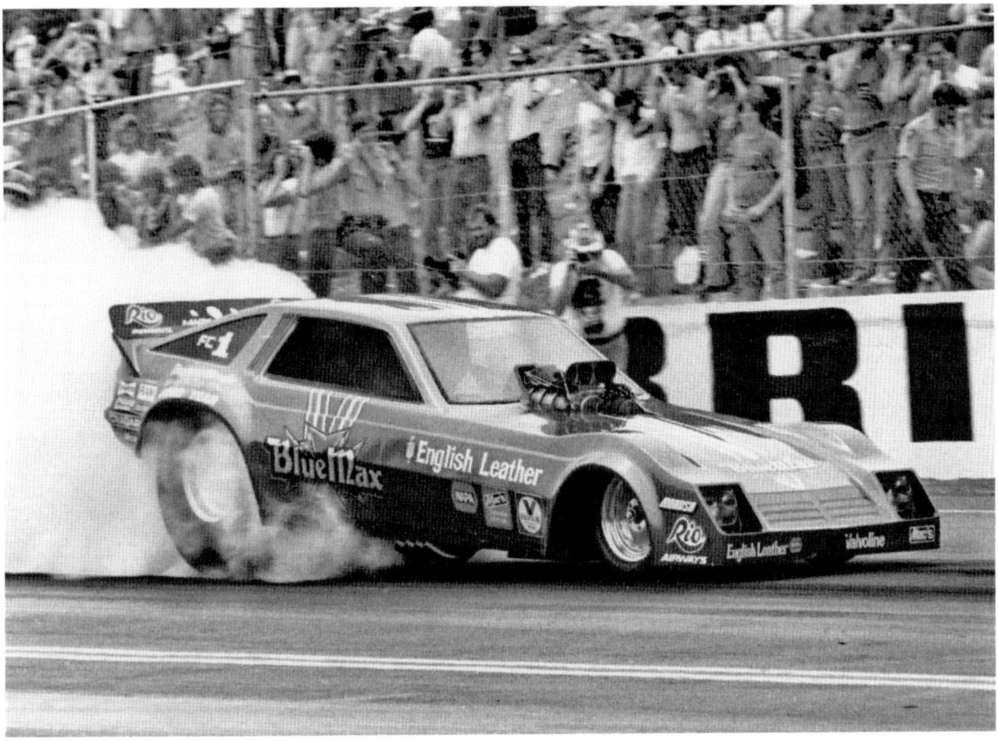

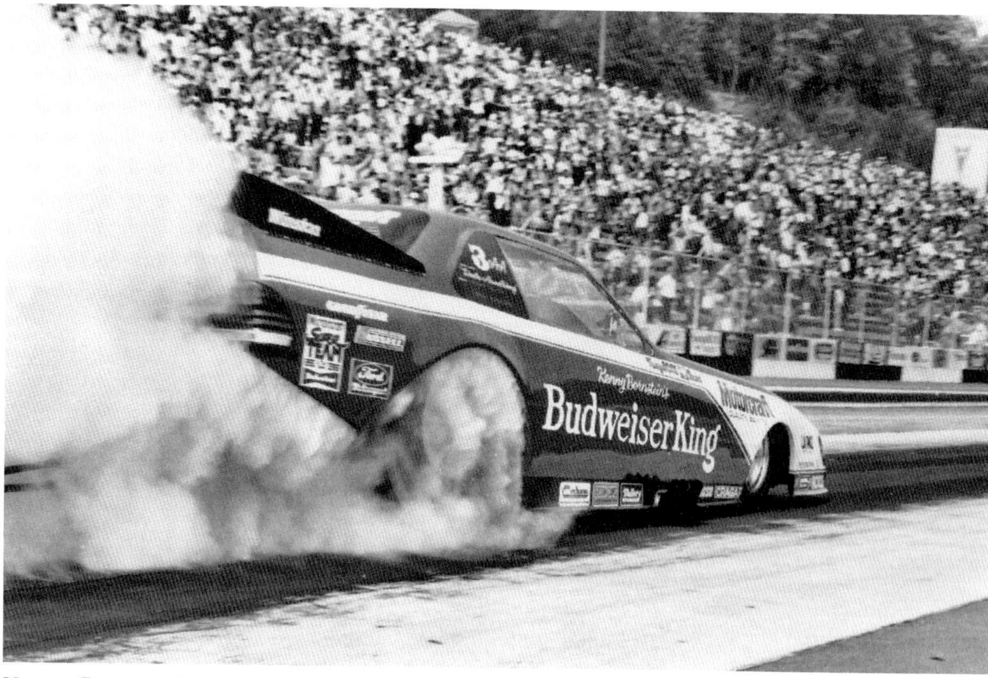

Kenny Bernstein's string of Budweiser King racers was consistently among the quickest and fastest at Bristol. Despite five final-round appearances, the six-time world champion failed to win at Thunder Valley between 1970 and his retirement in 2003. In the top photograph, Bernstein performs a burnout in his 1986 Ford-bodied entry. The overwhelming favorite broke the engine in that year's finals against underdog Tim Grose. In the bottom photograph, Bernstein burns out in his 1983 Mercury LN-7. (Photographs by David McGee.)

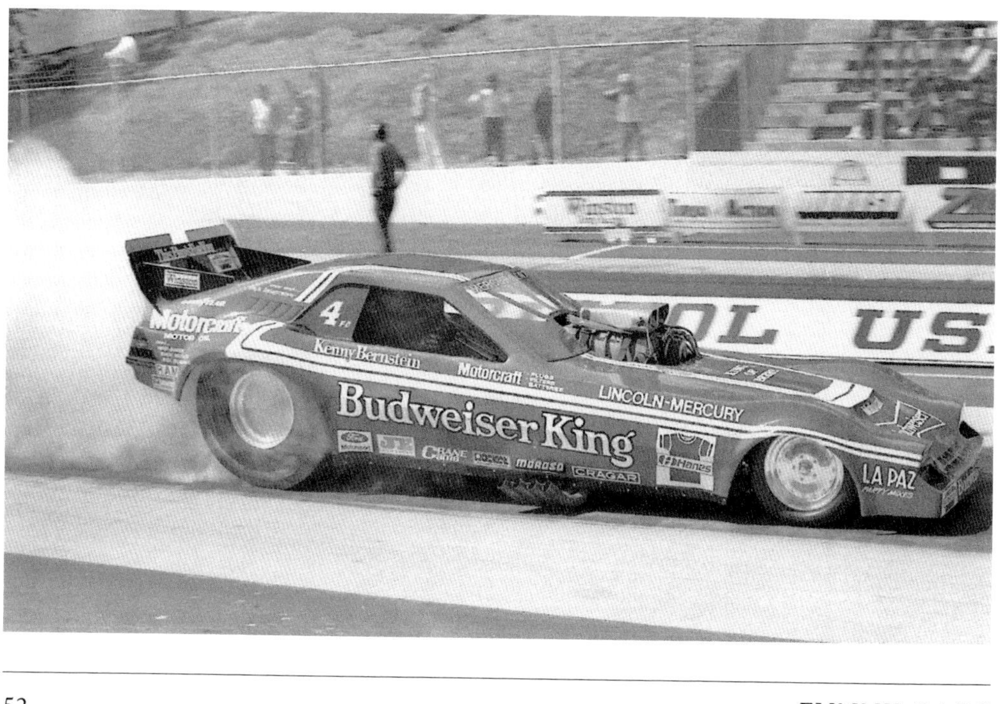

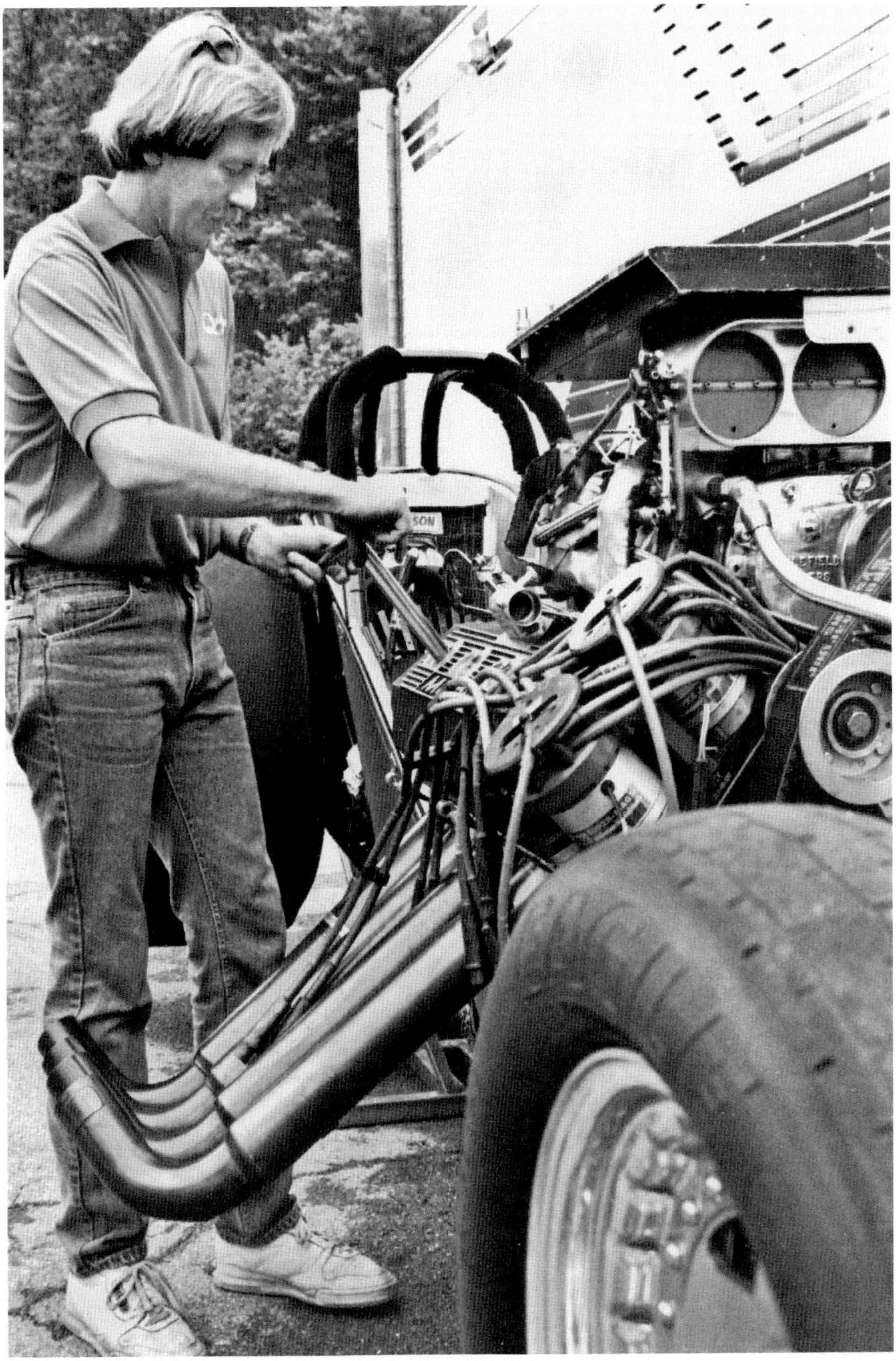

Independent Funny Car driver Tim Grose changes the 16 spark plugs on his engine. While sponsored teams usually have a half-dozen or more crewmembers, Grose and his wife Barbara typically performed all the maintenance on their car. His biggest win came at the 1986 Bristol Spring Nationals, when he beat four heavily-sponsored teams and collected a $30,000 payday. (Photograph by David McGee.)

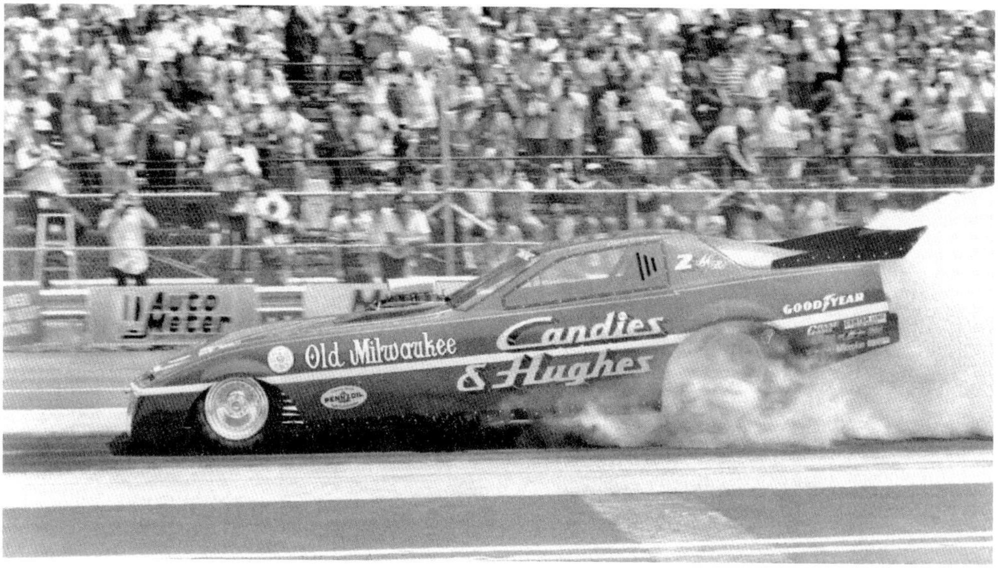

Mark Oswald wheeled the Candies and Hughes Pontiac to a sweep of both 1983 Bristol races and the 1984 Fall Nationals. The Louisiana-based team came within one round of also winning the 1984 Spring Nationals but lost in the finals to Billy Meyer. Oswald, who began his career in Top Fuel, also captured the 1988 Spring Nationals. (Photograph by David McGee.)

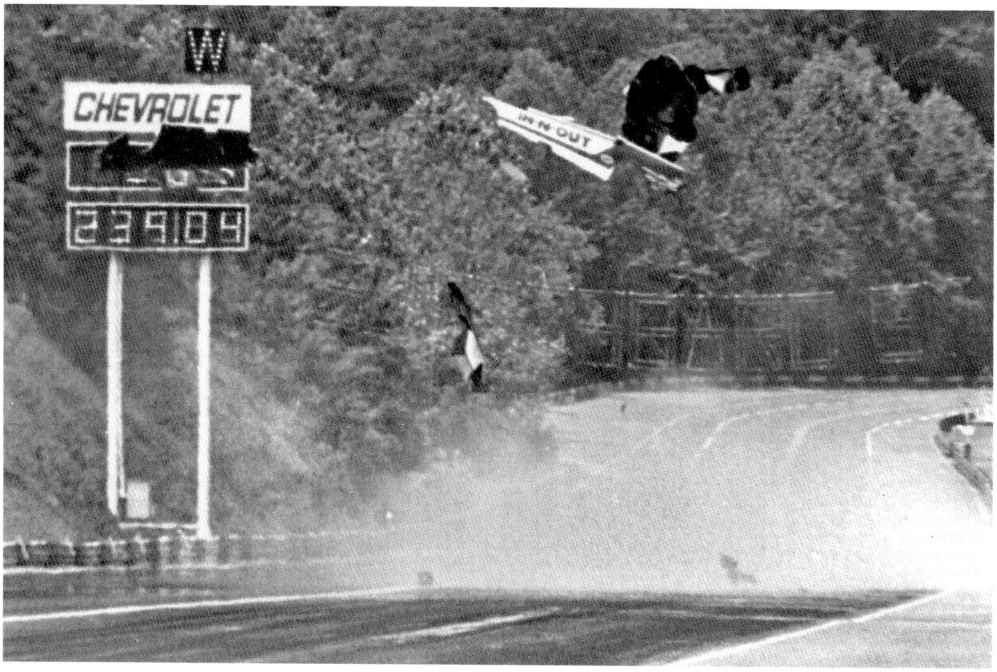

Bristol also provided some of the scariest highlights of Mark Oswald's career. Here a supercharger explosion sends the fiberglass body of his In-n-Out Burger machine some 30 feet into the air during a 1992 Fall Nationals qualifying run. The damage was so extensive, the team had to withdraw from the event. (Photograph by David McGee.)

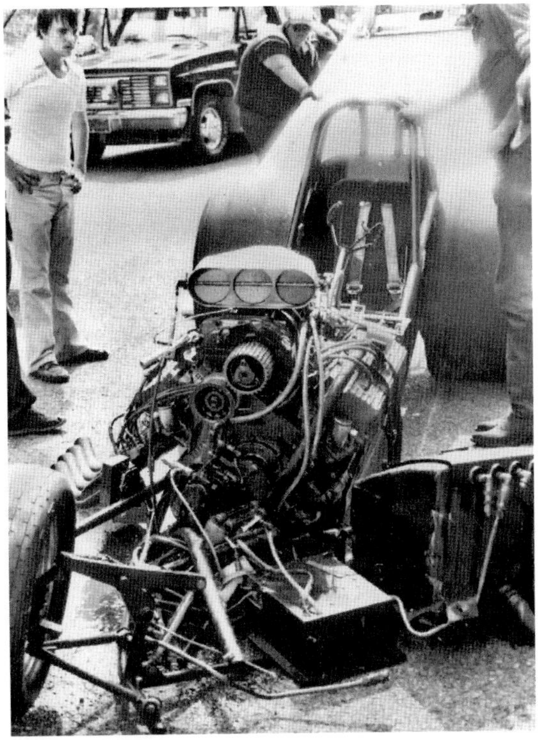

The battle for the 1985 IHRA world championship grew more intense when Mark Oswald suffered a Fall Nationals engine explosion and fire that sent the Candies and Hughes Pontiac crashing into the guardrail in the Bristol shutdown area. Besides ripping up the body, the chassis was also heavily damaged. Oswald (below) wipes his face after climbing from the damaged machine. The team made the final two races of the year to finish third in the championship. (Photographs by David McGee.)

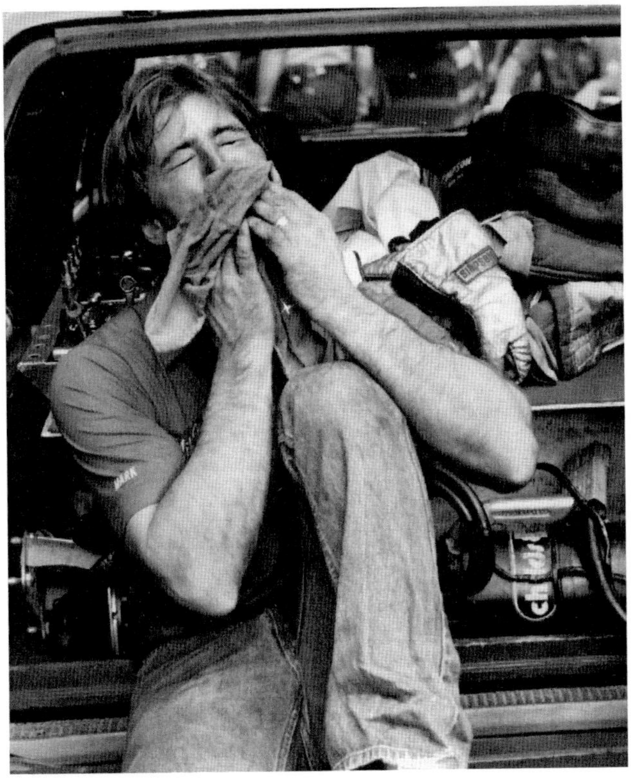

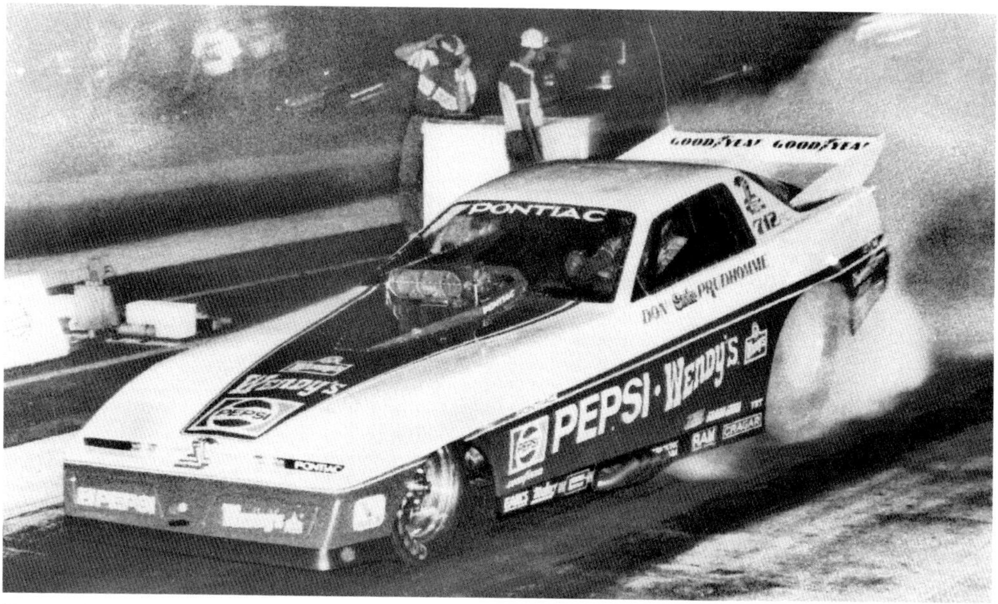

Don "The Snake" Prudhomme returned to Bristol in 1985 and recorded the sport's fastest speed, 266.27 miles per hour, during Funny Car qualifying. He made four runs above 260 miles per hour but lost the Spring Nationals to Dale Pulde when an inexpensive engine part broke on the final run. (Photograph by David McGee.)

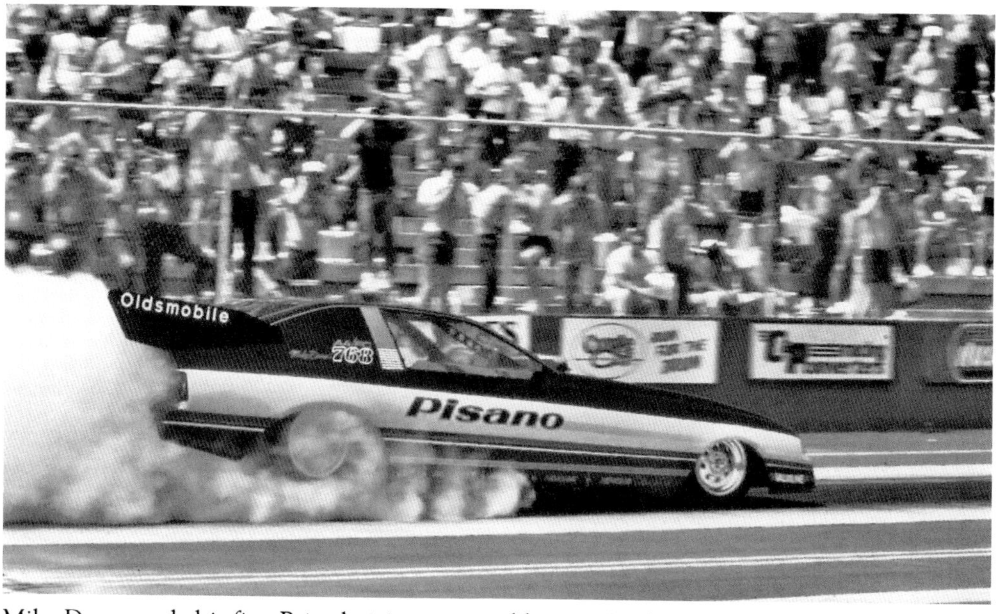

Mike Dunn made his first Bristol visit a memorable one. At the 1987 Spring Nationals, Dunn and car owner Joe Pisano set a national speed record of 270.27 miles per hour and defeated Mark Oswald to claim the final-round victory. After a successful career driving Top Fuel dragsters and Funny Cars, Dunn became a television analyst on NHRA's shows on ESPN. (Photograph by David McGee.)

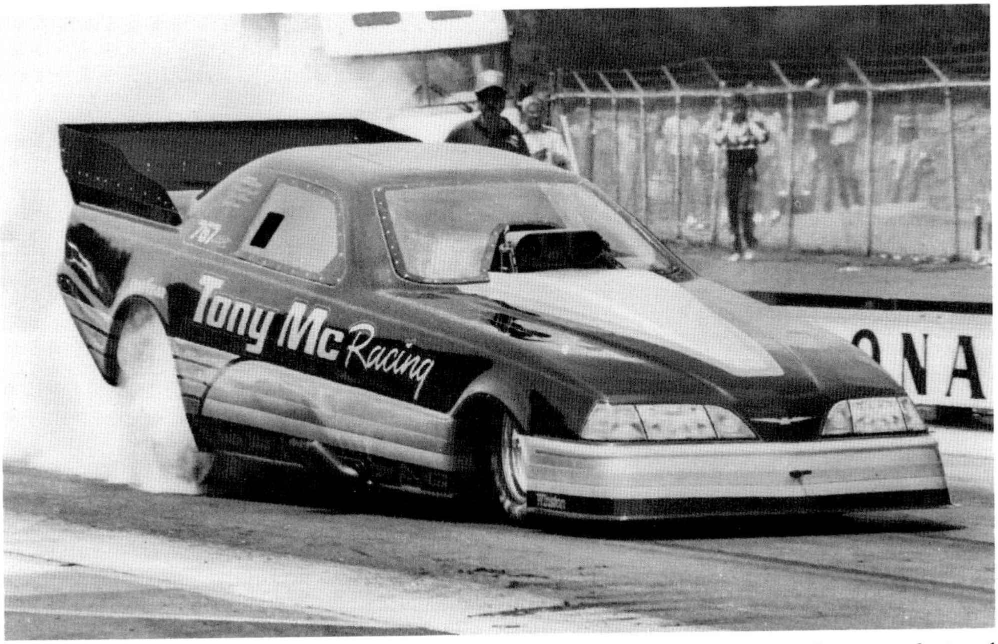

Unheralded rookie driver Tony McCallum became the first African American to claim a professional drag-racing title, winning Bristol's 1989 25th-anniversary Spring Nationals. McCallum's unsponsored Thunderbird made a final-round single when opponent Scott Kalitta was unable to repair the engine in his machine. In the lower photograph, McCallum talks with veteran driver Jim White prior to their first-round pairing. McCallum upset White and Roland Leong's "Hawaiian Punch" Dodge. (Photographs by David McGee.)

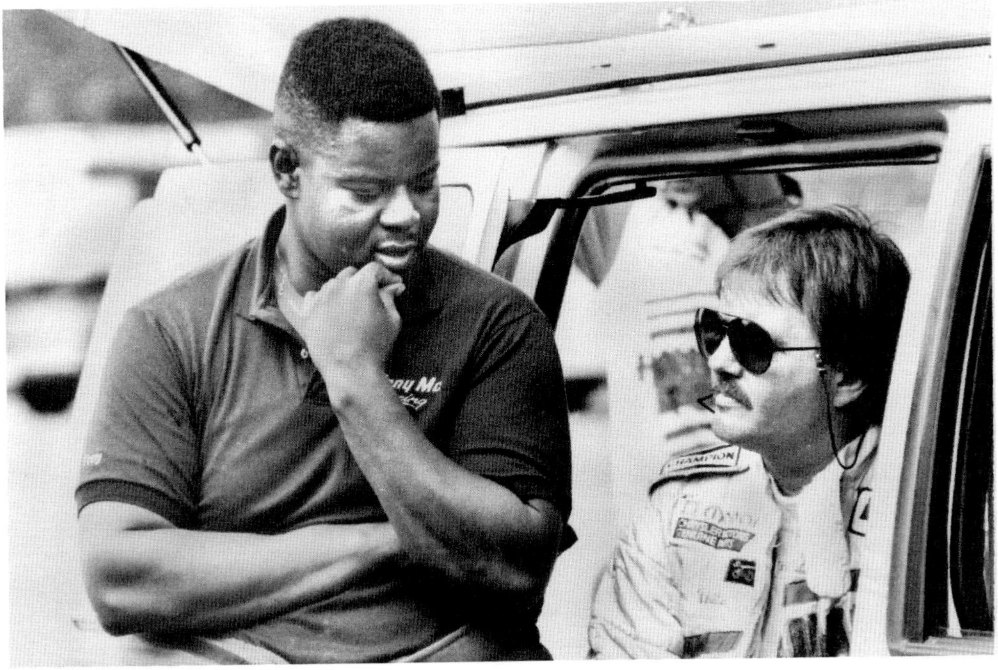

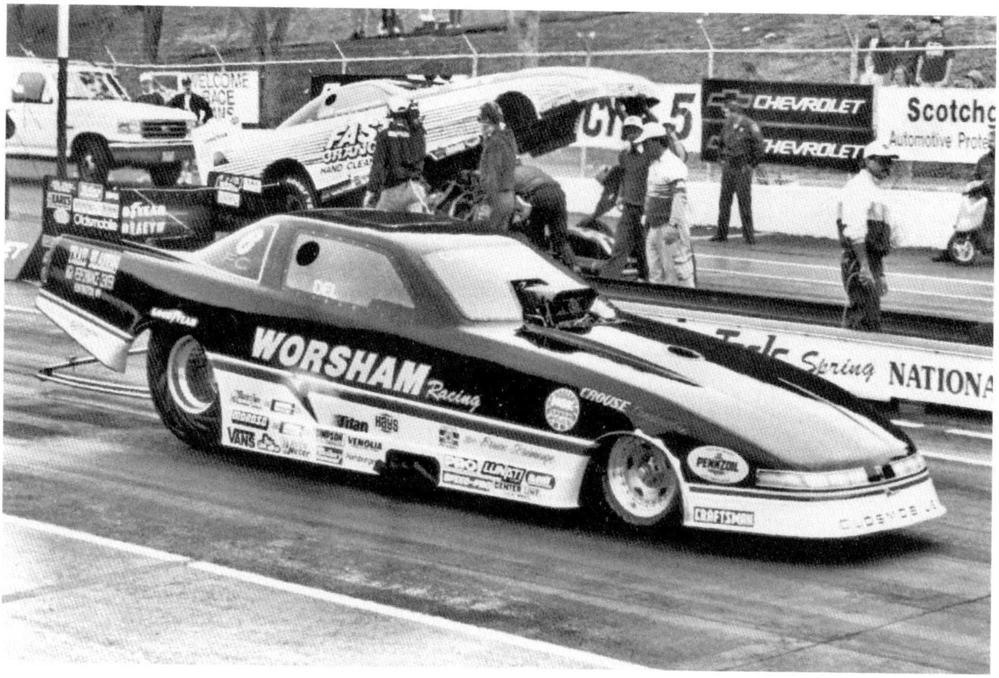

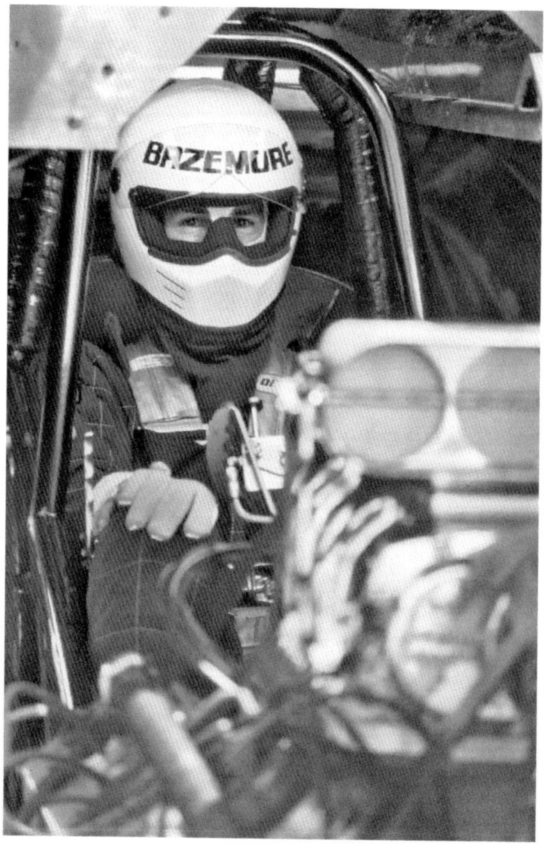

A pair of future stars met in the Funny Car finals of the 1992 Spring Nationals. Californian Del Worsham (near lane) made a single in his Oldsmobile when the engine in Whit Bazemore's Ford lost fire. Bazemore had been the event's top qualifier. It marked the only Bristol appearance of nitro Funny Car from 1991 to 1999. Both drivers later won NHRA races at Bristol. (Photograph by David McGee.)

Whit Bazemore, who once worked as a professional photographer, made his first national-event driving start in an alcohol Funny Car at the 1986 Spring Nationals. As his career progressed, Bristol would remain a favorite track. Bazemore later won the Funny Car category at the 2002 Thunder Valley Nationals. (Courtesy of *Bristol Herald Courier*; photograph by Earl Neikirk.)

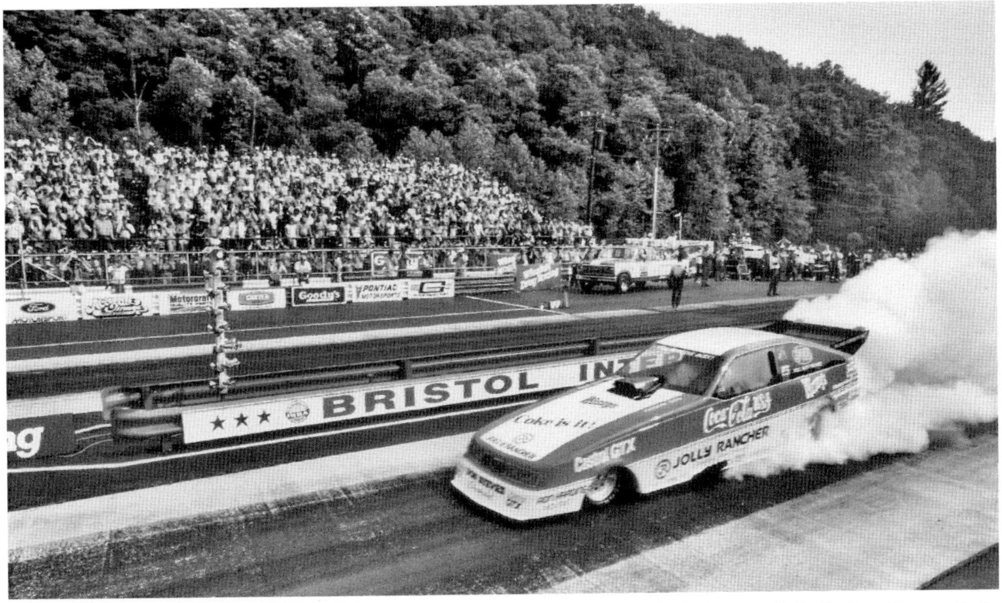

John Force struggled in his early visits to Thunder Valley. While he qualified this Coca-Cola Cavalier third in the 16-car show at the 1985 Spring Nationals, he lost a second-round race to Tom McEwen. That was a notch better than Force's 1984 Bristol debut, where he started 12th and lost to McEwen in round one. (Courtesy of *Bristol Herald Courier*; photograph by Earl Neikirk.)

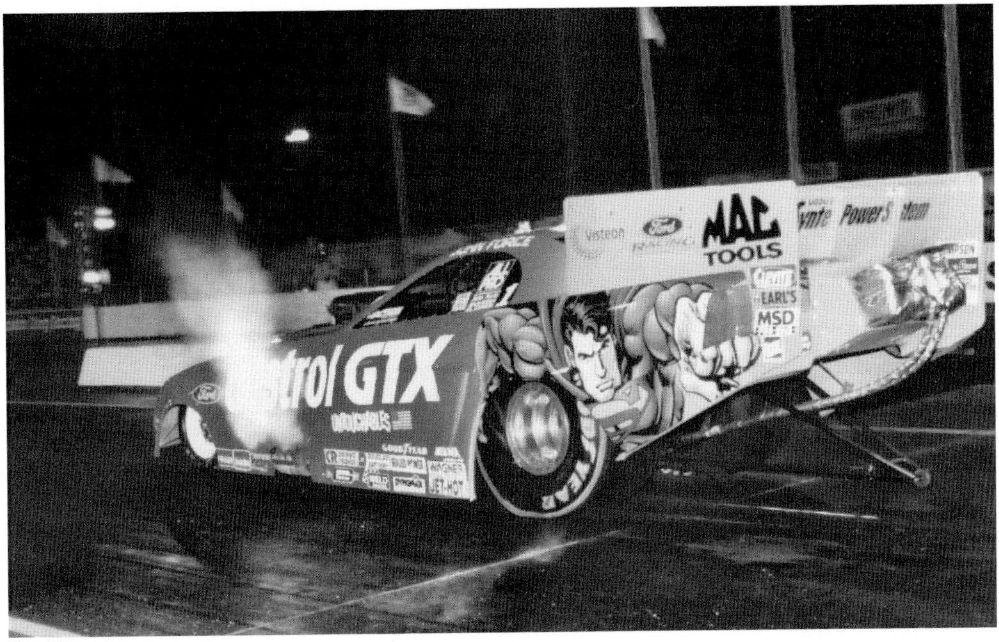

Force lived up to the Superman theme on his Ford Mustang during the first Winston Showdown in 1999. The unique all-star event pitted Funny Car drivers against Top Fuel racers for a $200,000 top prize. Force knocked out a quartet of dragster stars, beating Bob Vandergriff in the finals. (Photograph by David McGee.)

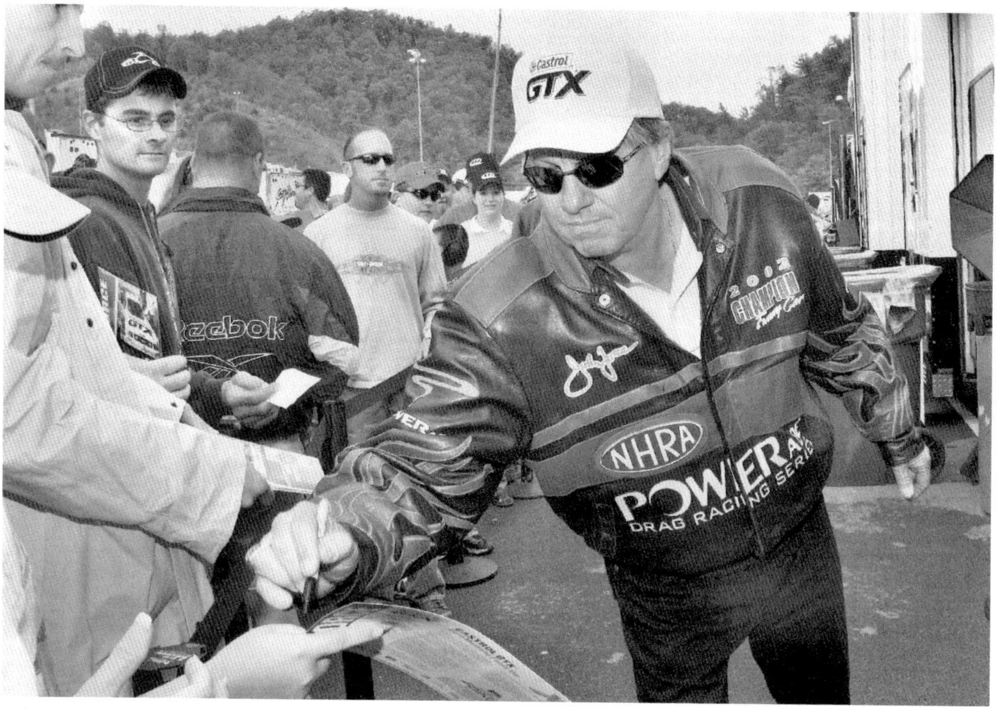

John Force is the undisputed king of the Funny Car division and a fan favorite. Despite his 14 NHRA championships, Force always takes the time to meet fans and sign autographs for the throngs who gather at his pit area on race weekends. (Photograph by David McGee.)

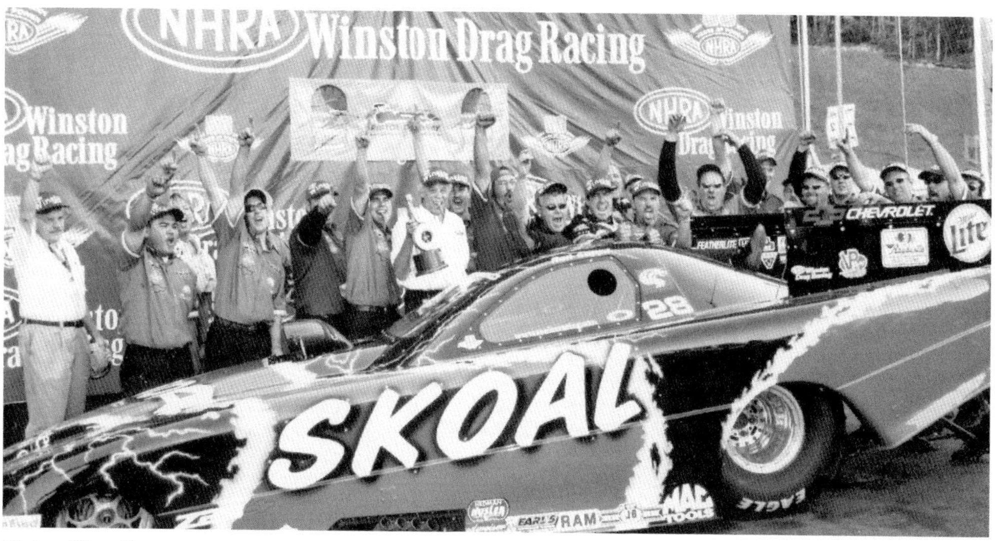

Driver Ron Capps, car owner Don Prudhomme (with trophy), crew chief Ed "the Ace" McCulloch, and members of their crew celebrate winning the Funny Car class at the inaugural 2001 Thunder Valley Nationals. It was the first NHRA national event at Bristol since 1967 and came during the association's 50th-anniversary season. Capps defeated Al Hoffman in the finals. (Photograph by David McGee.)

4

Pro Stock

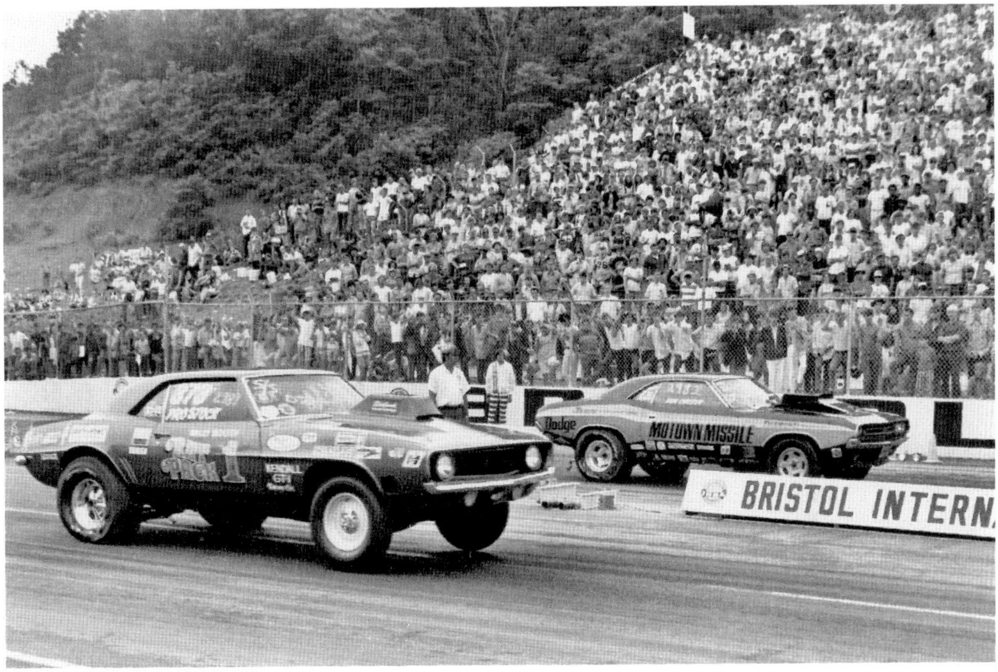

Few drag racing divisions command the fan loyalty of Pro Stock. The class features the distinct shapes and power plants of American carmakers Chevrolet, Ford, and Dodge and allows loyal fans a chance to cheer for their favorite manufacturer. The class evolved as a heads-up super stock division during the late 1960s. AHRA first ran the class in 1968, NHRA soon followed in 1970, and IHRA has always run the cars. In the early years, when Wally Booth (near lane) matched his Chevy Camaro with the factory-supported "Motown Missile" Dodge of Don Carlton, the cars began life as production-line machines. Modern Pro Stocks still burn gasoline and look like production cars but are highly sophisticated racecars with 1,400-horsepower engines. (Photograph by John Beach.)

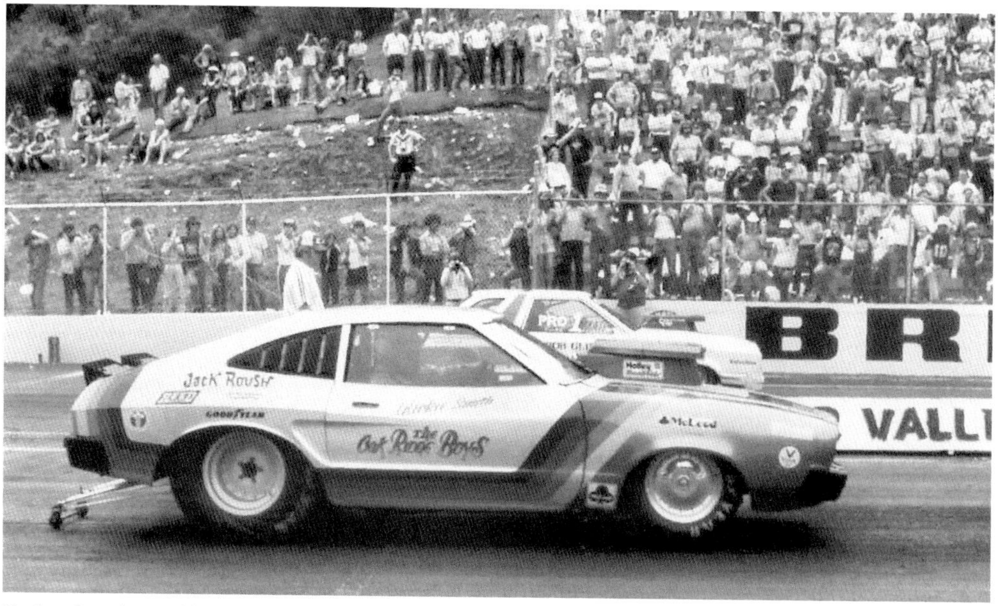

Rickie Smith established a Bristol success record that may never be matched. After two sportsman wins in the 1970s, Smith won Pro Stock 8 times during the 1980s and 1990s in 10 final-round appearances. Smith's first Bristol win, the 1980 Summer Nationals, came aboard Keith Fowler's Oak Ridge Boys Ford Mustang. The car featured an engine prepared by NASCAR icon Jack Roush. (Photograph by David McGee.)

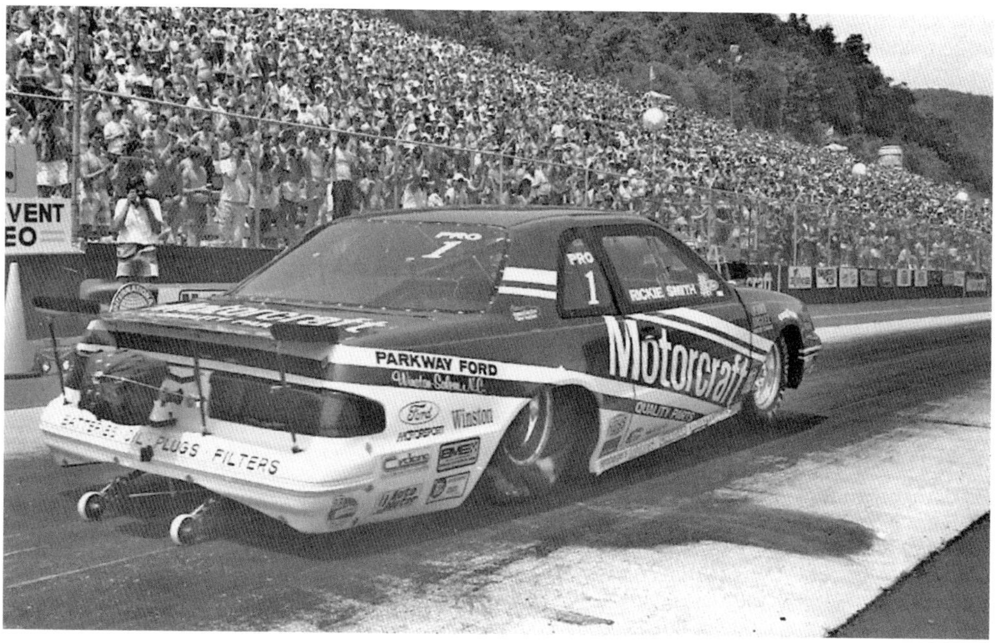

Some of Smith's greatest success came while driving a string of Motorcraft-backed Fords in the mid-1980s. He reached four final rounds in six seasons, earning two Spring Nationals titles and narrowly losing to Warren Johnson in the 1988 finals. (Photograph by David McGee.)

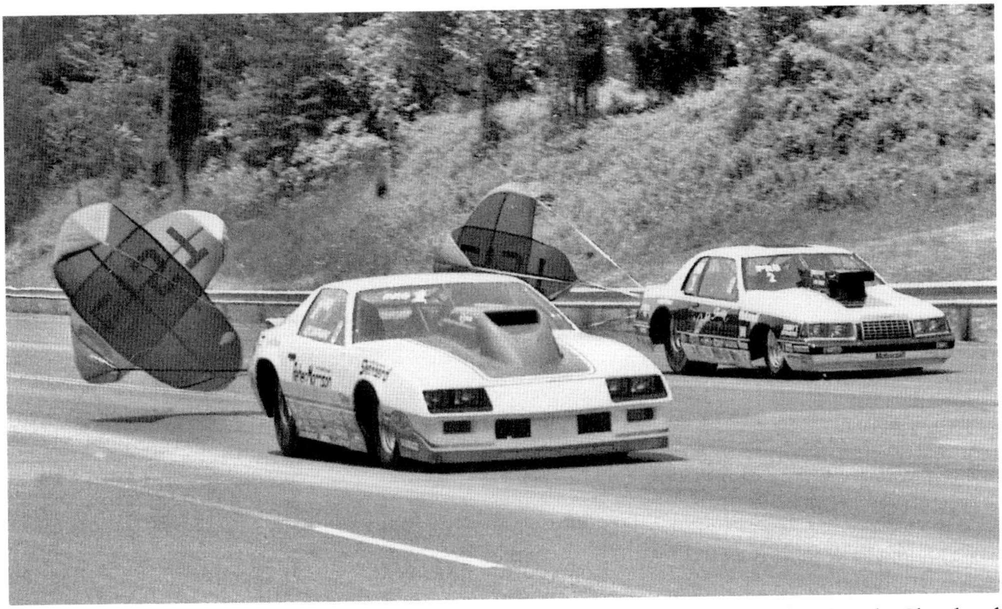

Parachutes help slow the Pro Stocks of Lee Shepherd (near lane) and Rickie Smith. Shepherd swept both Bristol races in 1984 en route to the IHRA championship. He was killed in a testing accident the following year, but replacement driver Bruce Allen won the 1985 Spring Nationals for the Texas team. (Photograph by David McGee.)

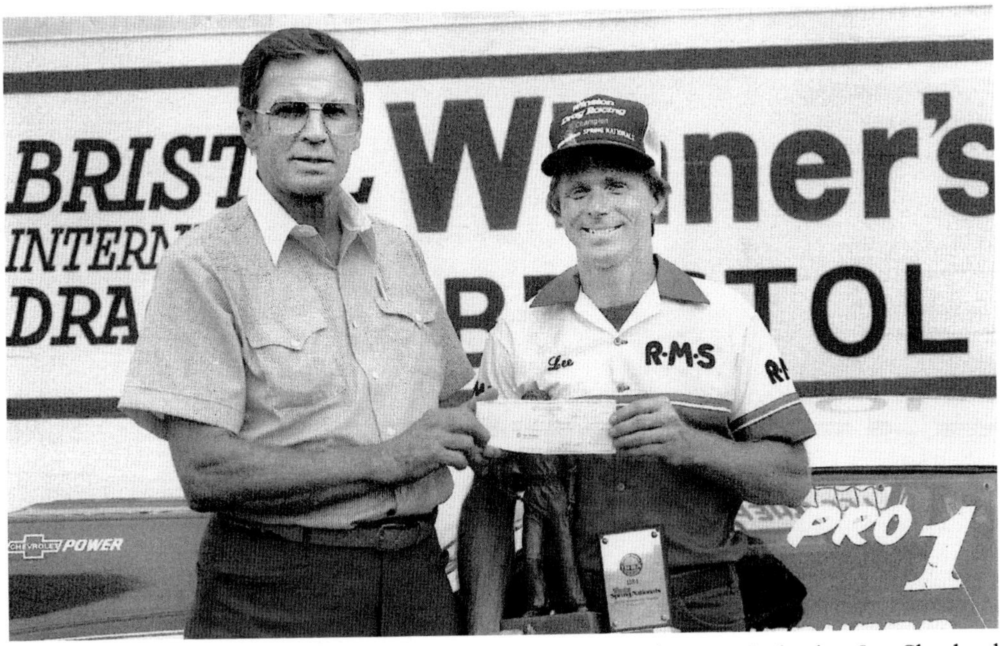

Bristol owner Larry Carrier (left) presents the $10,000 Pro Stock winner's check to Lee Shepherd after he captured the 1984 Spring Nationals. In only six Bristol races, Shepherd reached five final rounds and scored four victories. The team also earned IHRA and NHRA world championships. (Photograph by David McGee.)

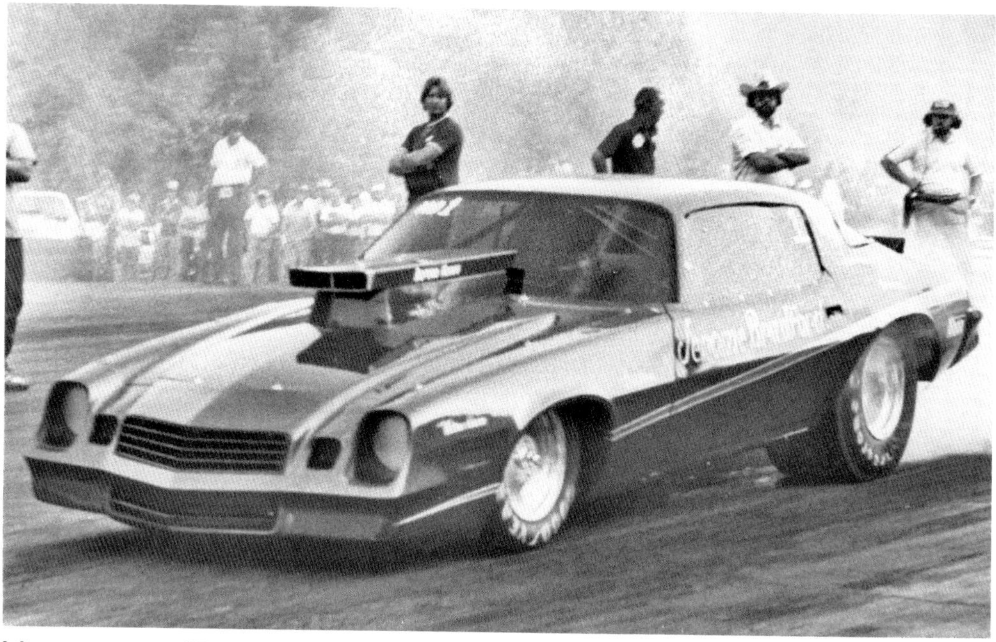

Minnesota native Warren Johnson moved his racing operation to Georgia in 1979 to drive a series of red-and-gold Chevrolets for Jerome Bradford. The team won three straight Spring Nationals titles, including the 1980 edition in this Camaro. (Photograph by David McGee.)

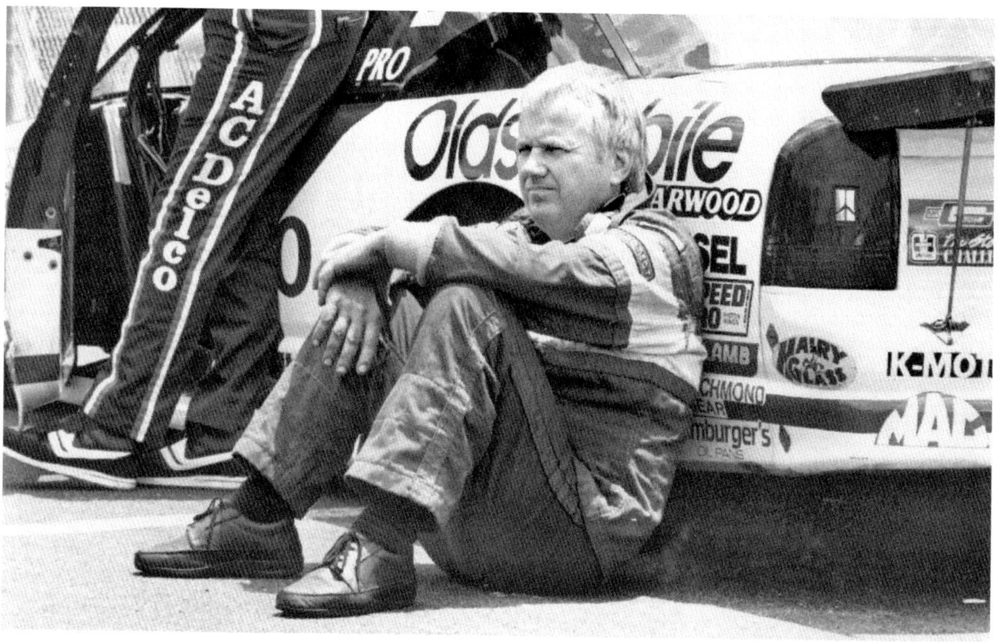

Warren Johnson sits beside his AC-Delco Oldsmobile in the Bristol staging lanes during the 1989 Spring Nationals. Some temporary rules changes made Johnson's 500-cubic-inch NHRA engine quite competitive against the larger IHRA engines. Johnson won Bristol races in 1988 and 1989. (Photograph by David McGee.)

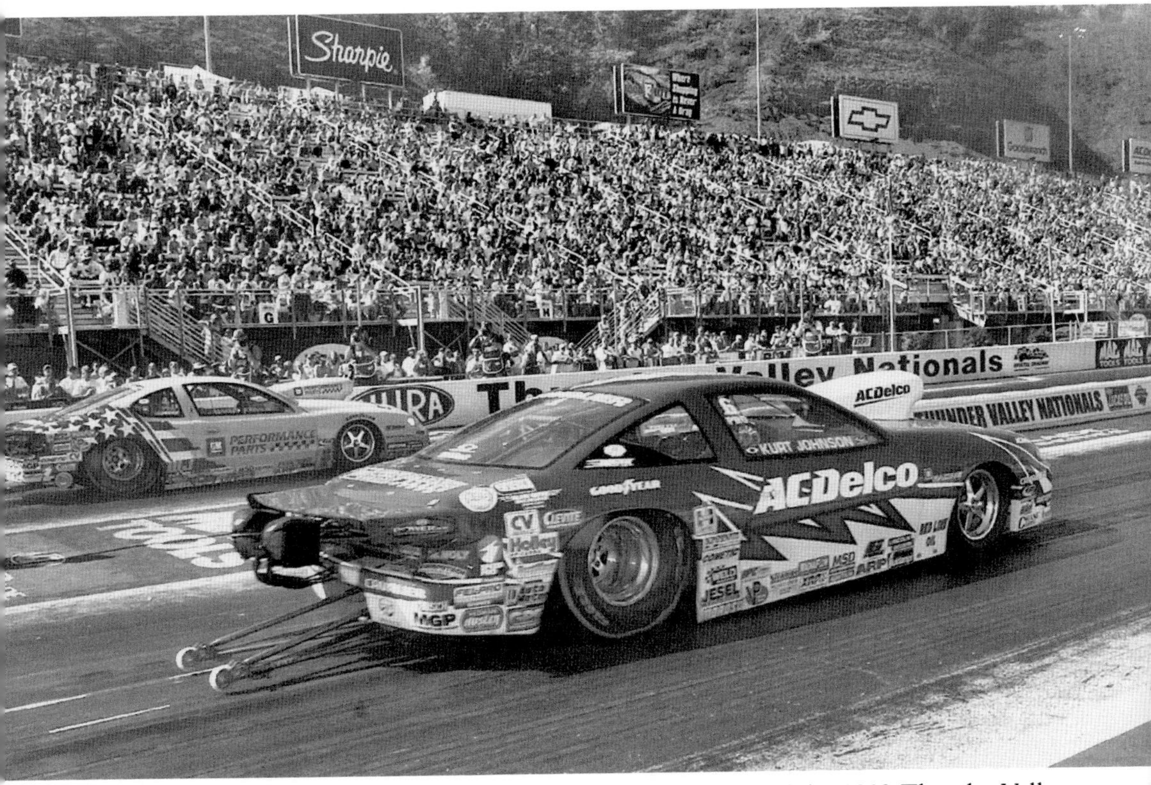

Warren Johnson (far lane) raced his son, Kurt, in the semifinals of the 2003 Thunder Valley Nationals. Kurt defeated his father en route to posting his first Bristol victory. The second-generation driver defeated Mike Edwards in the finals. Warren rebounded to win the 2005 event. (Photograph by David McGee.)

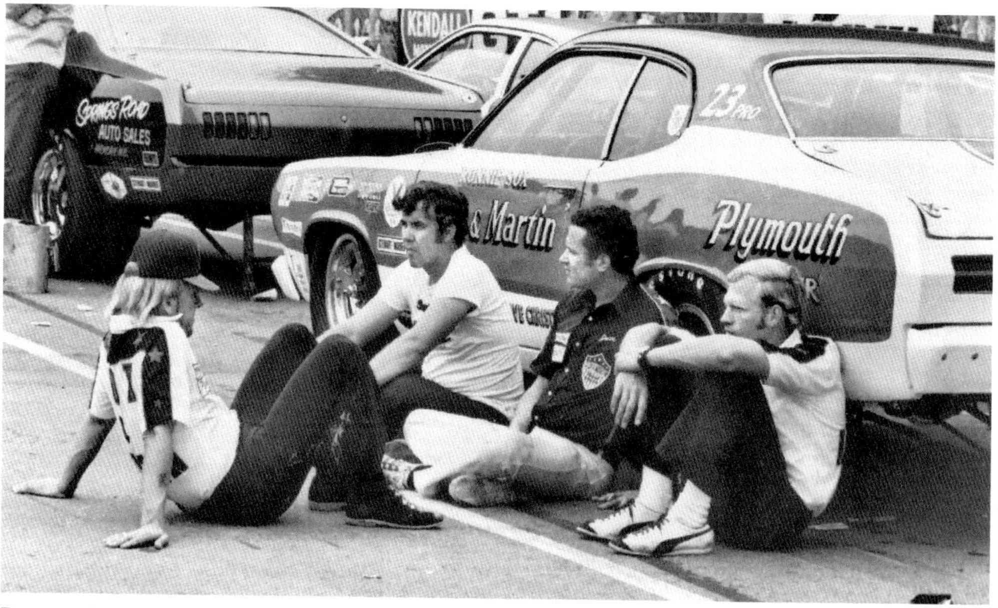

Ronnie Sox (seated at left) earned Bristol wins over four decades in two different professional and two sportsman classes. Here Sox and members of the Sox and Martin team wait to run their Hemi-powered Pro Stock Duster. Sox finished runner-up at the 1972 All-American Nationals with that car. (Photograph by John Beach.)

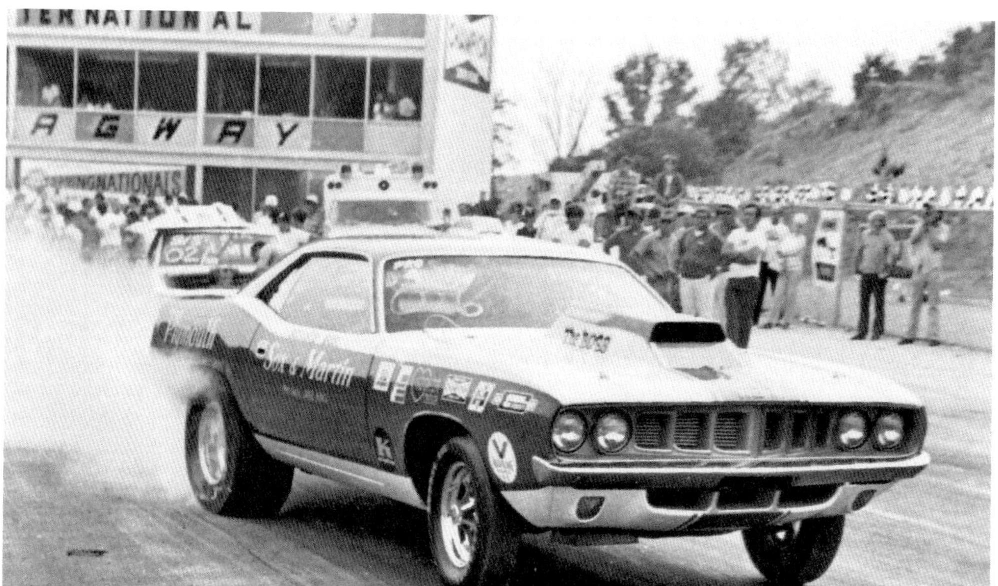

The Sox and Martin team was unbeaten at Bristol in 1971 as Sox wheeled "the Boss" Barracuda to wins in the Spring and All-American Nationals. The team was nearly unbeatable that entire year, winning the majority of races under the NHRA, IHRA, and AHRA flags. (Photograph by John Beach.)

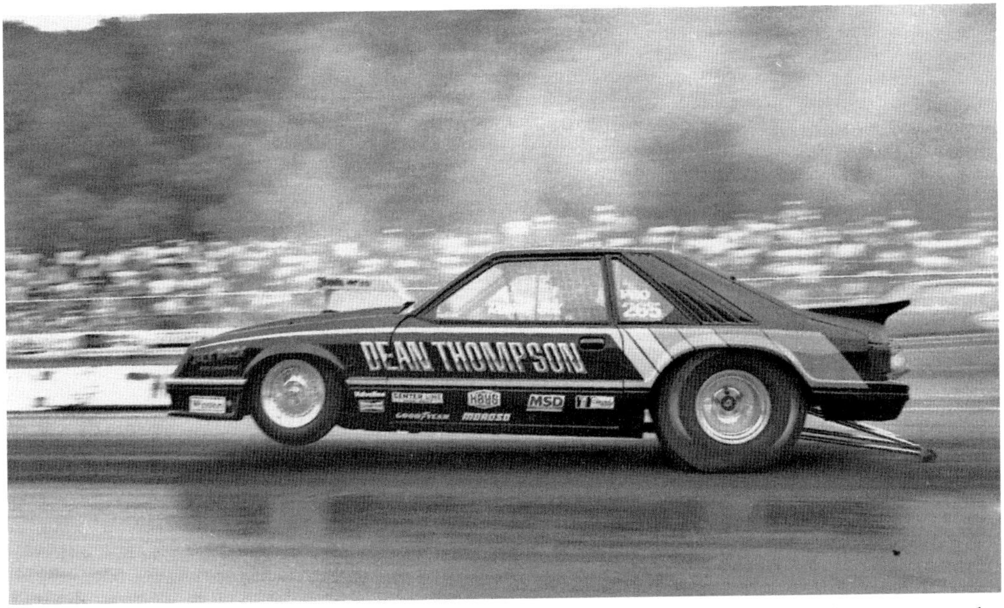

During the 1981 season, Ronnie Sox drove Dean Thompson's immaculate Ford Mustang to the Spring Nationals title, a new national elapsed-time record, and the IHRA series championship. It was his only Bristol win during the 1980s. (Photograph by David McGee.)

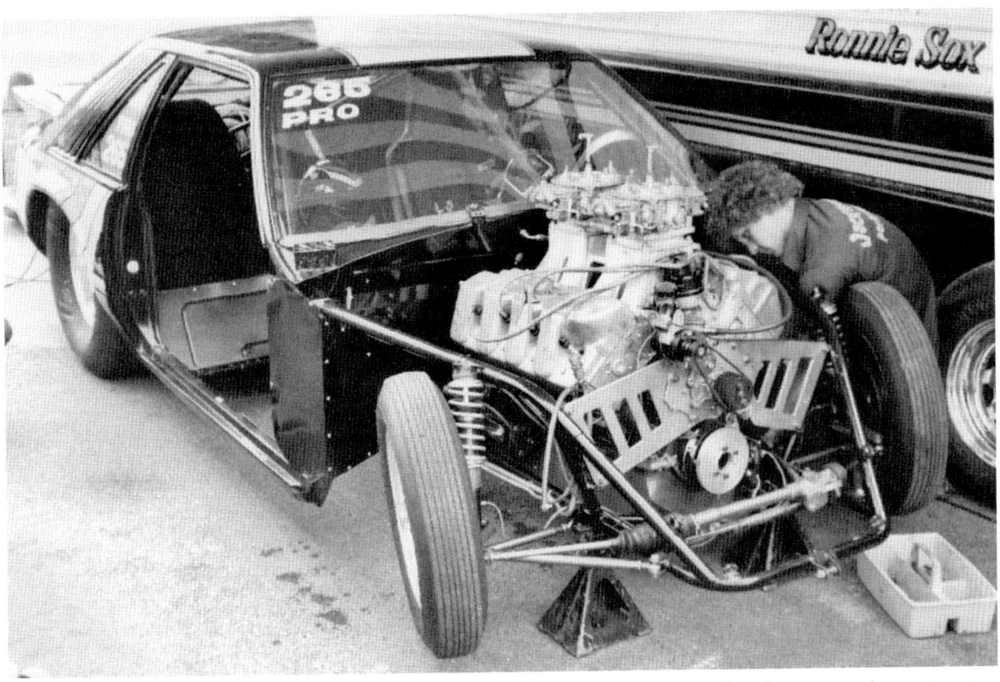

Dean Sox, son of the legendary driver, performs maintenance on the championship-winning Mustang. Pro Stock cars feature removable, lightweight front-end components so crewmembers can easily access the engine and chassis. The car's Ford engines were prepared by Jack Roush of NASCAR fame. (Photograph by Jeff Wright.)

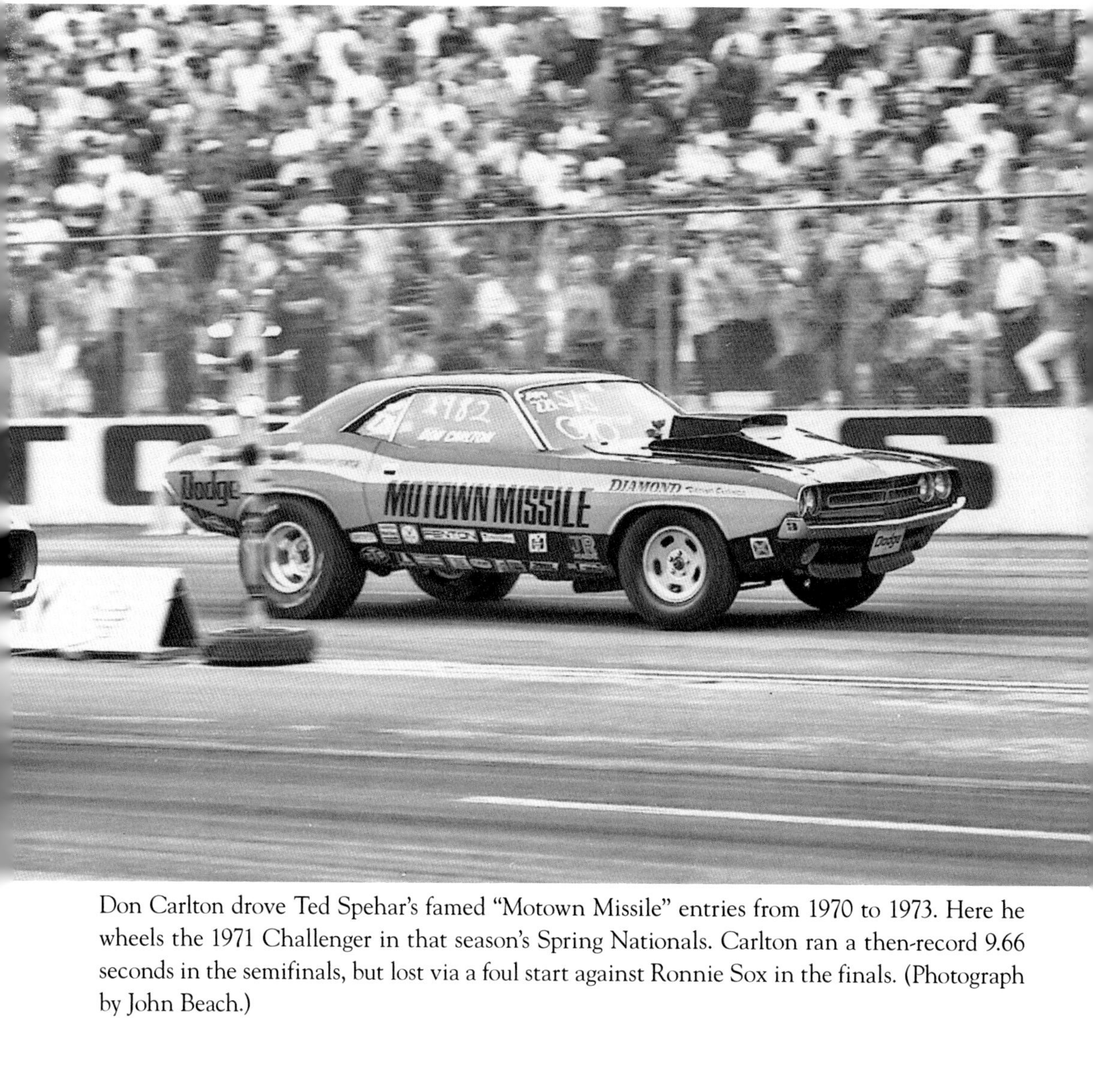

Don Carlton drove Ted Spehar's famed "Motown Missile" entries from 1970 to 1973. Here he wheels the 1971 Challenger in that season's Spring Nationals. Carlton ran a then-record 9.66 seconds in the semifinals, but lost via a foul start against Ronnie Sox in the finals. (Photograph by John Beach.)

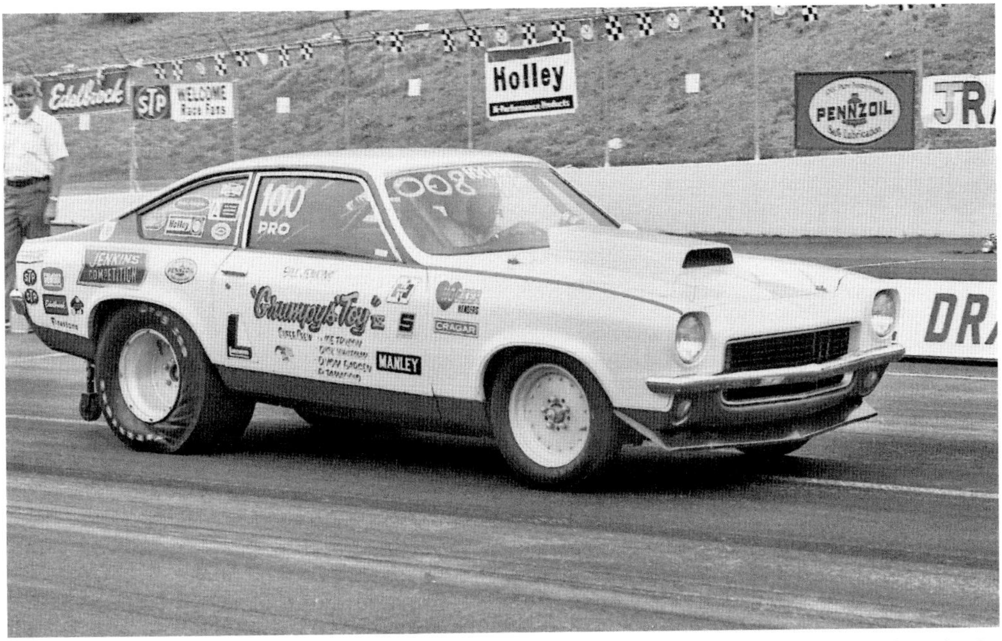

Widely regarded as genius for his ability to tune Chevrolet engines, Bill "Grumpy" Jenkins had a successful driving career in the 1960s and 1970s. His lightweight, small-block-powered Chevrolet Vega revolutionized Pro Stock and carried Jenkins to that year's Spring Nationals title over Butch Leal's Plymouth Hemi. Jenkins won the 1969 event aboard a Camaro. (Photograph by John Beach.)

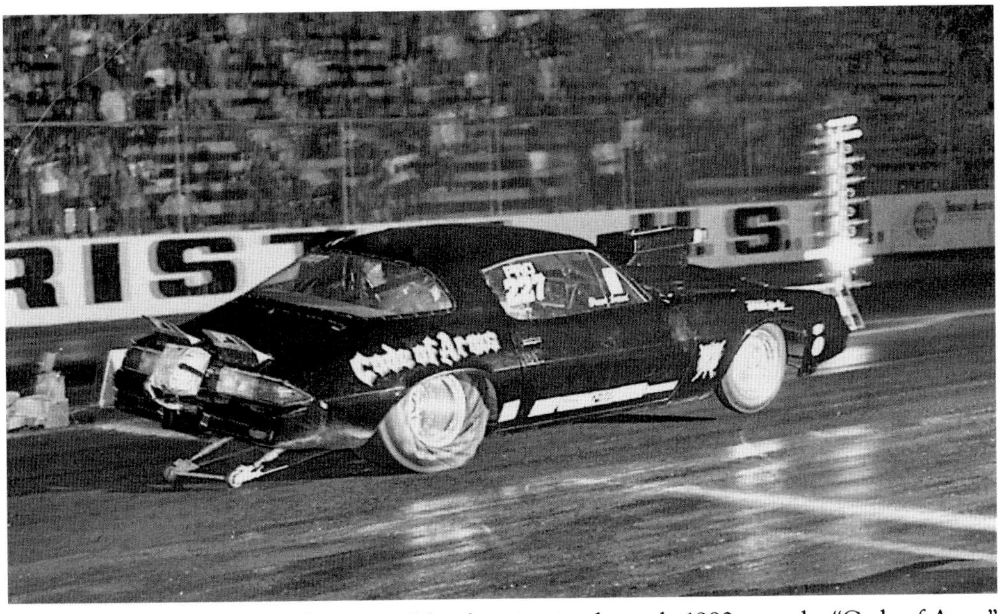

With its wild, twisting launches, one of fan favorites in the early 1980s was the "Code of Arms" Camaro raced by the father and son team of Charlie and Chuck Sneed. The car was among the first 16 into the 7-second range. (Photograph by David McGee.)

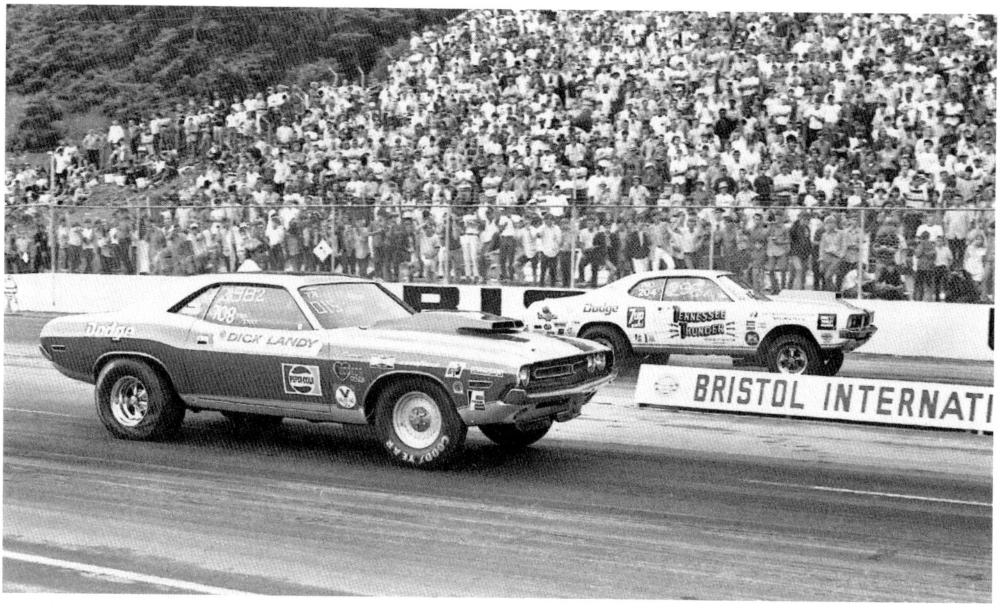

Californian "Dandy" Dick Landy's Dodge (near lane) squares off with John Livingston's "Tennessee Thunder" Dodge Demon from Nashville. Despite a storied career, Landy never added a Bristol trophy to his collection. Livingston, who competed at Bristol's first race in 1965, kept racing at Bristol in the 1970s, 1980s, 1990s, and into the 21st century. (Photograph by John Beach.)

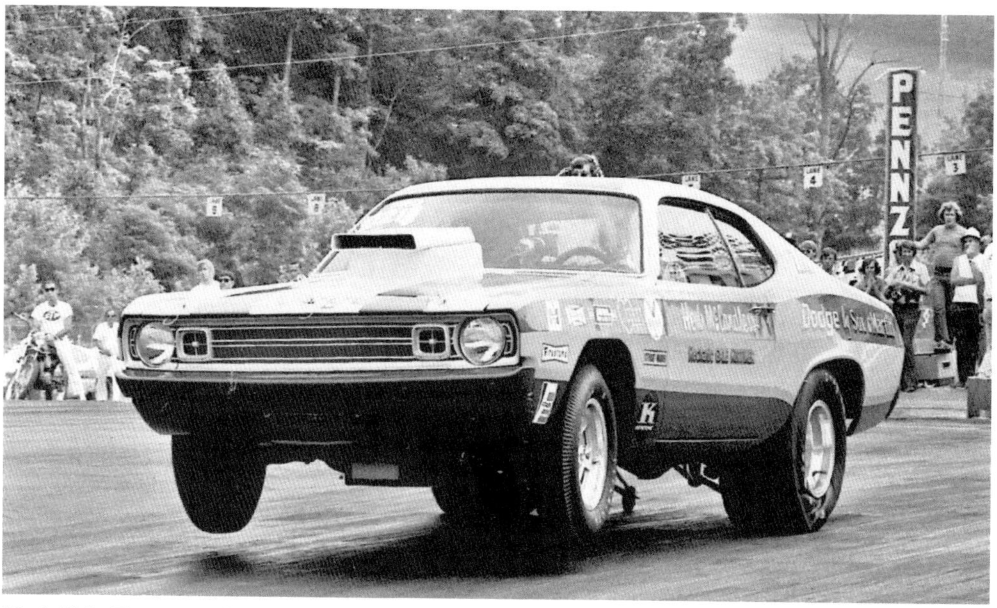

Herb "Mr. Four Speed" McCandless was a regular factor in Pro Stock eliminations but failed to win the category at Bristol. Here he launches a Hemi Dodge Demon prepared by the Sox and Martin team. At the 1977 Spring Nationals, McCandless defeated Rickie Smith in the finals of the short-lived Super Modified class, which served as a springboard for Smith's professional career. (Photograph by John Beach.)

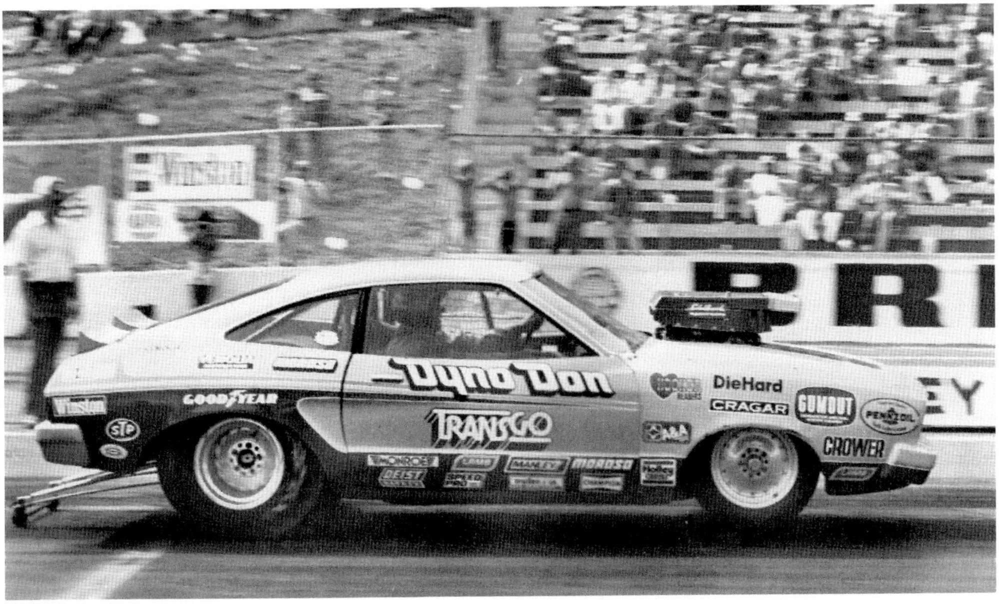

Former world champion "Dyno Don" Nicholson reached the final rounds at Bristol five times during his illustrious career. He won the 1970 and 1973 All-American race. This Mustang carried him to his last Bristol final, the 1980 Summer Nationals, which he lost to Rickie Smith. (Photograph by David McGee.)

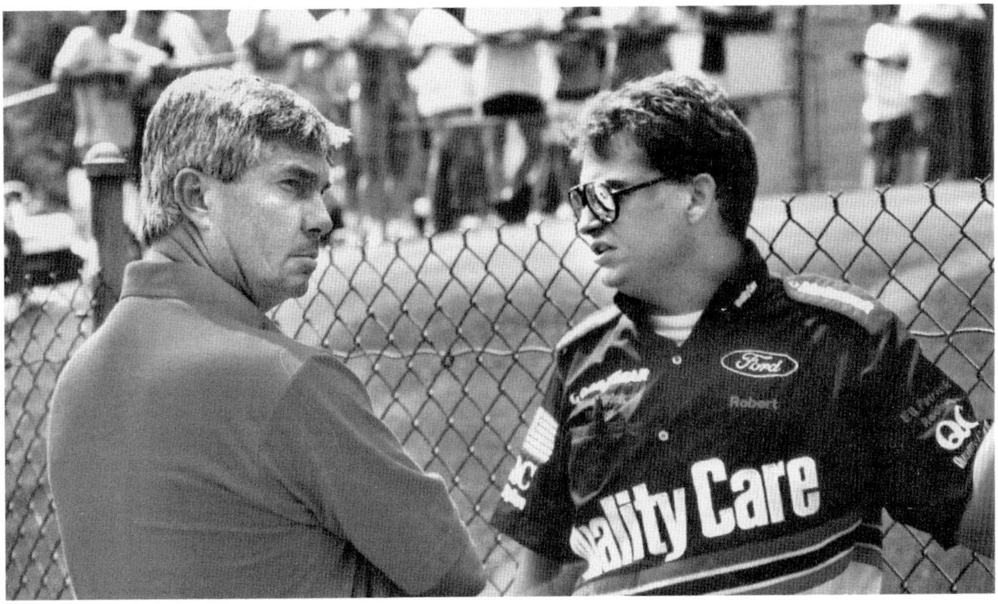

Veteran Roy Hill (left) and Robert Patrick both enjoyed success at Bristol. Hill earned Pro Stock victories in the 1993 and 1995 Spring Nationals. Mike Bell and Richie Stevens also drove Hill-owned Fords to Bristol victories. Patrick drove his family's Ford to the 1994 Spring Nationals title and later that year became the first Pro Stocker to exceed 200 miles per hour at Bristol, running 200.17. (Photograph by David McGee.)

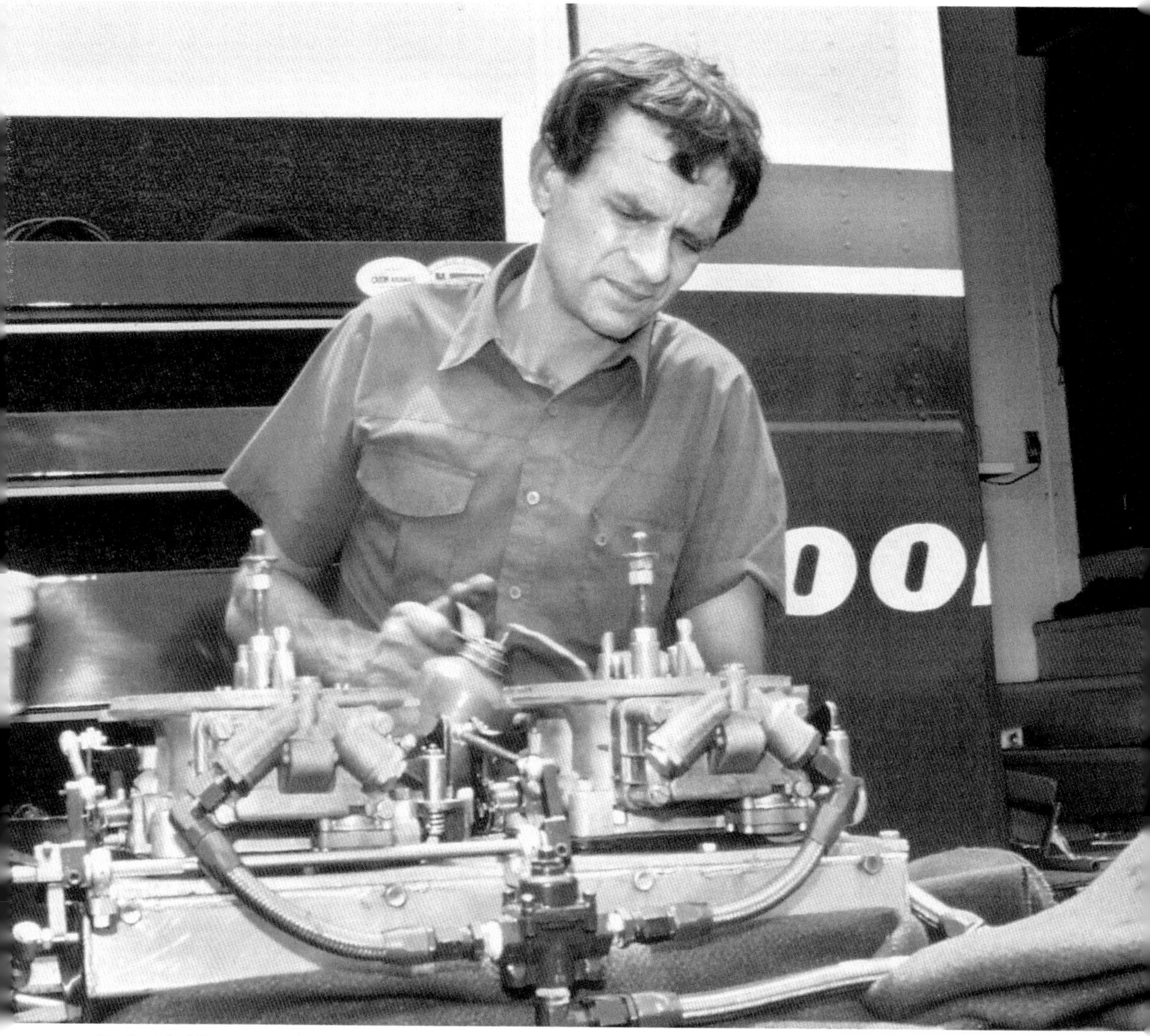

Bob Glidden earned the nickname "Mad Dog" for his relentless pursuit of additional horsepower. Here he works on the engine of his Ford Thunderbird. Glidden scored four Bristol wins during his career, including a sweep of both 1976 events and the 1985 and 1986 Fall Nationals. (Courtesy of *Bristol Herald Courier*; photograph by Earl Neikirk.)

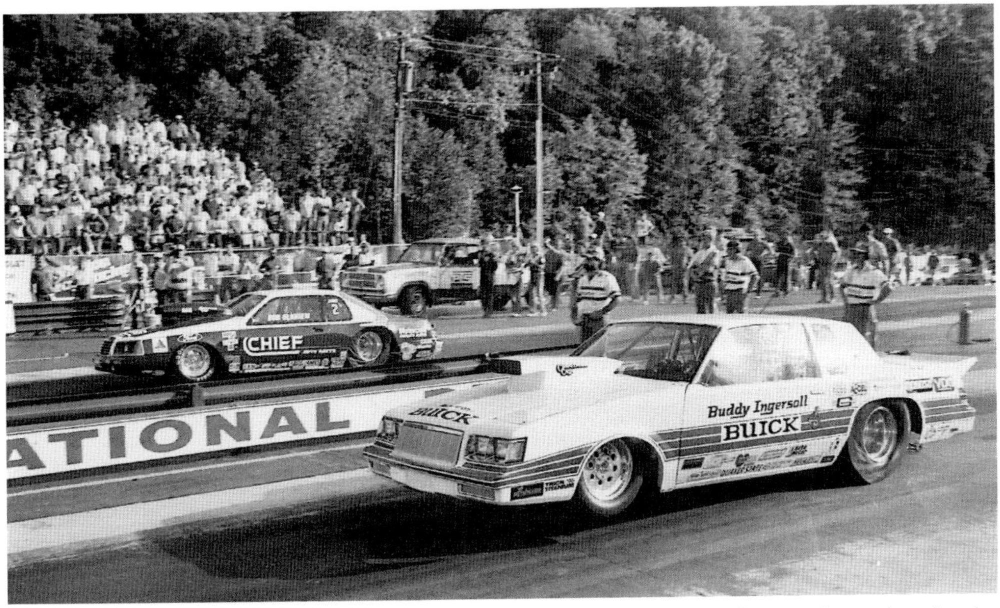

Bob Glidden's last Bristol win, at the 1986 Fall Nationals, was especially significant for what he defeated in the finals. IHRA allowed Buddy Ingersoll (near lane) to race his controversial twin-turbocharged 260 cubic inch Buick against the normally aspirated cars for that season, despite numerous protests. Glidden's traditional 700-cubic-inch Ford needed a 7.28-second run at 193 miles per hour to stop Ingersoll's amazing 7.37 at 189 miles per hour. (Photograph by David McGee.)

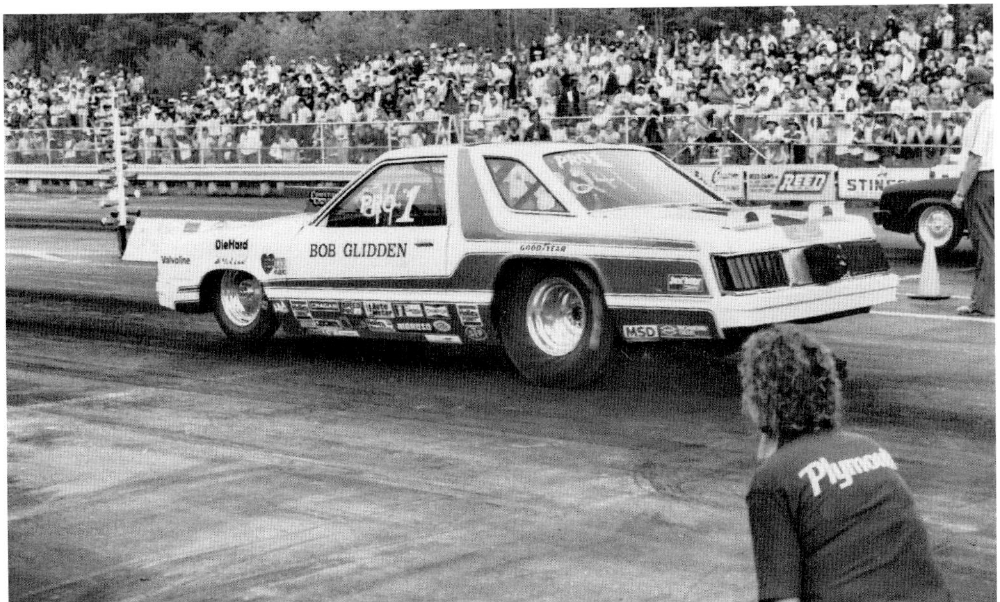

Glidden unveiled a new Ford Fairmont Pro Stocker during the 1980 Spring Nationals. The team had just switched back to Ford from its previous Plymouth entry but hadn't had time to replace the crew shirts, sported here by Bob's wife, Etta. (Photograph by David McGee.)

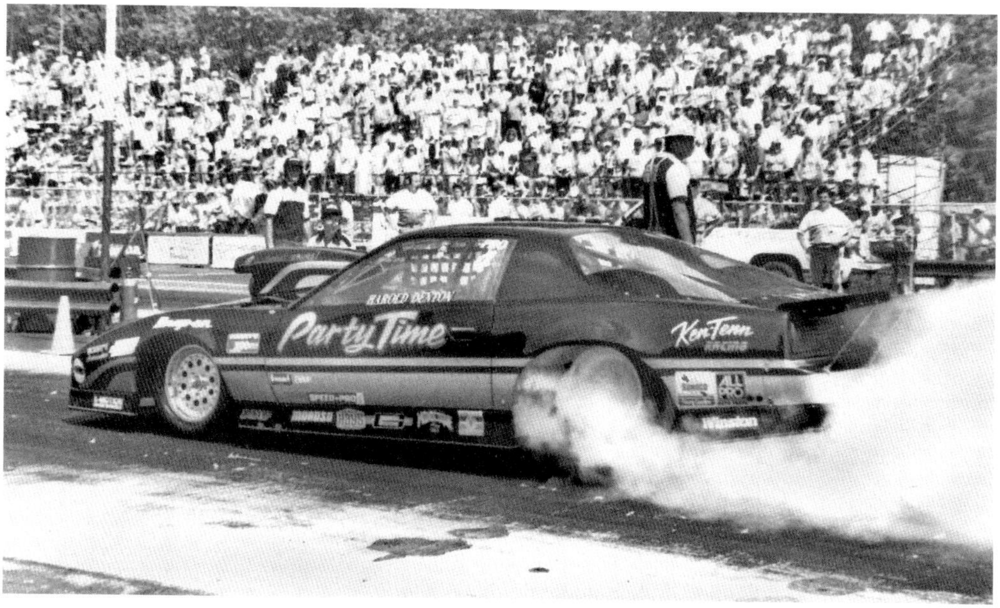

Harold Denton scored one of the most emotional victories in Bristol history when he piloted the Ruth family's "Party Time" Pontiac to the 1991 Spring Nationals crown. The race marked the team's first trip to Bristol since the death of former track and car owner Jim Ruth the previous December. (Photograph by David McGee.)

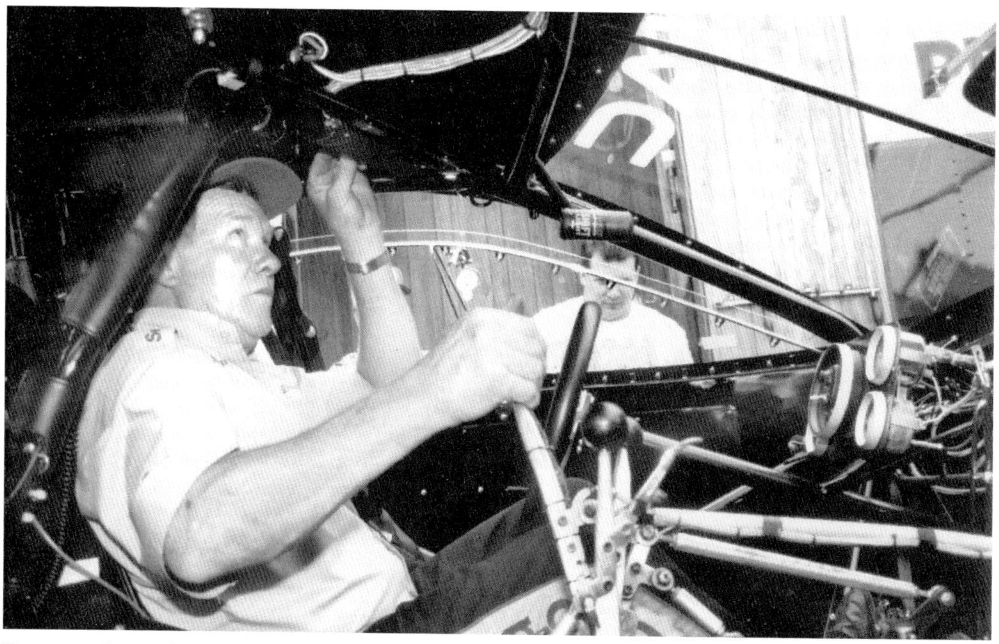

Denton, shown here checking the electrical system on the sport's first six-second Pro Stocker, just missed a Bristol sweep at the 1991 Fall Nationals. He qualified first and won that weekend's $20,000 Sunoco Shootout, a special eight-car event for the top cars in the country. A first-round upset loss knocked him out of Sunday's eliminations. (Photograph by David McGee.)

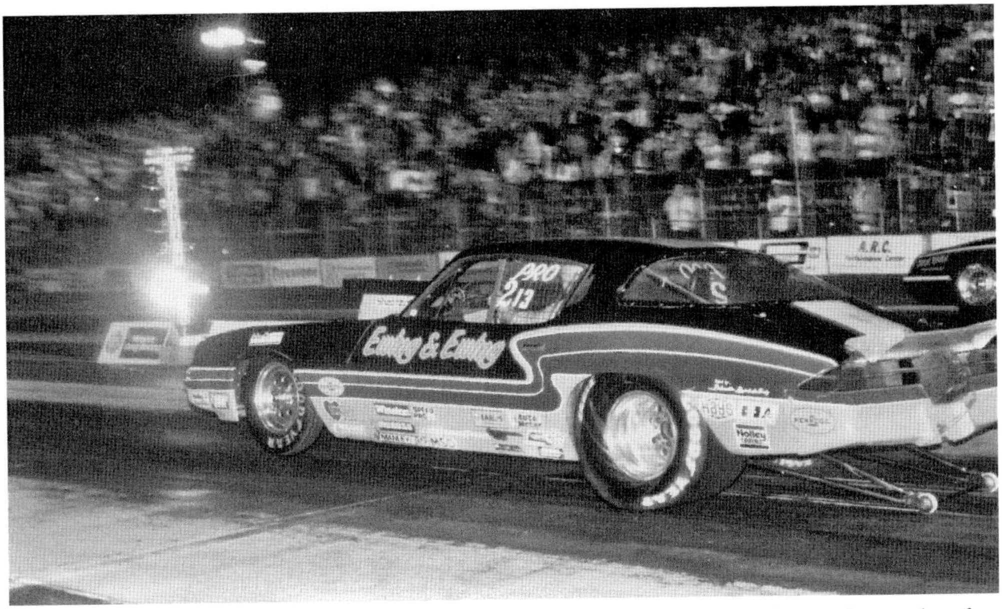

Georgia veteran Billy Ewing enjoyed a string of successful runs at Bristol. He advanced to five final rounds and won the 1991 Fall Nationals. He and brother Lamar raced a series of brightly painted Camaros like this one, but their lone Bristol win came in an Oldsmobile. (Photograph by David McGee.)

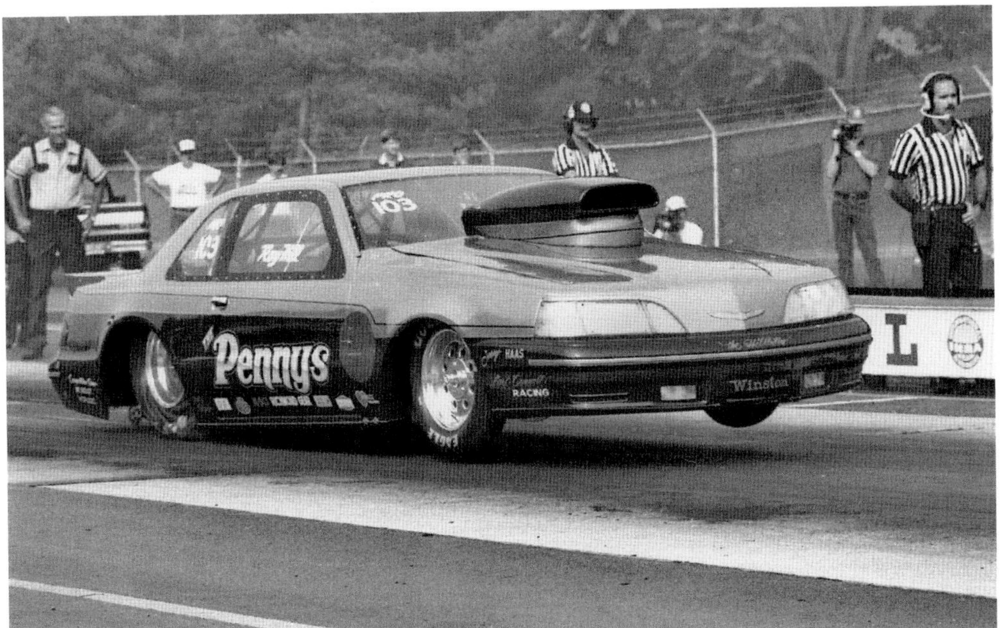

Doug Kirk won IHRA Pro Stock championships in 1991 and 1993 driving his family's Oldsmobiles. But his only Bristol win occurred in 1987 behind the wheel of Joe Penny's Ford Thunderbird. The second-generation racer captured two straight national events after replacing Roy Hill in the seat midway through the season. (Photograph by David McGee.)

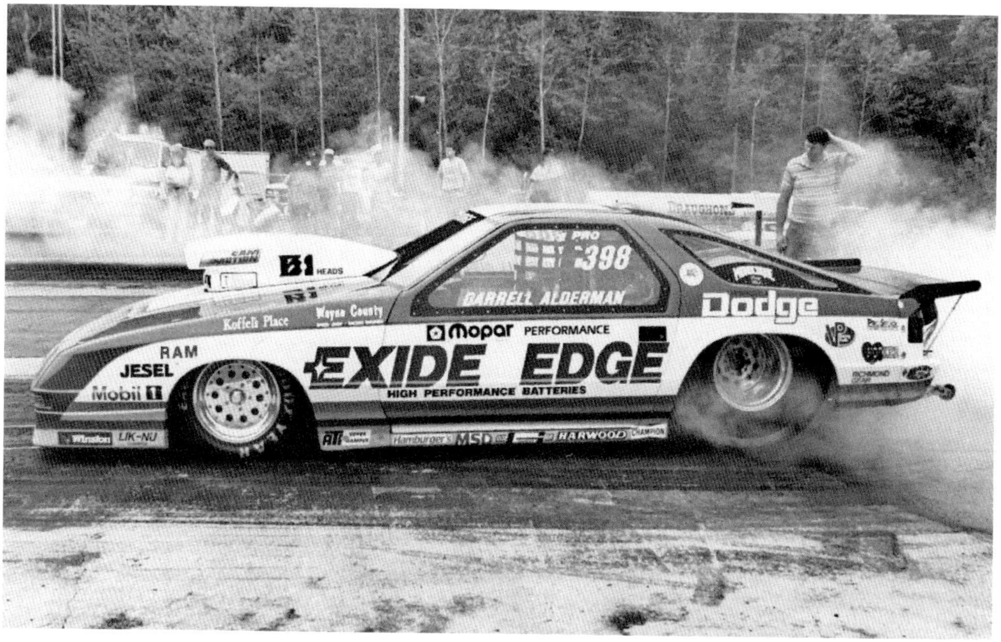

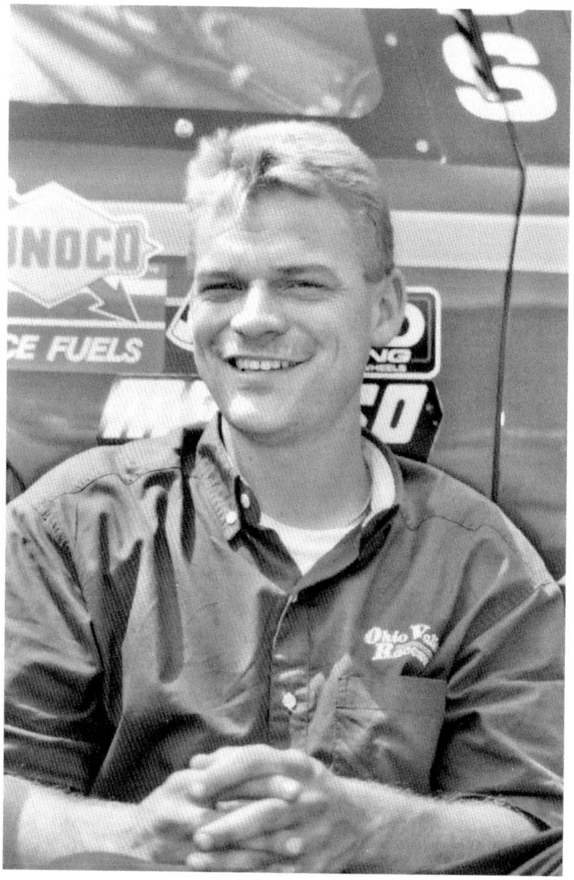

Darrell Alderman began his Pro Stock driving career in a car owned by fellow Kentuckian Jim Ruth. But his NHRA world championships in 1990, 1991, and 1994 came aboard Dodges campaigned by Wayne County Speed Shop. Alderman earned a runner-up in 1989, when the team brought this Dodge to Bristol. He won the 1986 Spring Nationals in Jerry Haas's Chevrolet. (Photograph by David McGee.)

Billy Huff is another Kentucky racer who posted a career highlight at Thunder Valley. Locked in a tense 1994 IHRA championship battle with Robert Patrick, Huff qualified atop the field at the season-ending Fall Nationals. Winning the race meant winning the title, which is exactly what Huff did by beating Roy Hill in the finals. (Photograph by David McGee.)

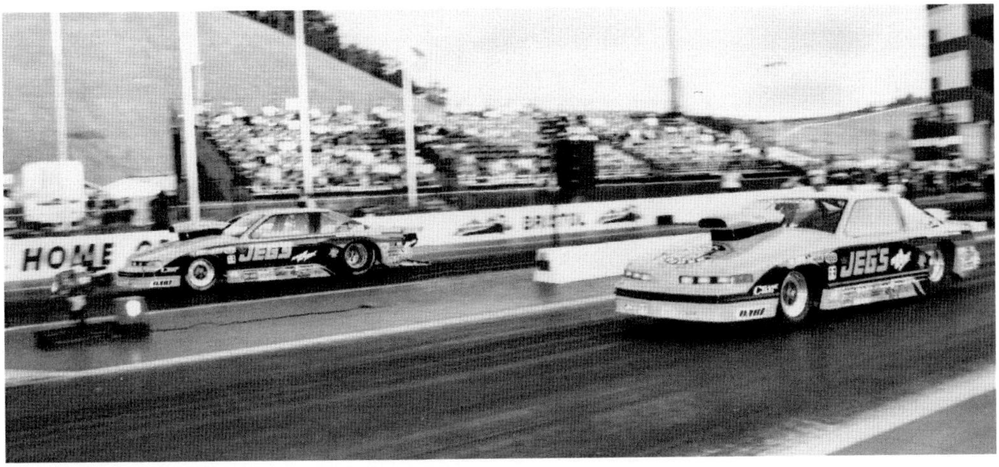

In a battle of matching Oldsmobiles, Jeg Coughlin Jr. beat his brother, Troy, in the Pro Stock finals at the 1999 Winston Showdown all-star race. Troy (near lane) returned the favor the next year, downing his brother (far lane)and winning the 2000 event, pictured. He defeated Mark Pawuk in the finals. Each win was worth $50,000. Their father, Jeg Coughlin Sr., owned the winning Funny Car at Bristol's 1973 All-American Nationals. (Photograph by David McGee.)

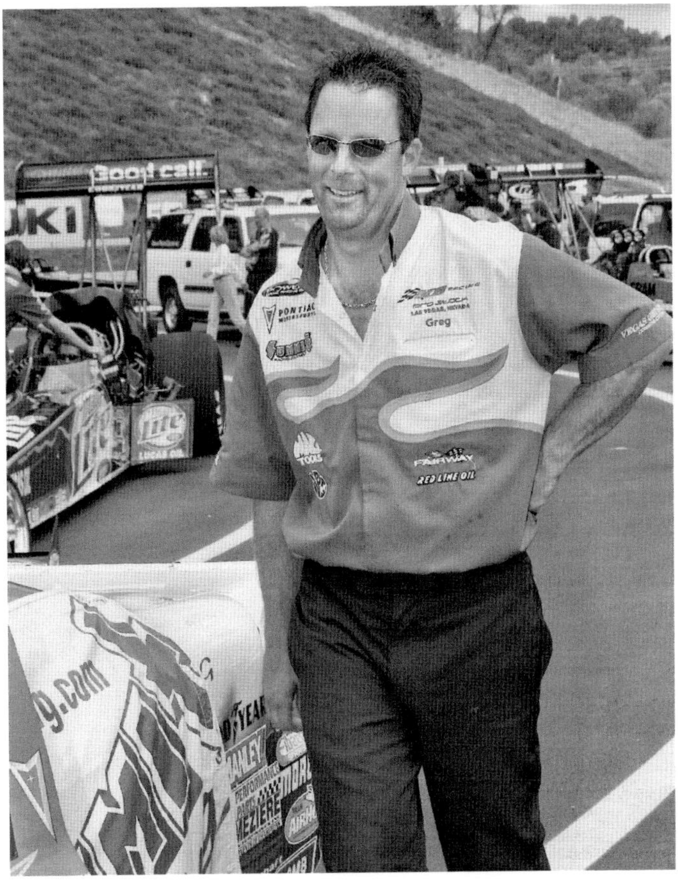

Two-time NHRA Pro Stock champion Greg Anderson earned his first national-event win at the 2001 Thunder Valley Nationals. He drove Ken Black's Pontiac past former world champion Jim Yates in the final round. (Photograph by David McGee.)

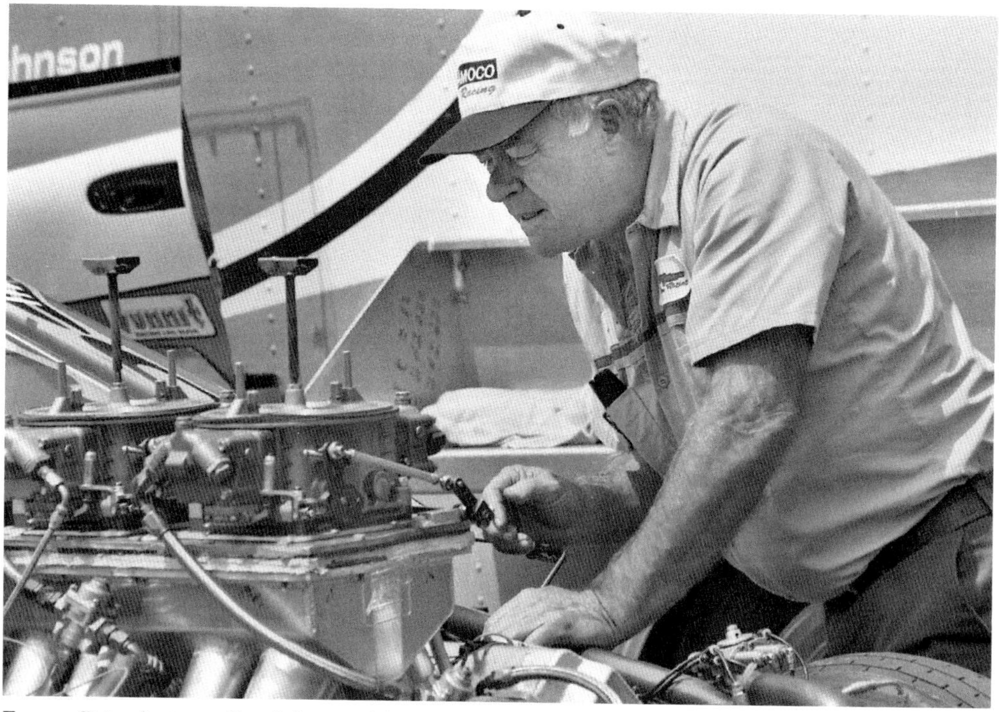

Former Bristol winner Roy Johnson (above) returned to Thunder Valley in the 1990s as crew chief and engine builder for his son Allen's Pro Stock Dodge team (below). The East Tennessee–based operation is regularly among the top qualifiers at NHRA national events and has posted a series of top-10 finishes in the season points battles. Allen's first national-event win came at his home track, when he won super stock at the 1982 Spring Nationals. (Photographs by David McGee.)

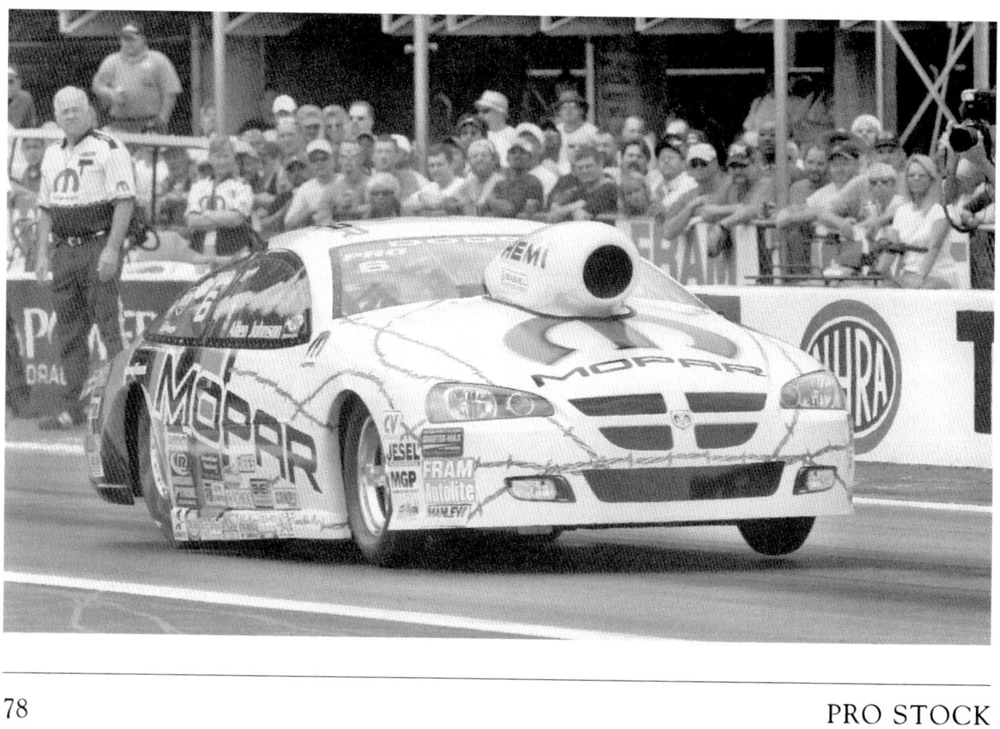

5

Pro Modified and Top Sportsman

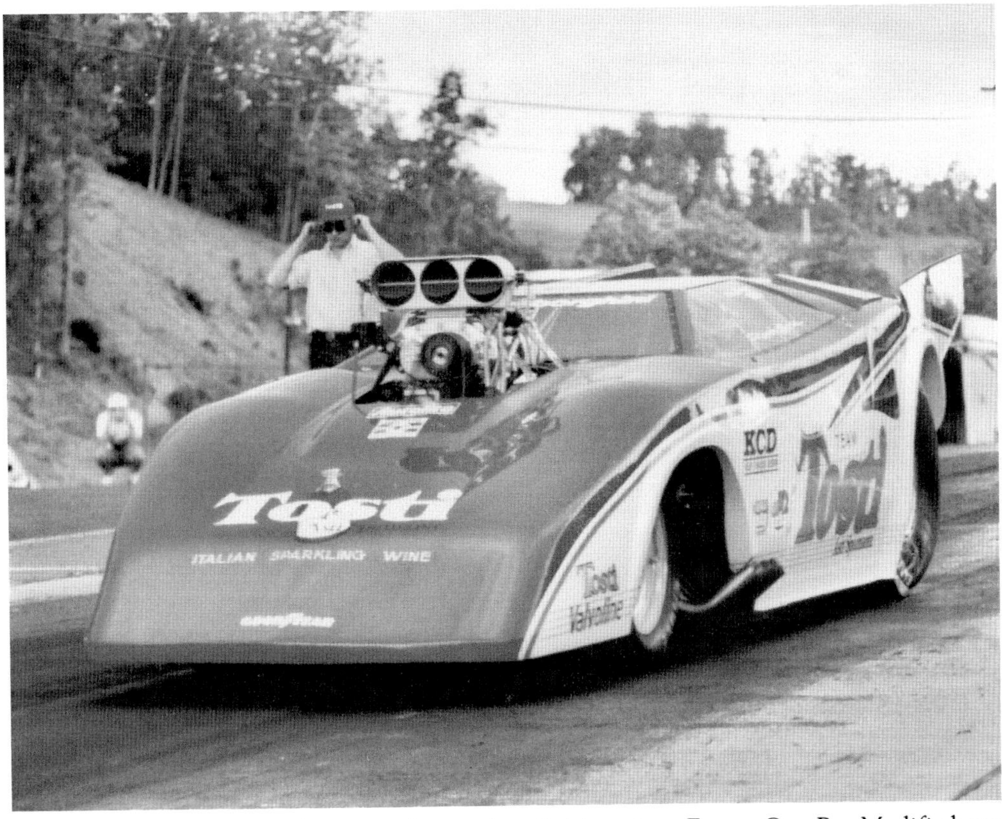

Regarded as the most revolutionary drag-racing division since Funny Car, Pro Modified was established in 1990 after evolving from the 1980s Top Sportsman class. The fans loved the machines for a diverse range of body styles, wild paint, and a mixture of supercharged engines versus 700-cubic-inch Mountain Motors with nitrous oxide injection. Perhaps none of drag racing's wild bunch was wilder than the Lamborghini of Bristol driver Randy Moore. Randy, the son of dragway cofounder Carl Moore, competed in 1991–1992 and established an elapsed time record of 6.63 seconds. After his engine combination was outlawed, the team qualified first at the 1991 Fall Nationals with a 6.75-second time at 205 miles per hour, followed by a winning 6.74 at 209 miles per hour. (Photograph by David McGee.)

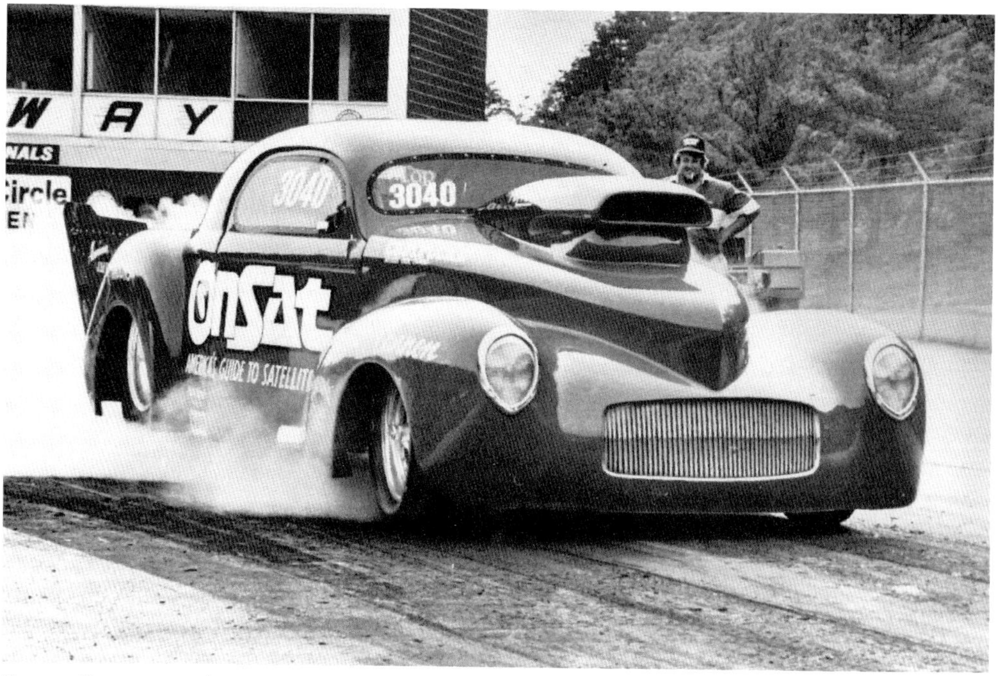

Scotty Cannon ranks as Bristol's all-time Pro Modified winner with four career victories. The South Carolina native first came to prominence aboard a series a boxy, bright red Willys-bodied Top Sportsman machines. His supercharged Corvette (below) carried him to the 1993 Spring Nationals title. (Photographs by David McGee.)

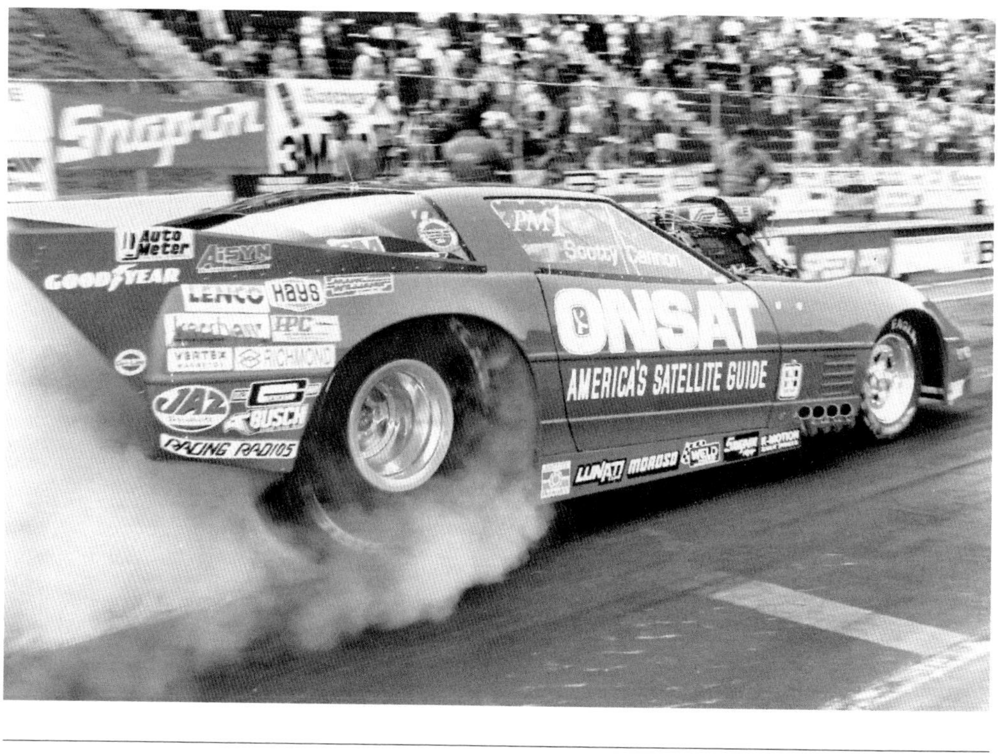

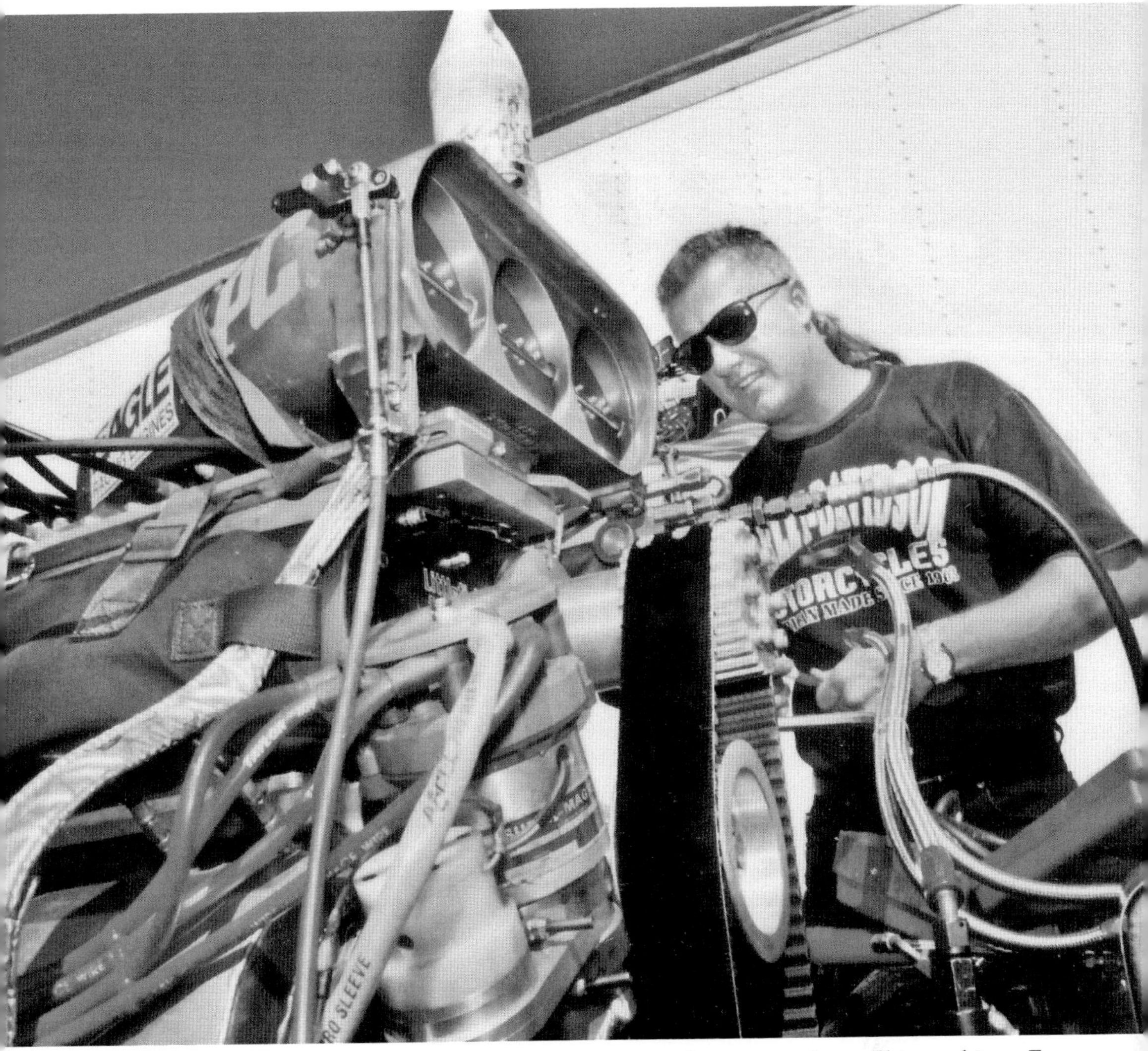

An experienced tuner and driver, Scotty Cannon works on the engine of one of his machines. For many years, Cannon's cars were sponsored by *OnSat*, a satellite television magazine. Cannon won five IHRA world championships in 1991, 1992, 1993, 1994, and 1998. The bright-red machines were nicknamed the "Killer Red Mater"—or tomato, for anyone not familiar with the slang term. (Photograph by David McGee.)

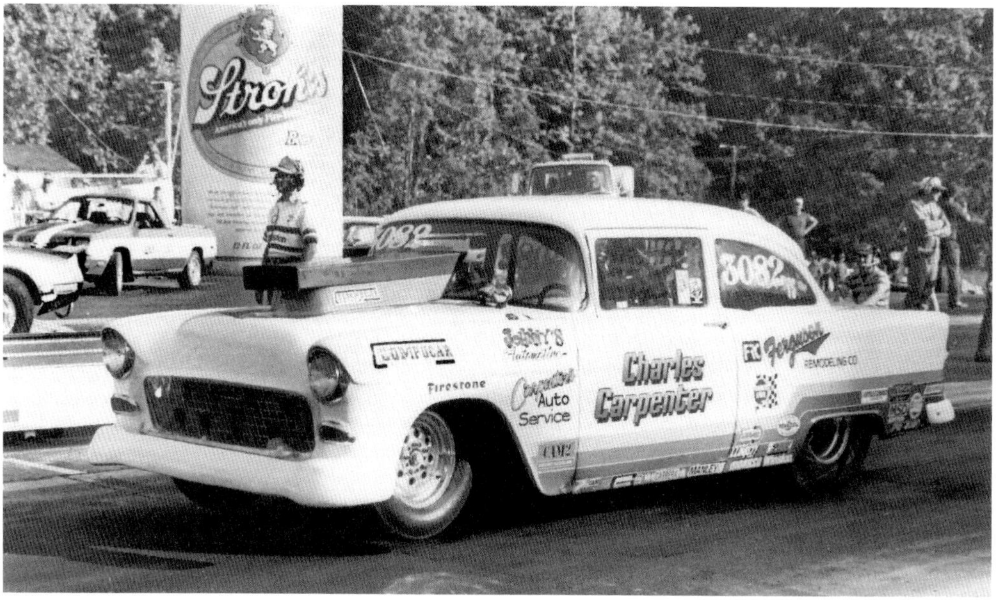

Charles Carpenter influenced sweeping changes across the sport of drag racing with his unconventional 1955 Chevrolet Top Sportsman car (above). The mostly steel machine shocked the sport in the early 1980s with runs in the 7-second zone at 185 miles per hour. Carpenter relied on heavy doses of nitrous oxide, which injected hundreds of horsepower into the engine. Subsequent versions (below) were sleeker, lighter, and featured Pro Stock–style chassis technology. In addition to national events, Carpenter increased his considerable reputation on the Super Chevy Show circuit and by match-racing similar machines across the country. (Photographs by David McGee.)

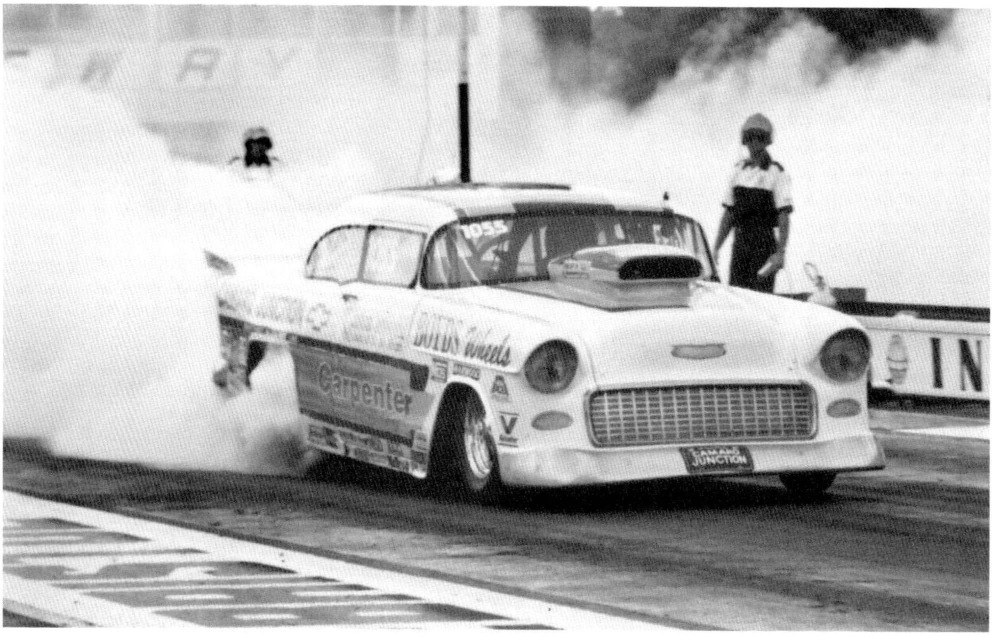

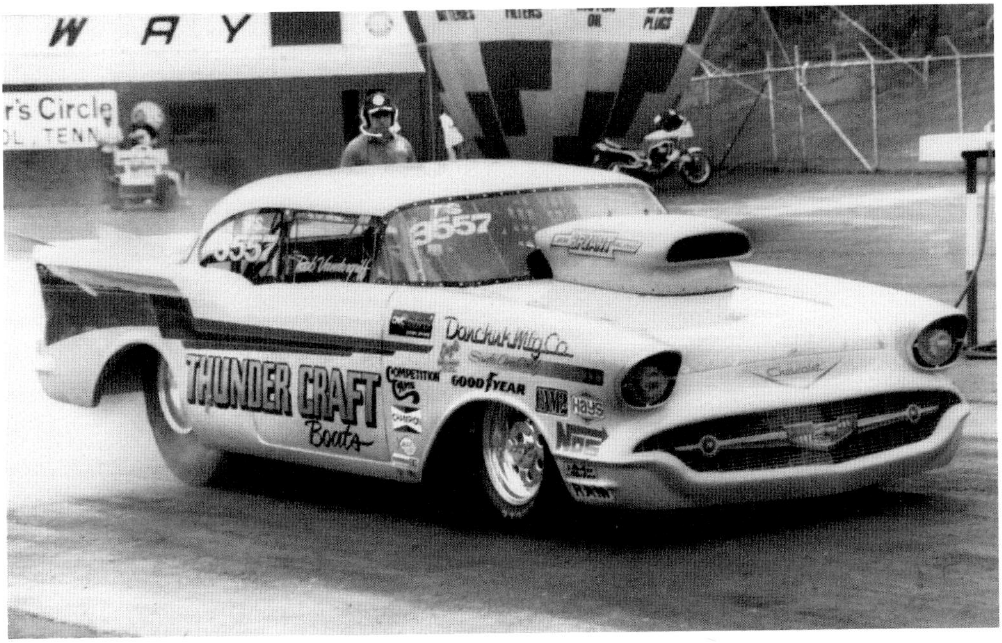

The first answer to Carpenter's shoebox Chevy was the 1957 Chevrolet raced by Tennesseans Jim Bryant and Rob Vandergriff. The duo burst onto the Top Sportsman scene in 1985 with the fiberglass-bodied racer shown above. Vandergriff (near lane below) drove this radical, more aerodynamic machine to a Pro Modified runner-up showing to Scotty Cannon at the 1991 Spring Nationals. (Photographs by David McGee.)

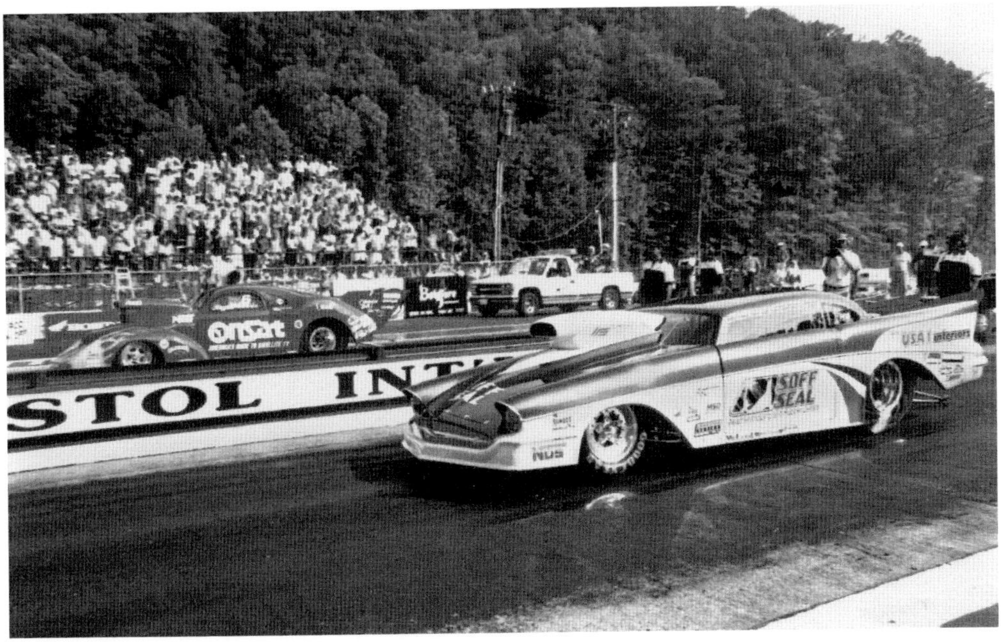

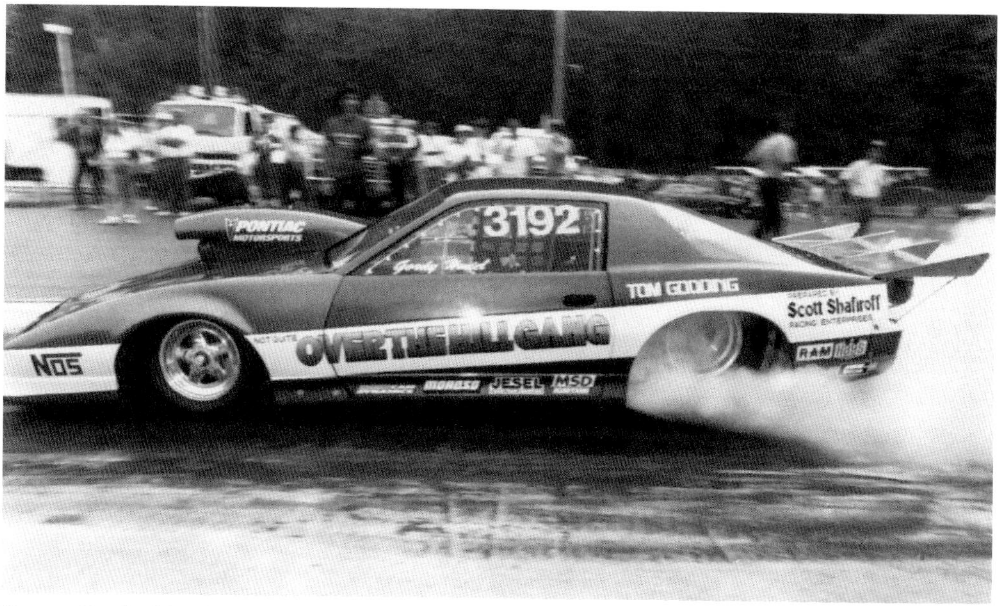

Driver Gordy Hmiel and car owner Scott Shafiroff made drag-racing history at the 1988 Fall Nationals. Hmiel became the first Top Sportsman car in the 6-second zone, running 6.99 seconds in an elimination-round win over Ronnie Hood. Ironically the driver and car owner had to catch a plane flight before eliminations could be completed. (Photograph by David McGee.)

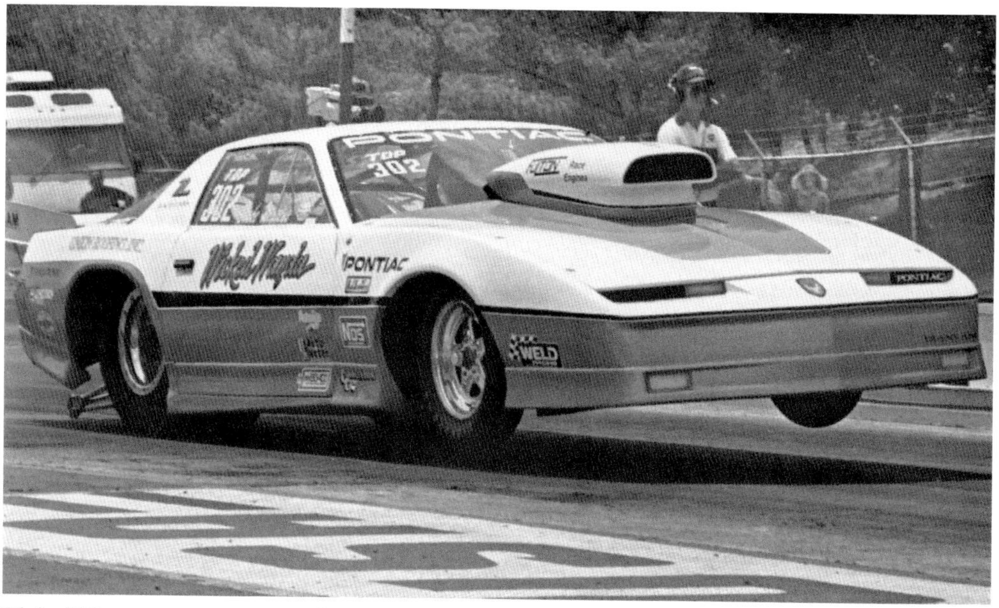

Blake Wiggins was a terror in his series of "Wicked Wanda" Corvettes and Pontiacs. The cars, named for his wife, always qualified near the top of the chart and were factors on race day. Wiggins pocketed $5,000 at Bristol by winning the 1988 Ram Top Performer Challenge. Three years later, he won the Ram Pro Modified Challenge and $10,000. He was also runner-up in Bristol's first Pro Modified final. (Photograph by David McGee.)

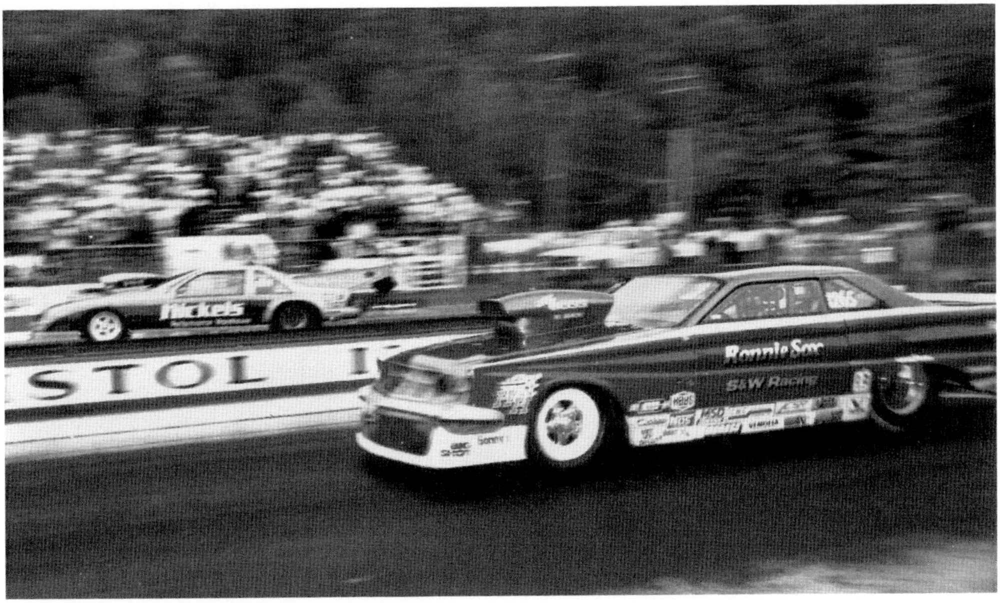

When the Pro Modified class began, it attracted a mixture of the Top Sportsman standouts, new drivers, and many veterans from other classes. The first two winners at Thunder Valley were newcomer Mike Ashley (far lane), who won the Spring Nationals, and Ronnie Sox, who beat Ashley in the Fall Nationals finals for his last Bristol win. (Photograph by David McGee.)

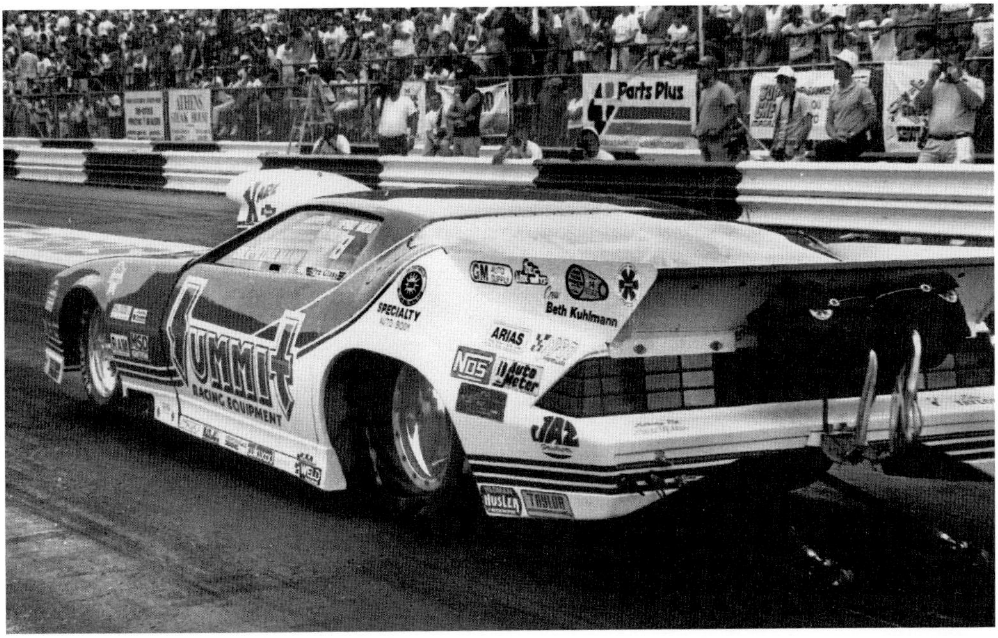

The first Top Sportsman racer to reach 200 miles per hour, Bill Kuhlmann won the 1993 Pro Modified crown at the Spring Nationals. The Missouri driver raced a variety of unique Chevrolet products, including this Camaro with a massive rear spoiler that extended into the rear window. Kuhlmann also won at a Bristol Super Chevy event. (Photograph by David McGee.)

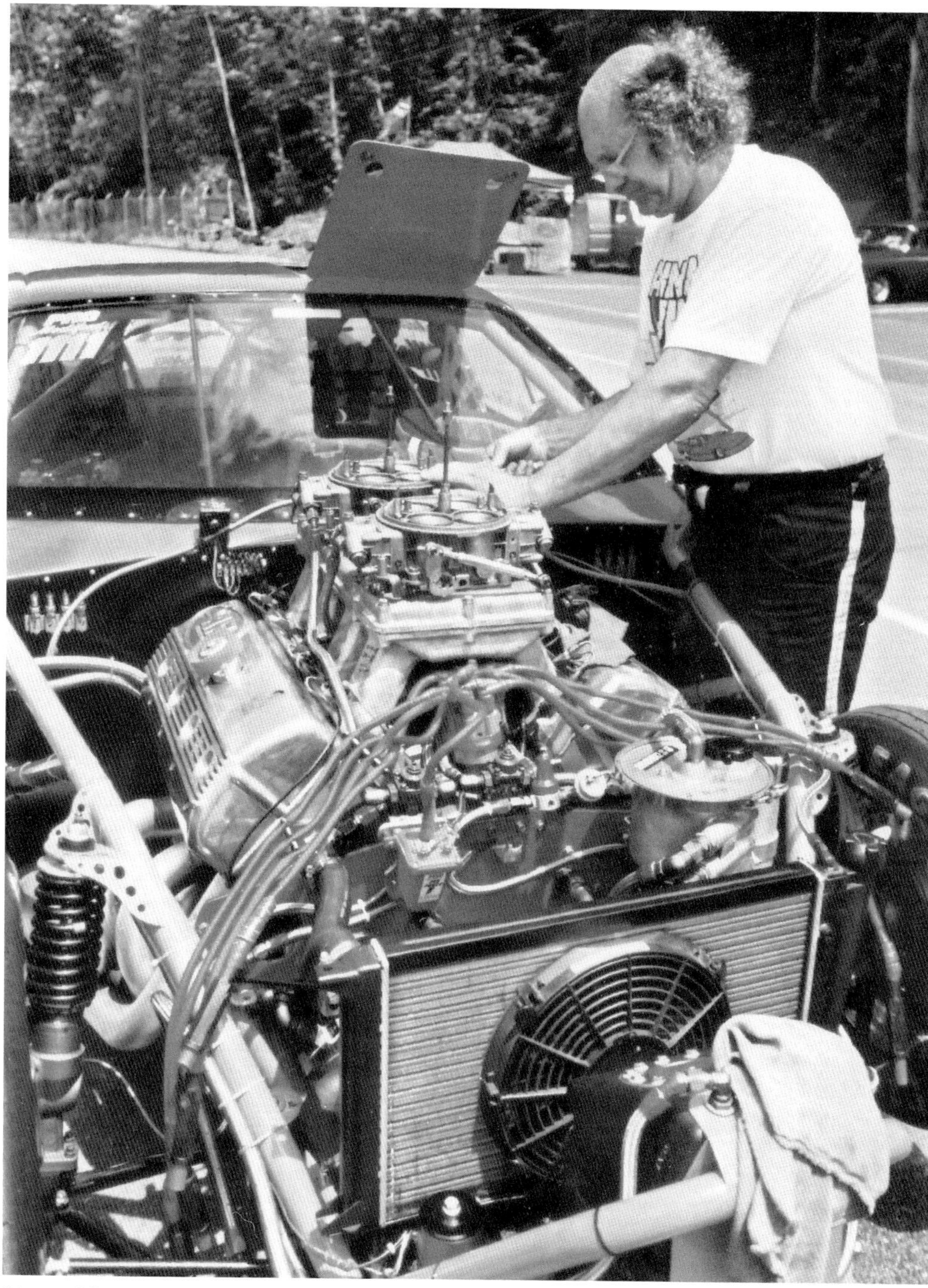

"Animal Jim" Feurer was a star in the Top Sportsman class whose fame grew in Pro Modified. A fan favorite for his wild antics, colorfully painted cars, and his loyalty to Ford products, Animal Jim works on the massive engine in his Ford Probe. The Illinois racer was also a strong advocate for continuing the search for prisoners of war and soldiers missing in action and displayed those sentiments on his cars. (Photograph by David McGee.)

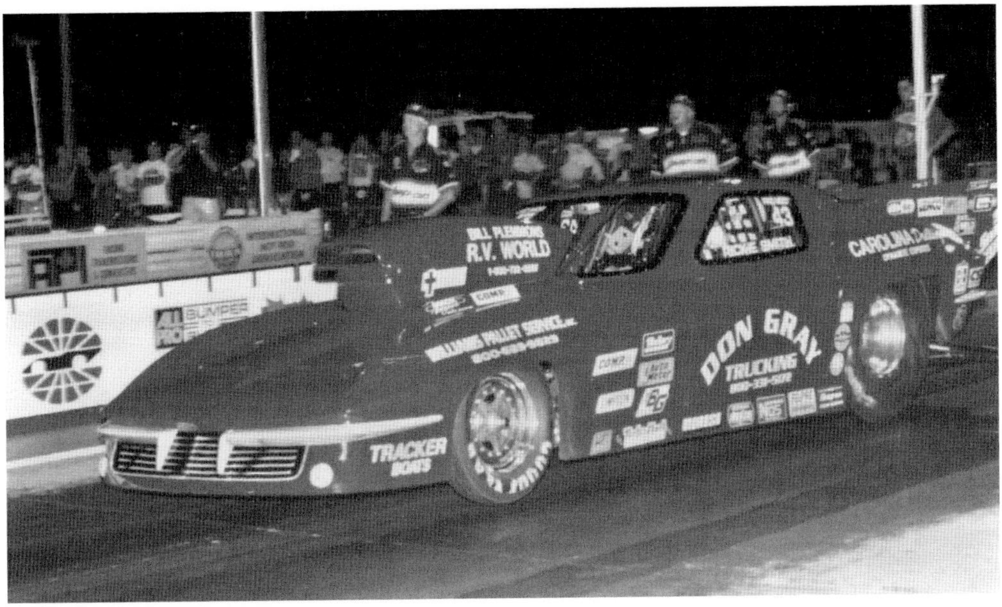

Pro Stock star Rickie Smith has raced the Pro Modified class on a part-time basis with a series of 1963 Corvettes. He won Pro Modified at the 1997 IHRA Spring Nationals and earned a runner-up to Thomas Patterson at the 2002 NHRA Thunder Valley Nationals. (Photograph by David McGee.)

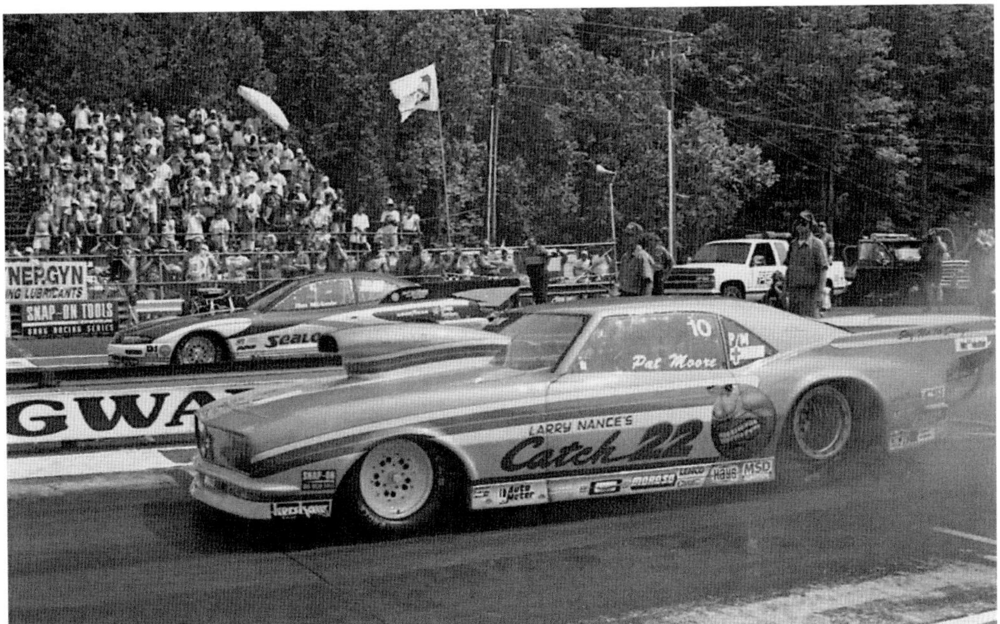

Another favorite of the Bristol fans was Pat Moore aboard the "Catch 22" Camaro owned by former NBA all-star Larry Nance. While he never scored in Pro Modified at Bristol, the 1989 Top Sportsman world champion first gained prominence by winning the IHRA Grand Bracket championship title at Thunder Valley in 1985. (Photograph by David McGee.)

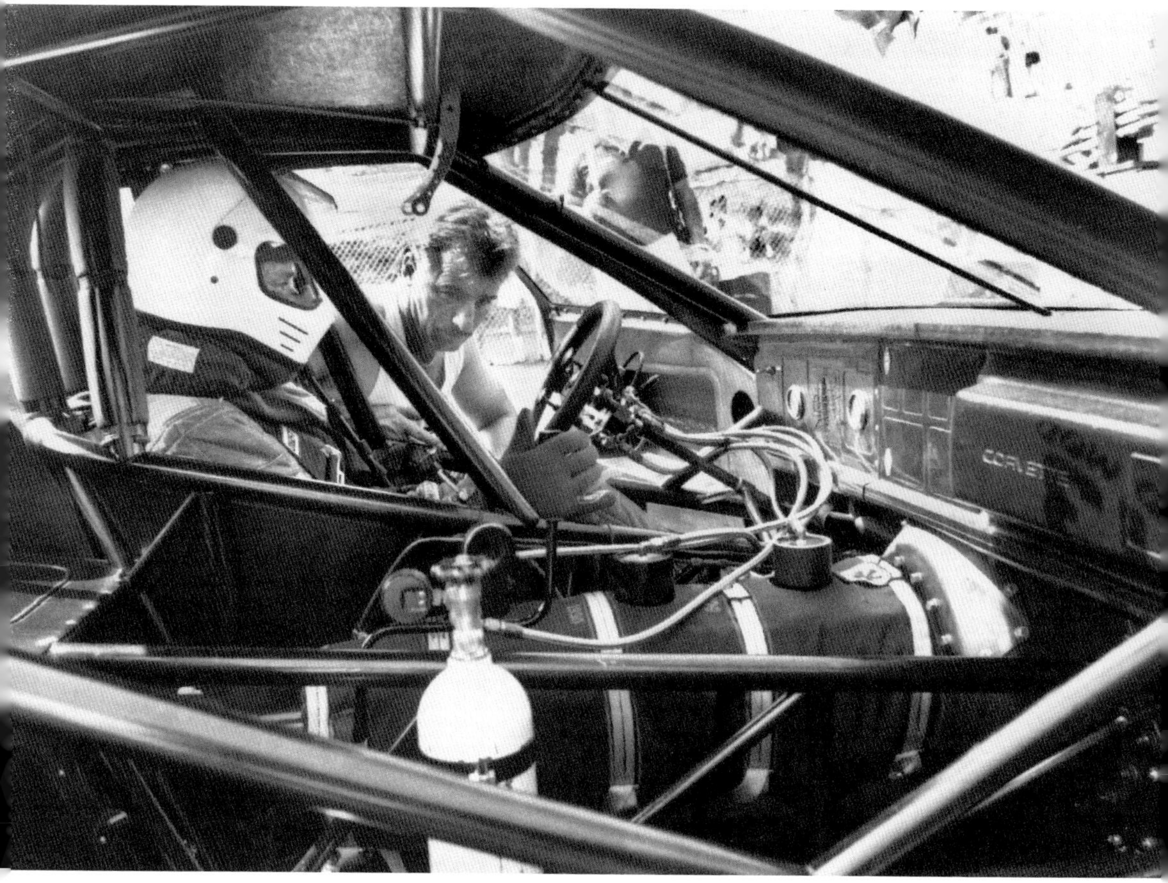

Fred Hahn was a factor in Top Sportsman and Pro Modified for decades, driving a series of supercharged Corvettes for New Yorker Jim Oddy. The team eventually found the Bristol winner's circle at the 2003 Thunder Valley Nationals. Hahn is shown here strapped into the cockpit of the machine. (Photograph by David. McGee.)

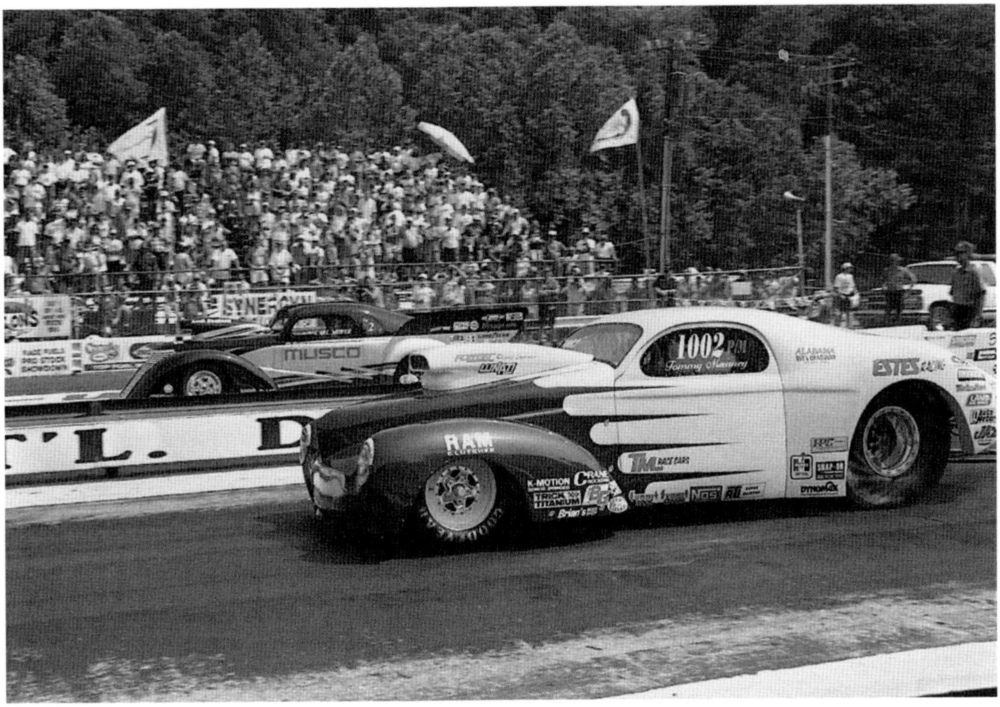

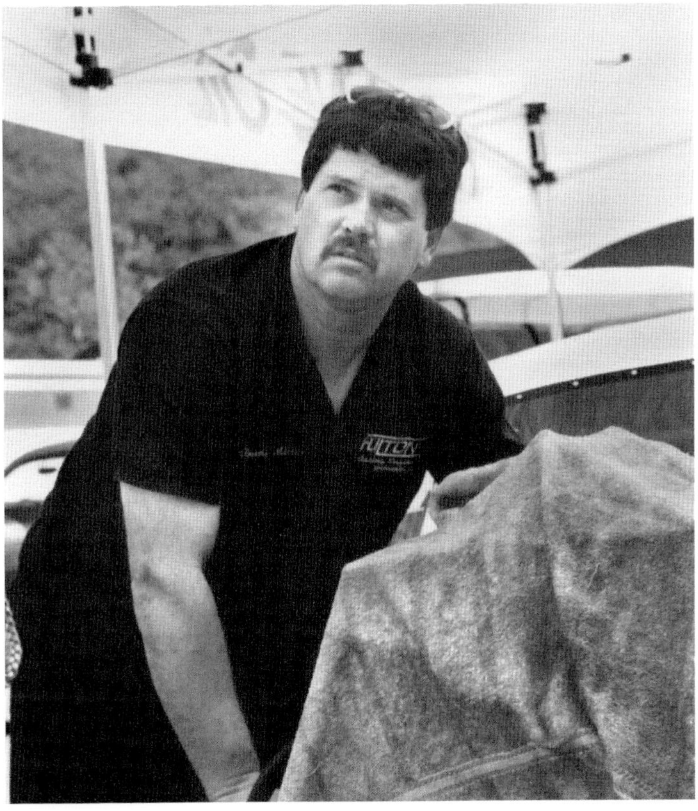

Tommy Mauney became the third driver to win in two different professional classes at Bristol when he captured the 1995 Spring Nationals Pro Modified title in this Willys owned by the Parsons brothers. He is also a former Spring Nationals Pro Stock winner. A professional chassis builder, Mauney wrapped up the 1995 world championship at that year's Fall Nationals. Following Mauney's success, Shannon Jenkins replaced him in the driver's seat of the Willys and won two straight Fall Nationals titles. (Photographs by David McGee.)

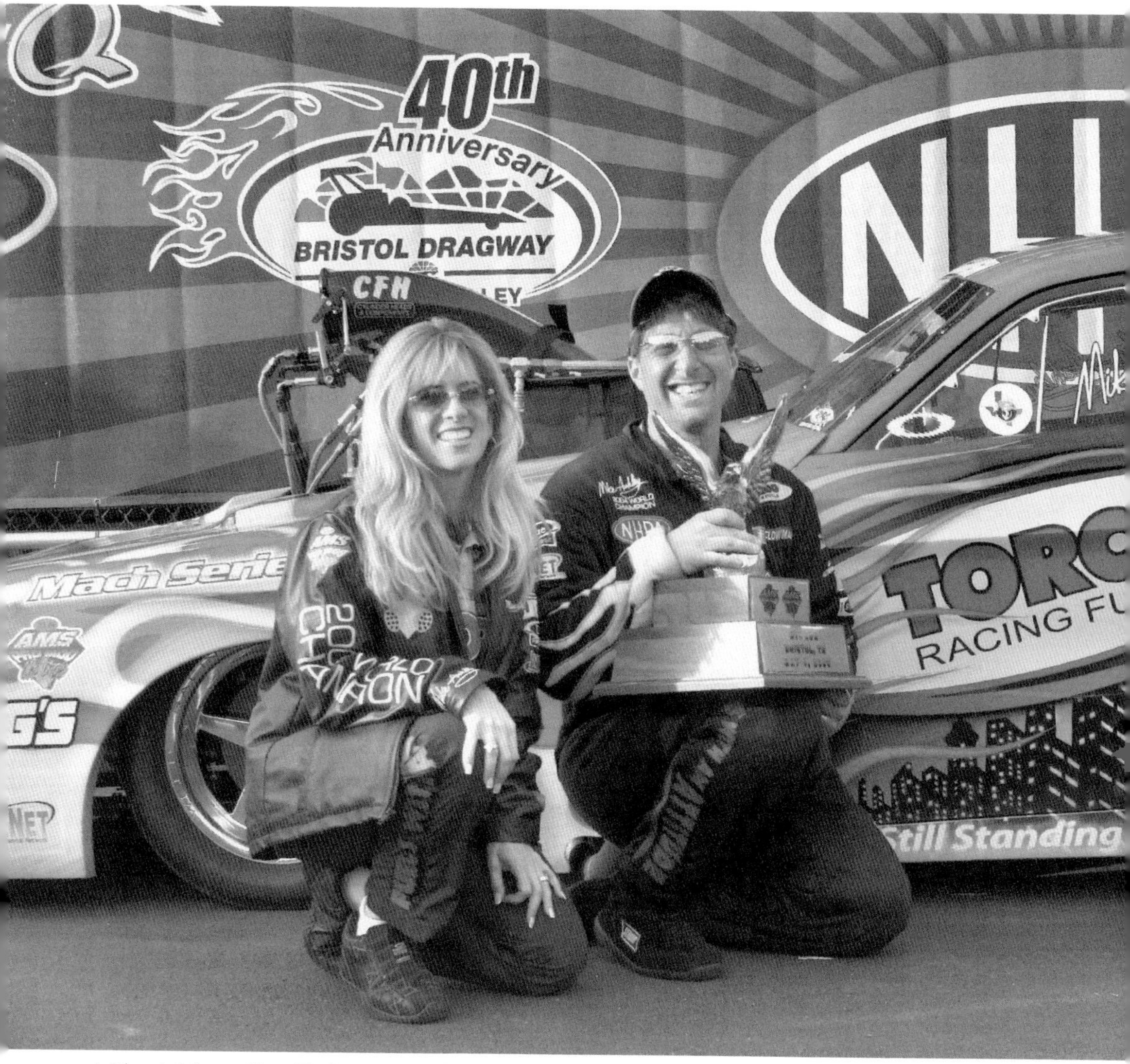

Mike Ashley, a New York mortgage banker, returned to Bristol 15 years after his first Pro Modified win and captured the class at the 2005 Thunder Valley Nationals. He is pictured with his wife, Mindy, in the winner's circle. Ashley's colorful supercharged Mustang was maintained by Bristol's Adkins brothers and painted at their Illusions Custom Paint shop about a mile from Thunder Valley. He began competing in the nitro Funny Car class in late 2005. (Photograph by David McGee.)

6

A Place to Race Everything

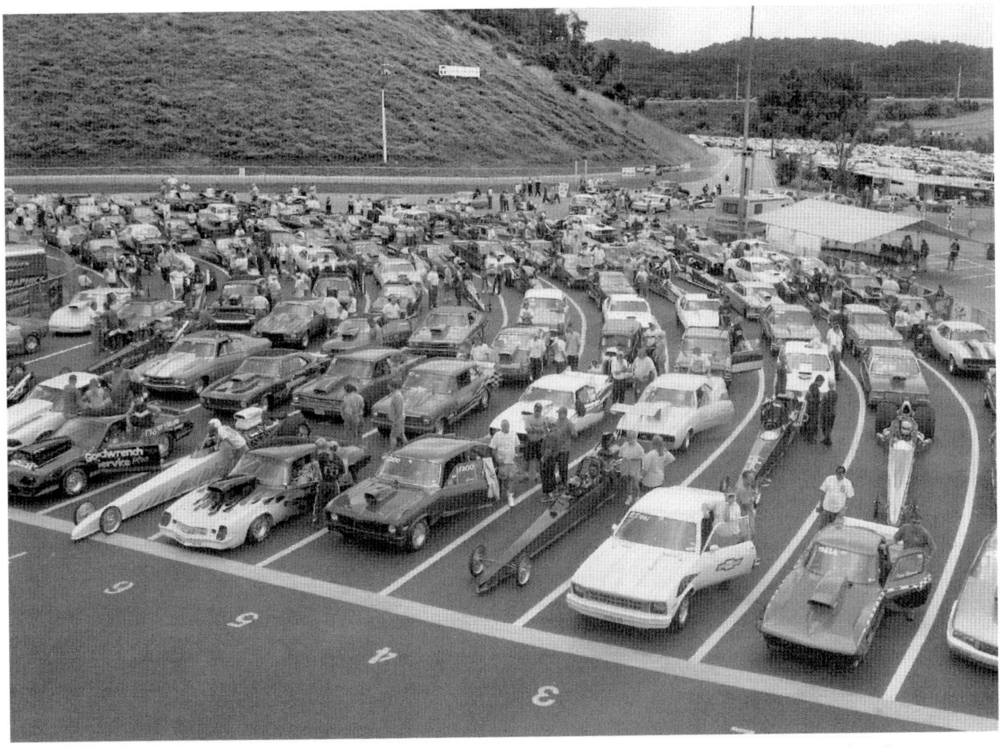

For every professional driver who has traversed the Bristol quarter-mile, thousands of sportsman racers have completed that same journey in every type of vehicle imaginable. From the diverse variety of national-event sportsman classes, brand-specific events, and weekend bracket-racing warriors of all ages to teens in street machines out for fun—Thunder Valley has catered to them all. In this photograph from the 2004 Super Chevy Show, the staging lanes are jammed with racers eager for their shot at the legendary racetrack. (Photograph by David McGee.)

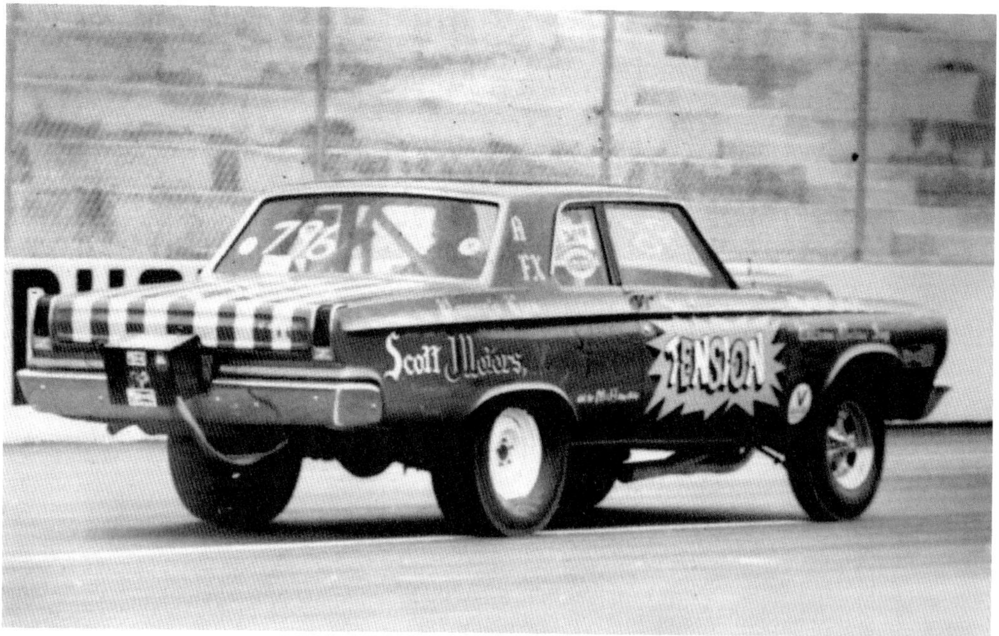

Shirl Greer, from nearby Kingsport, Tennessee, raced his "Tension" Dodge at the first Spring Nationals in 1965. As his career advanced into nitro Funny Cars, Greer won two Bristol national events and the 1974 NHRA world championship. (Courtesy of BMS archives.)

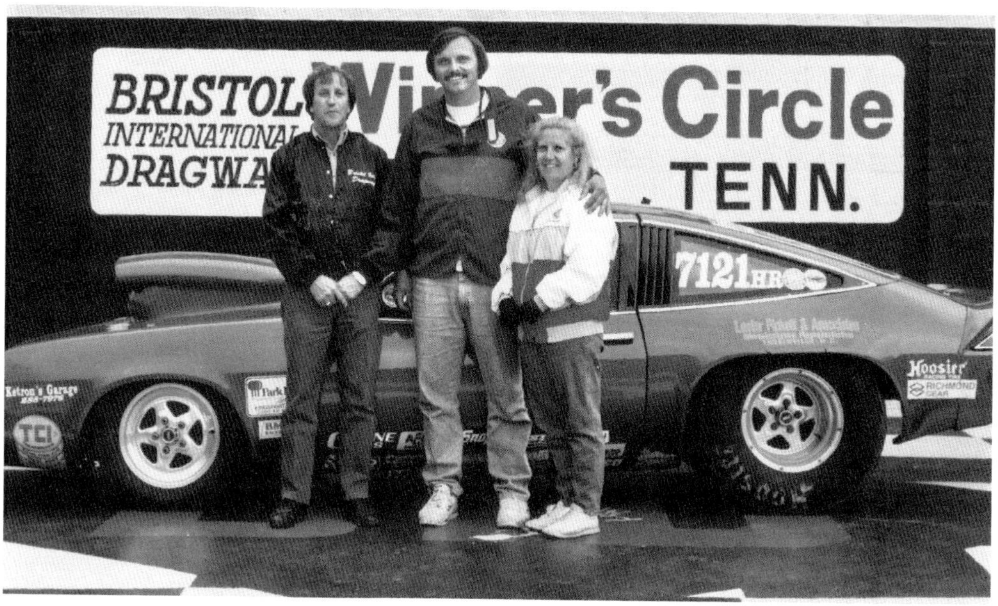

Many of Van Greer's career highlights have come at Bristol. The son of Shirl Greer won IHRA's Grand Bracket world championship title there in 1991. Pictured here with wife Christy and former track manager Gene Barker, Greer also won the 1996 Spring Nationals Super Rod title and was runner-up at two other national events. He has also captured numerous Thunder Valley bracket wins and championships. (Photograph by Chris Barker.)

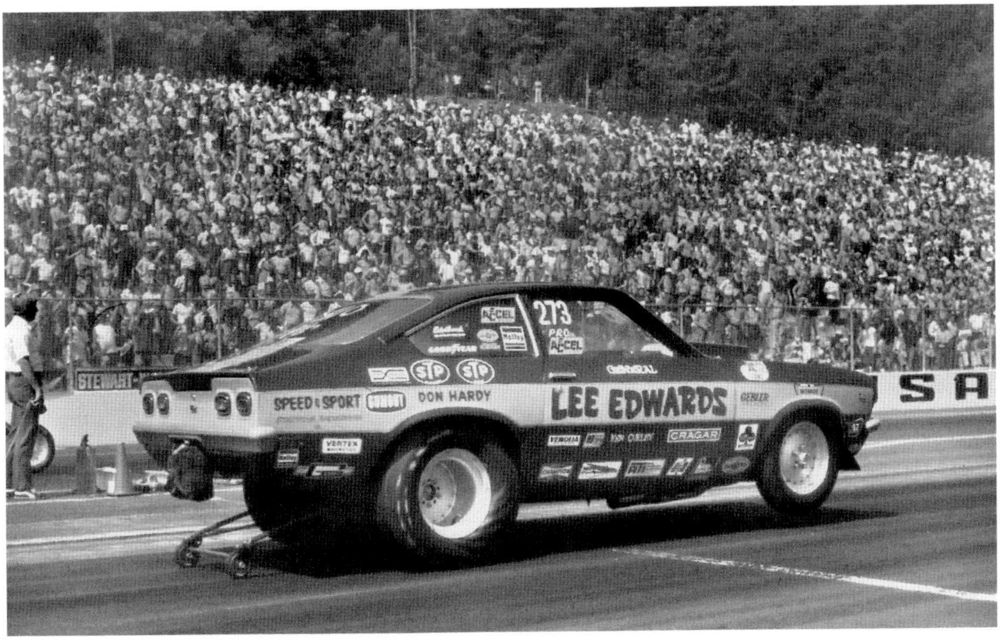

Virginia native Lee Edwards is best known as a Pro Stock standout, but his first national-event win came in Competition Eliminator at the 1973 All-American Nationals. Edwards was the 1977 Spring Nationals Pro Stock champion. (Photograph by John Beach.)

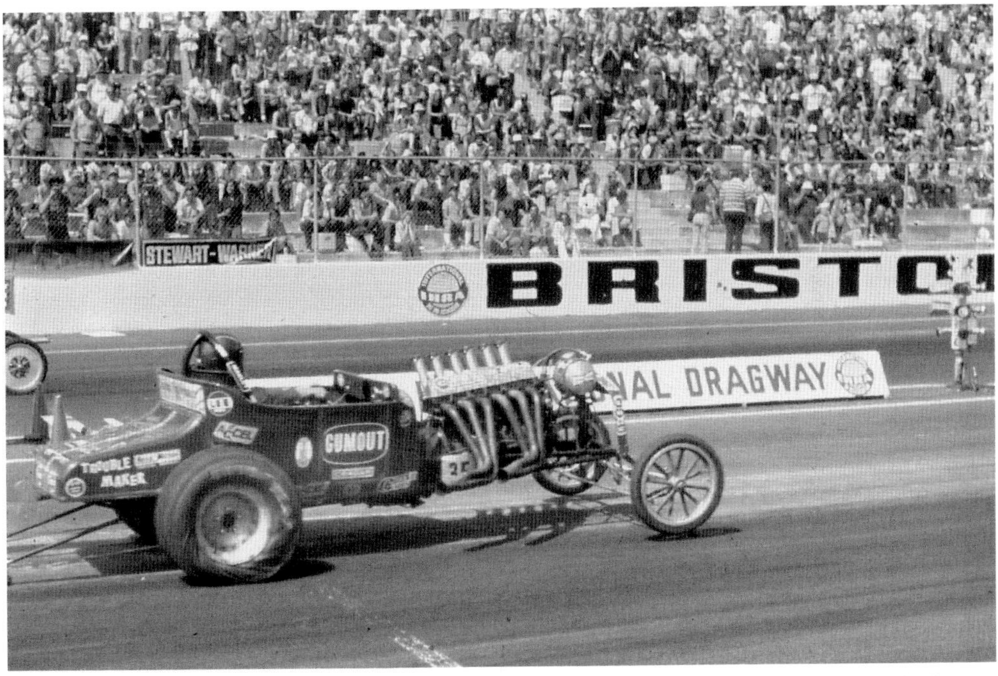

Joe Williamson drove his wild Kentucky-based "Trouble Maker" machine to the 1974 Spring Nationals title. The unique six-cylinder altered-class car captured Competition Eliminator. (Photograph by John Beach.)

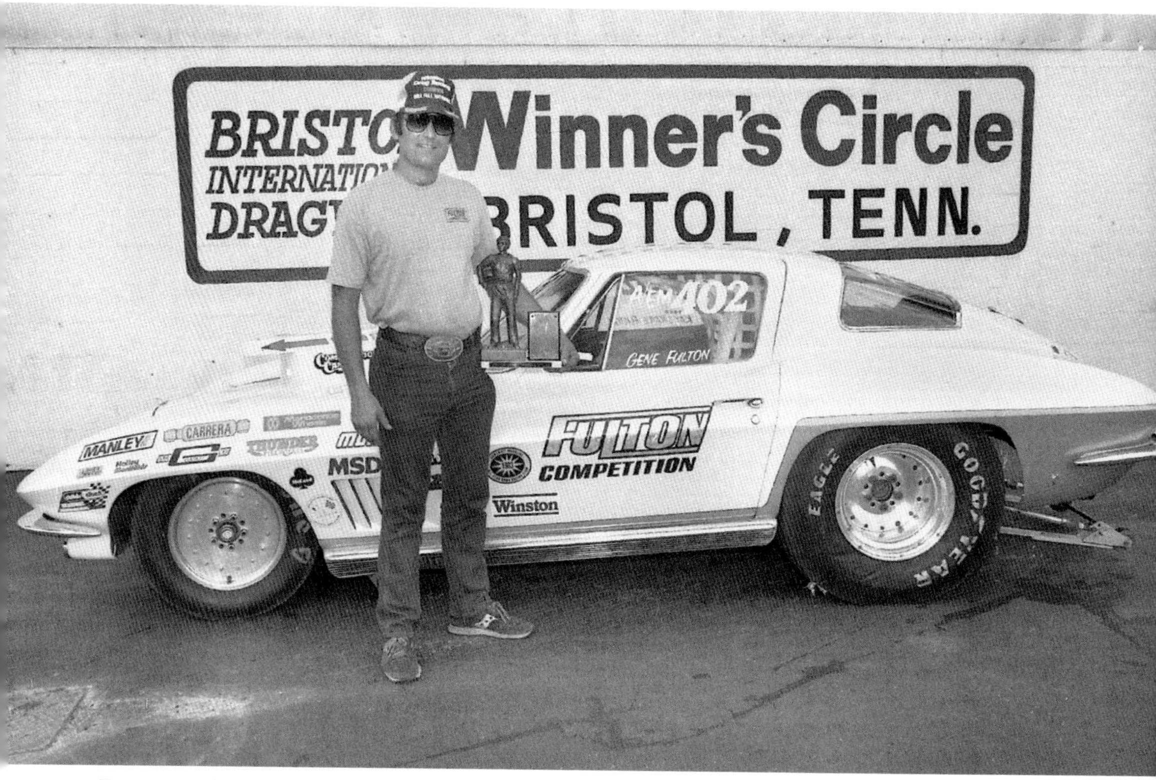

Few racers have experienced the highs and lows of Thunder Valley quite like Gene Fulton. The South Carolina engine builder won six national events at Bristol between 1974 and 1988. In 1978, however, Fulton escaped a harrowing top-end crash with another car that destroyed his Nova station wagon. (Photograph by David McGee.)

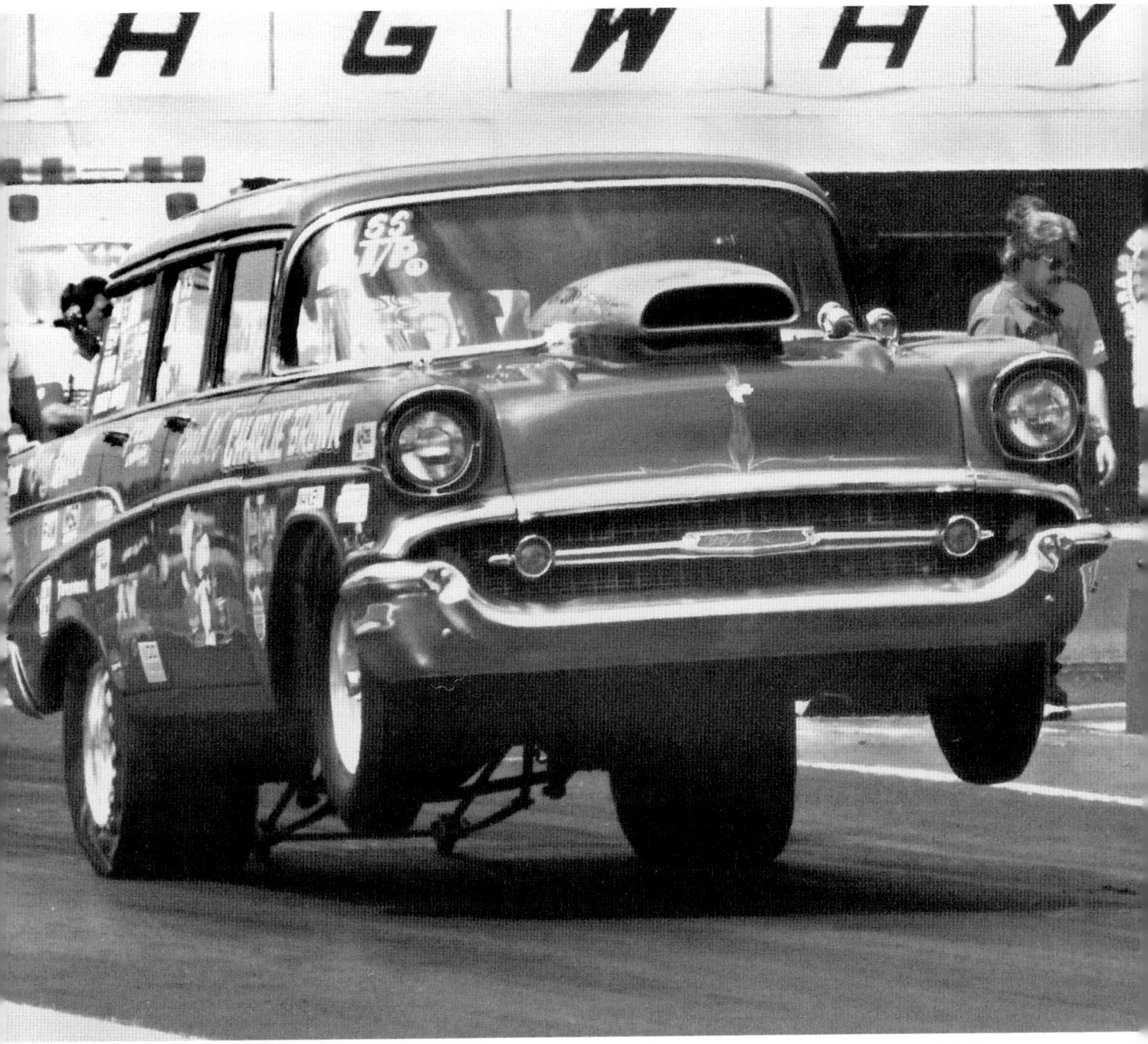

The only driver with more Bristol sportsman wins than Fulton is eight-time IHRA world champion Mike Boyles. His crowd-pleasing 1957 Chevy station wagon, dubbed "Good Ole Charlie Brown," has reached the Bristol winner's circle on eight occasions. In 1991–1992, Boyles won four straight national events by going unbeaten through more than 25 elimination rounds. He owns wins in the 1970s, 1980s, and 1990s. (Photograph by David McGee.)

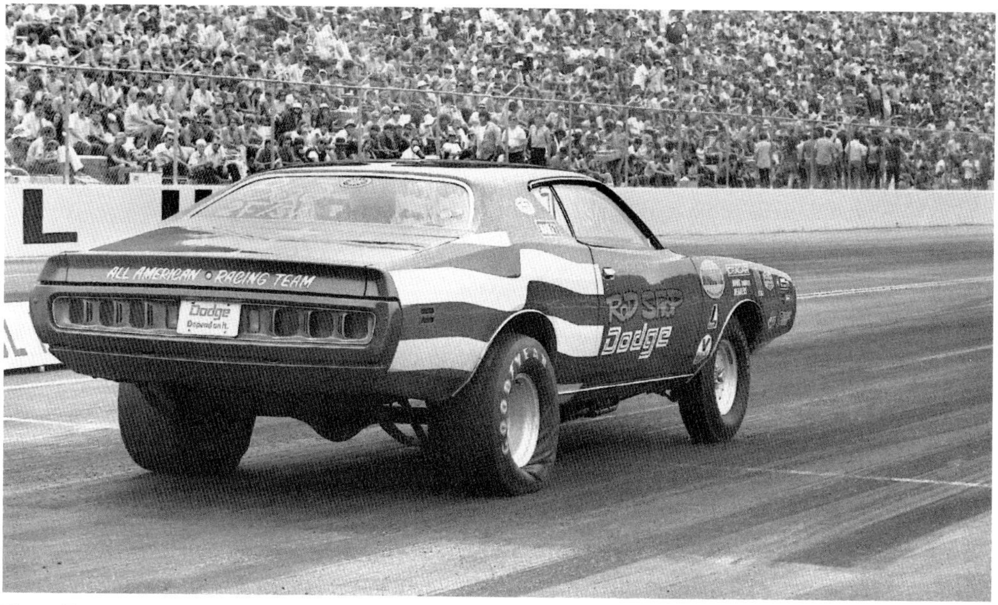

Dave Boertman is widely regarded as one of the best drivers to ever race in the Stock and Super Stock classes. The two-time NHRA world champion enjoyed lots of success at Bristol, racking up five wins in the Super Stock and Junior Stock classes while driving for the Columbus, Ohio–based Rod Shop team. (Photograph by John Beach.)

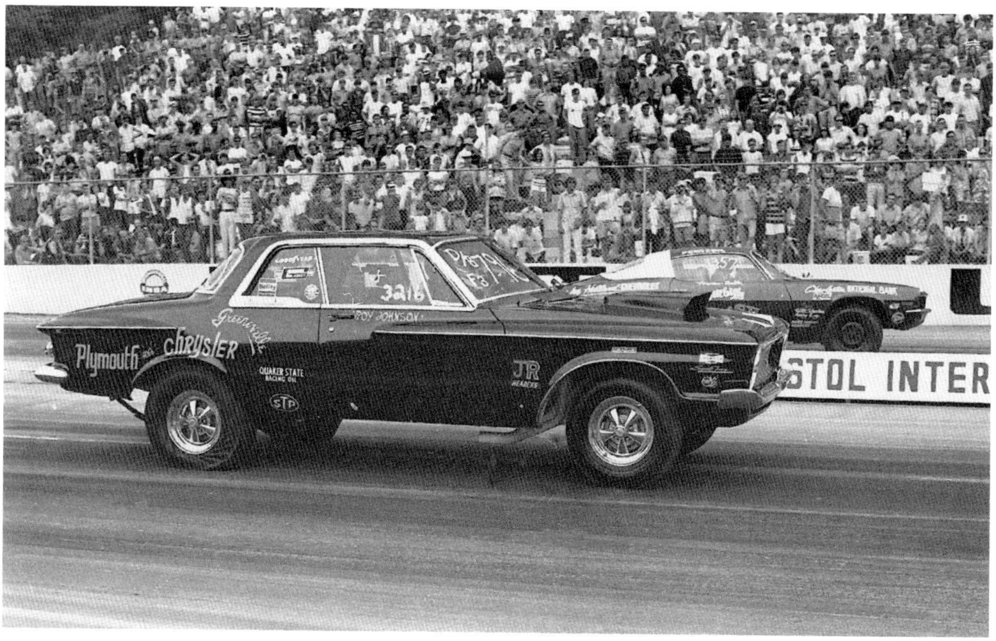

Past world champion Roy Johnson's first visit to the Bristol winner's circle happened at the 1972 All-American Nationals, as he drove this Plymouth to the Top Stock win. He also won Formula Stock at the 1974 Spring Nationals, and his son, Allen, captured the 1982 Spring Nationals Super Stock title. (Photograph by John Beach.)

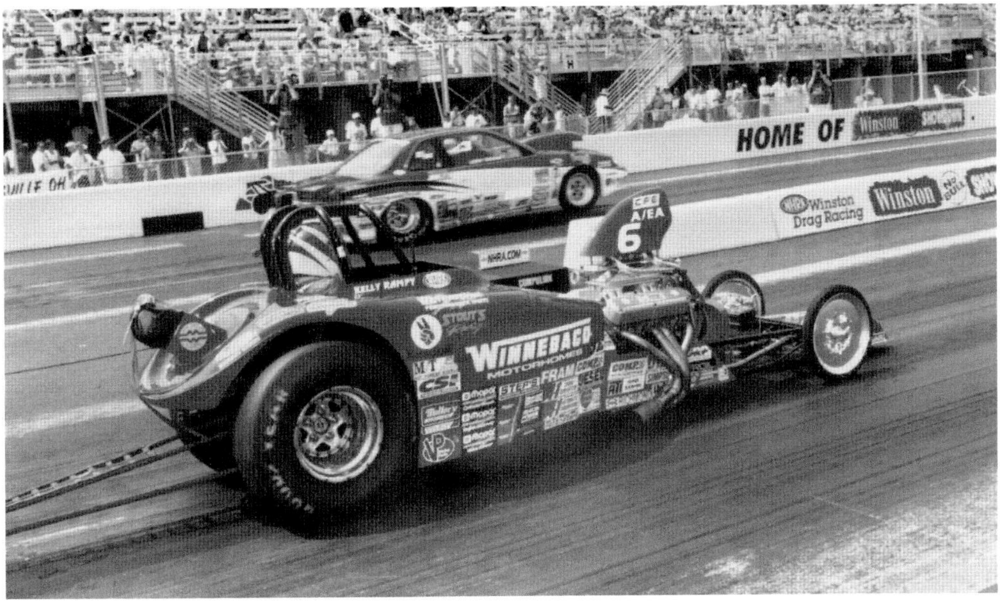

David Rampy (near lane) has won three NHRA national events, reached two divisional-race final rounds, won an IHRA national, and won the 1985 IHRA Bracket Finals title at Bristol over a 21-year span. Tennessean Larry Pritchett (far lane) won at the 1999 Winston Showdown and then racked up two wins in four final rounds at Bristol's NHRA Southeast Divisional races. (Photograph by David McGee.)

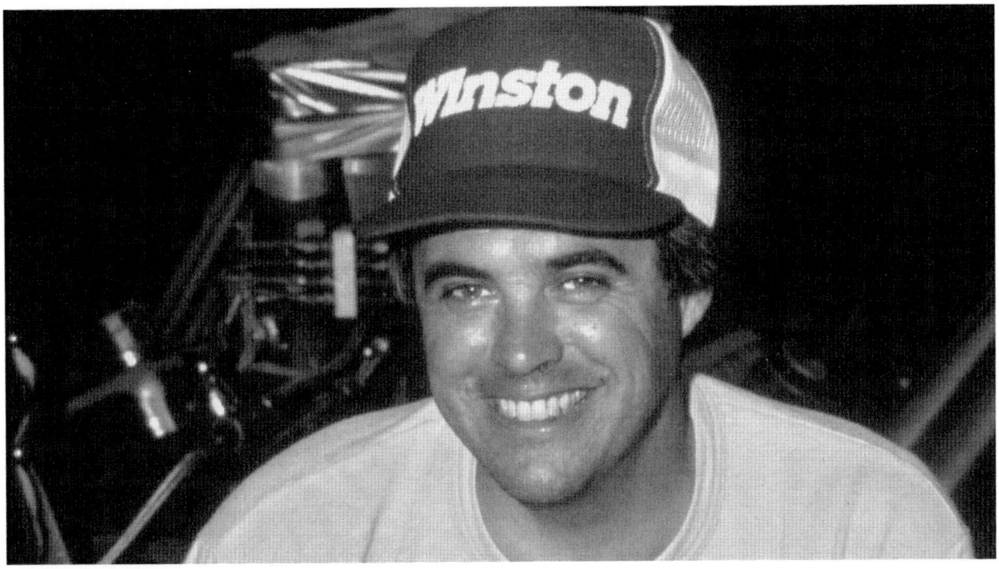

In more than 40 years of operation, only one driver has been fatally injured racing at Bristol. World champion Don Young died after his short-wheelbase dragster crossed the track and struck the guardrail at more than 150 miles per hour during the 1985 Fall Nationals. Because Young held a commanding lead in that season's points, he was honored posthumously with a second world championship. (Courtesy the author's collection.)

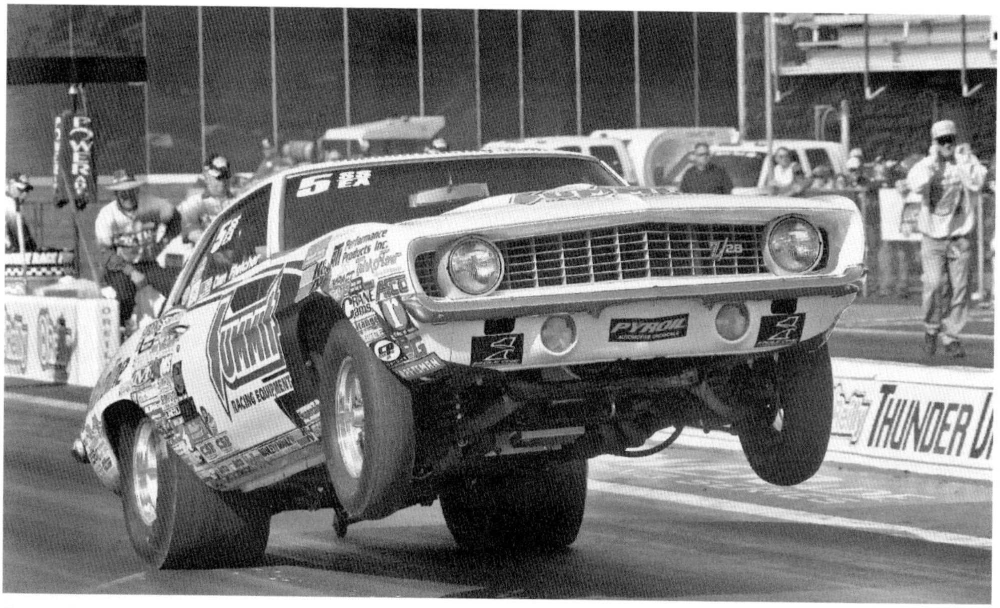

Dan Fletcher is one of two drivers to win the Super Stock class at Bristol under two different sanctioning bodies. The other is legendary driver Ronnie Sox. Fletcher won the track's final IHRA race in 1997 and the inaugural NHRA Thunder Valley Nationals in 2001 driving the same 1969 Camaro. Sox won the class at NHRA and AHRA races in 1967 and 1968. (Photograph by David McGee.)

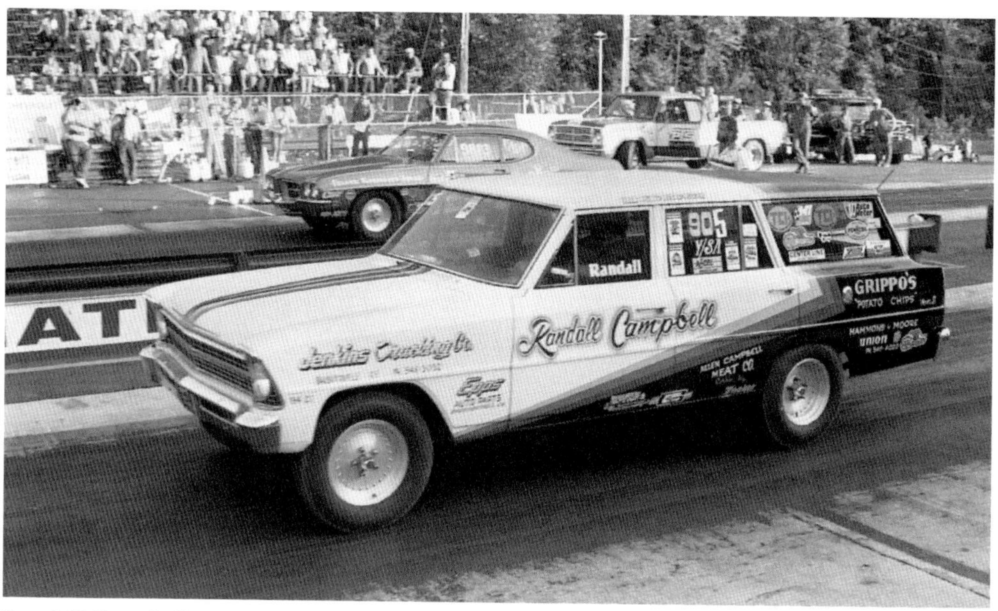

Randall Campbell, a two-time IHRA Stock world champion, has three career wins at Bristol in his six-cylinder-powered Chevrolet station wagon. While it was one of the slowest cars at any national event, in staggered-start sportsman racing, the slower car leaves first. Few could overcome Campbell's head starts. (Photograph by David McGee.)

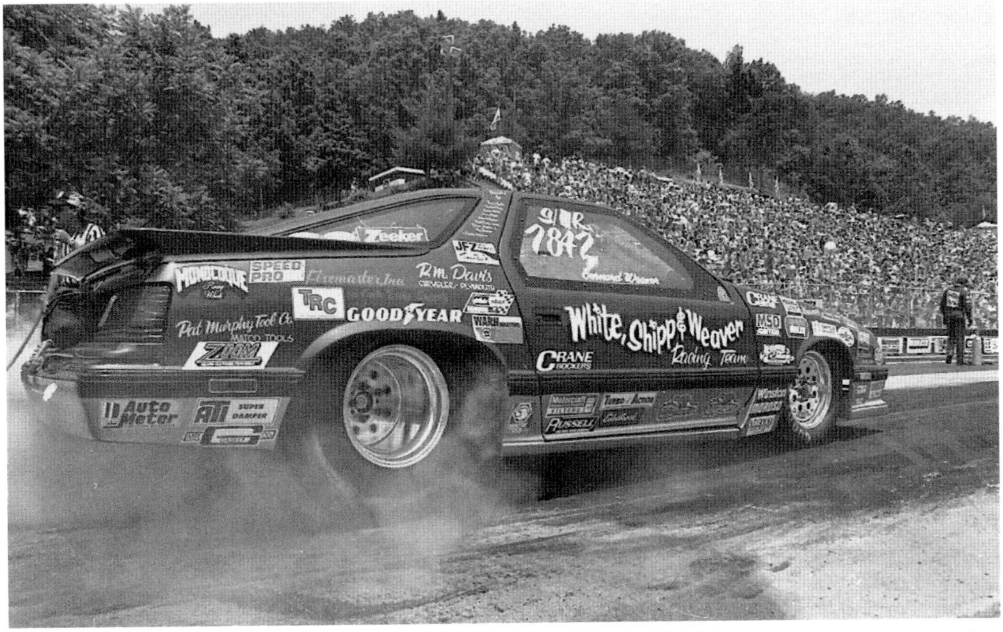

Bernard Weaver's Bristol success transcends two decades, as the Virginia racer has driven his Dodge to three wins in the 9.90 class. Called Super Gas in NHRA and Super Rod in IHRA, the aim is to run right on, or closest to, a preset 9.90-second index. (Photograph by David McGee.)

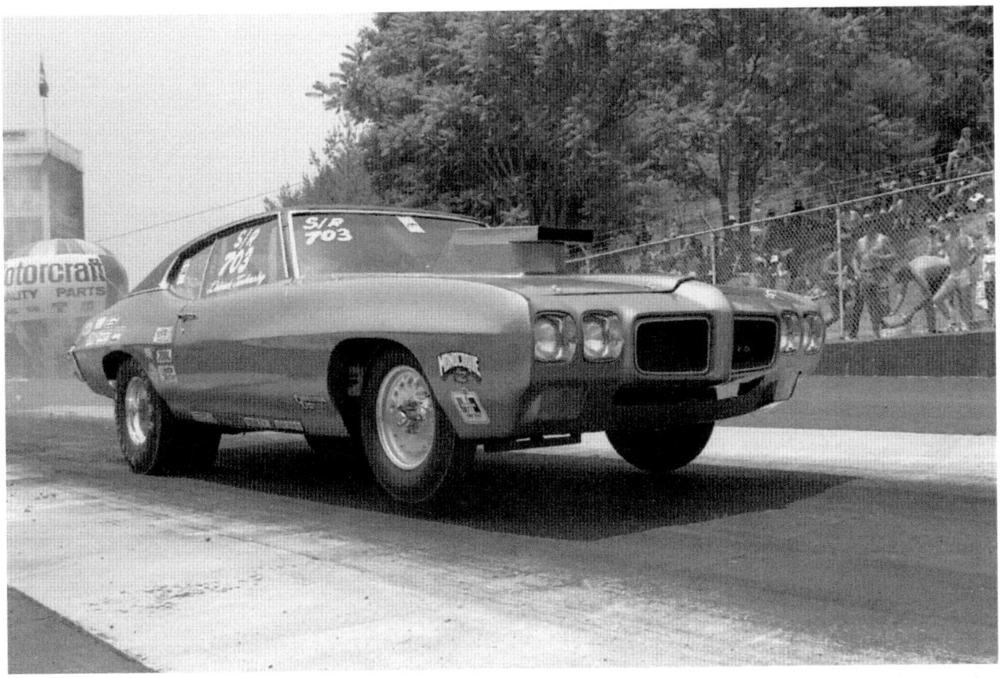

Two-time world champion Joe Tankersley collected four national-event wins at Bristol during the 1980s. The Tennessee racer won the 1983, 1984, and 1987 Fall Nationals, along with the 1986 Spring Nationals, in his Pontiac GTO. (Photograph by David McGee.)

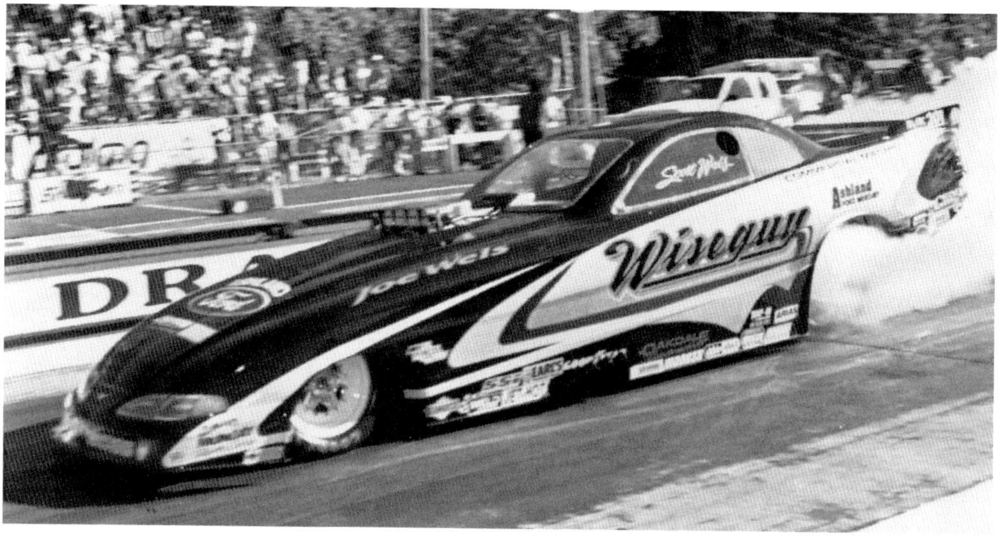

Slower and somewhat less noisy than their nitro-fueled big brothers, alcohol Funny Cars have intermittently been part of the Bristol landscape since the 1970s. During the first 21 races after IHRA established a professional class for the cars in 1986, no driver was able to repeat a Bristol win. Scott Weis broke that streak, winning three times in four seasons. (Photograph by David McGee.)

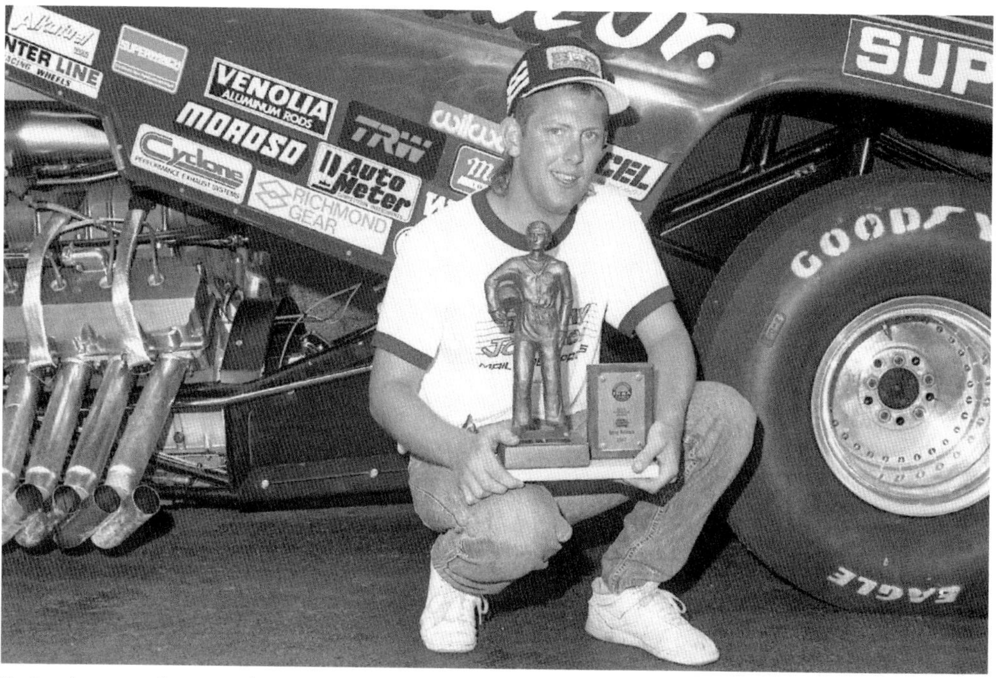

Before he posted national event wins and top 10 performances in Funny Car and Top Fuel, Tommy Johnson Jr. cut his teeth in an alcohol Funny Car. Johnson's first national-event win came at age 19 during the 1987 Spring Nationals. The Iowa teenager defeated multi-time world champion and mentor Bob Newberry in the final round. (Photograph by David McGee.)

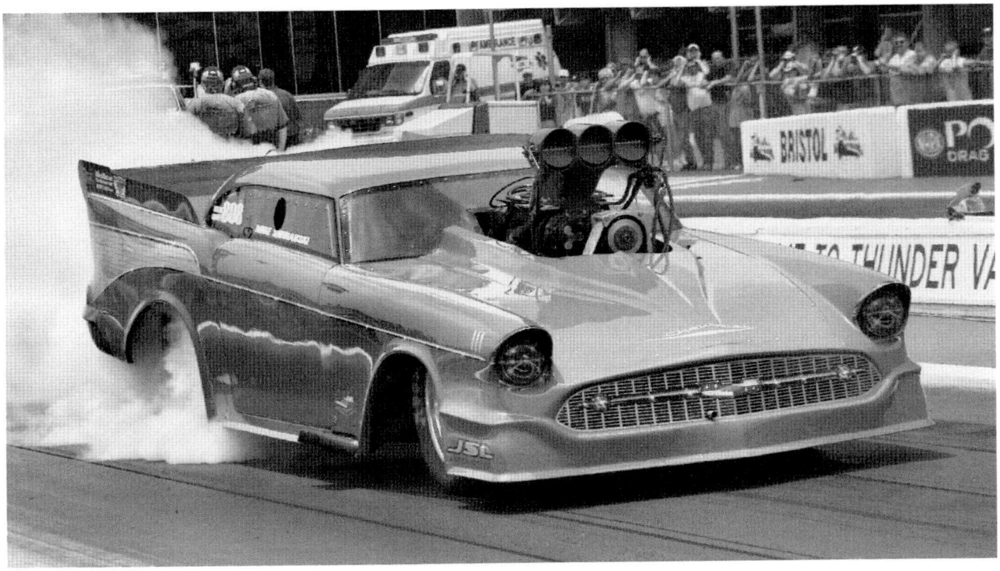

Bristol has hosted the Super Chevy Show nearly every year since 1986. The national series caters to Chevrolet and General Motors fans with an expansive car show, swap meet, vendor area, and lots of drag racing. Mike Swinarski races his radical 1957 Chevrolet in the signature Nitro Coupe class. Created by promoter Roger Gustin, the cars blend Pro Modified styling while burning a mixture of nitromethane and alcohol fuel. (Photograph by David McGee.)

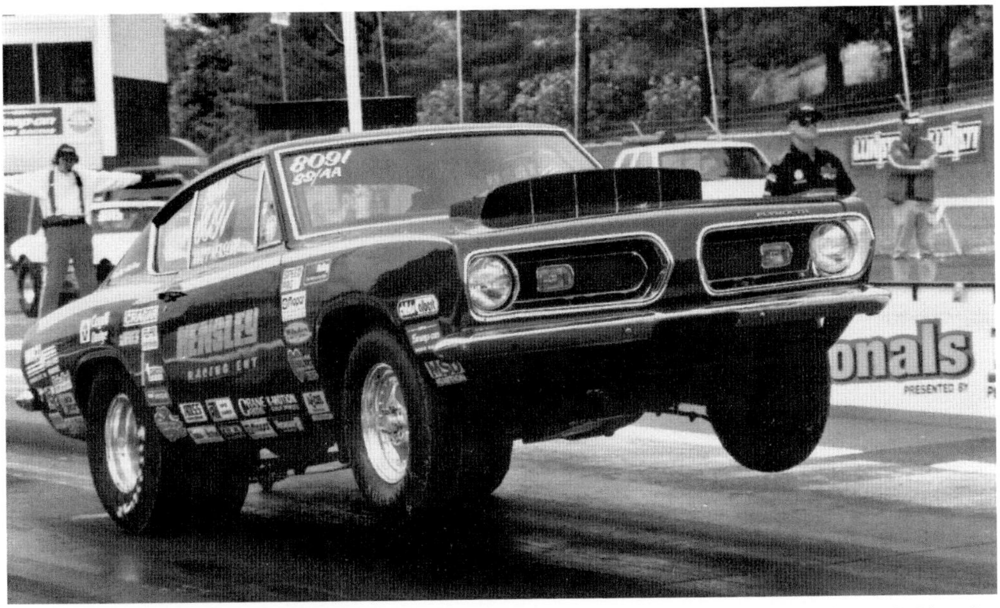

Since the early 1990s, Bristol has also catered to fans of the Dodge, Plymouth, and Chrysler machines with an annual series of Mopar-themed events. Among the regular supporters and sponsors has been the Hensley Racing team of Ken and Matt Hensley from nearby Knoxville, Tennessee. Matt is also a former Spring Nationals Super Stock champion with his popular Hemi-Cuda. (Photograph by David McGee.)

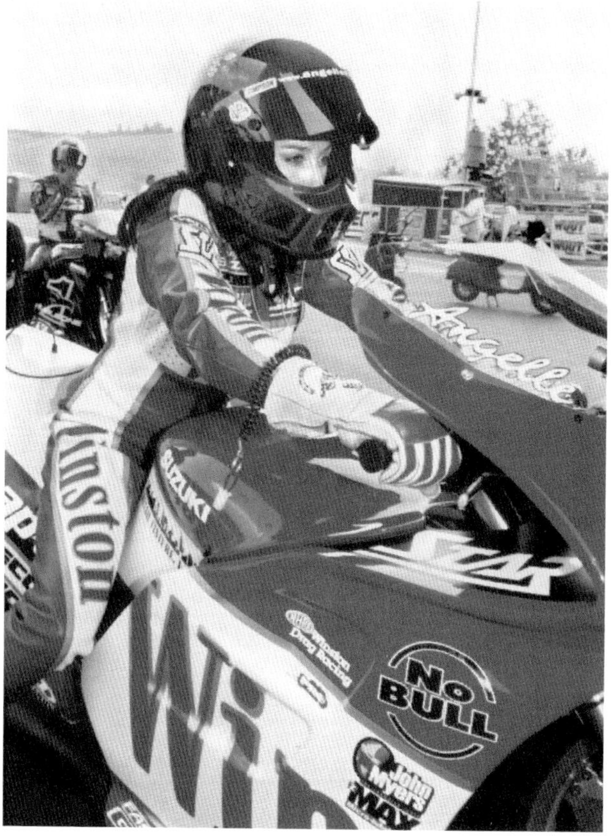

The Pro Stock Motorcycle class hasn't been contested at the Thunder Valley Nationals, but the radical 6-second, 190-mile-per-hour machines ran during the 1999 and 2000 Winston Showdowns. Angelle Sampey (left) prepares to leave the staging lanes aboard her Suzuki. Sampey lost to eventual winner Matt Hines (below) in 2000 but won the first of three world championships later that season. Hines was undefeated in two events at Bristol, riding his family's Suzuki to both showdown wins. (Photographs by David McGee.)

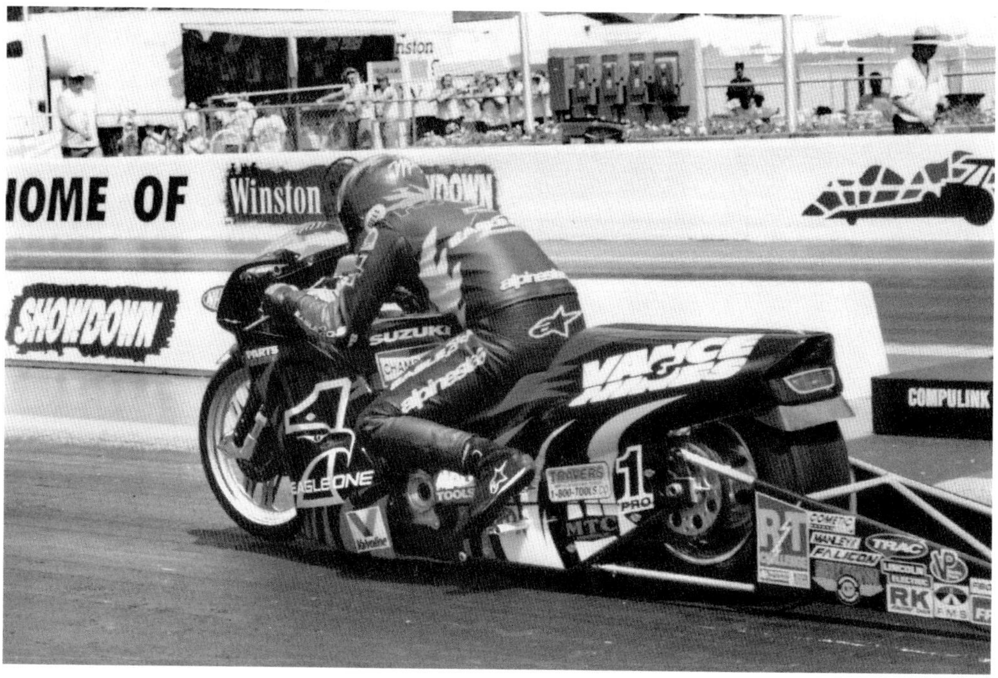

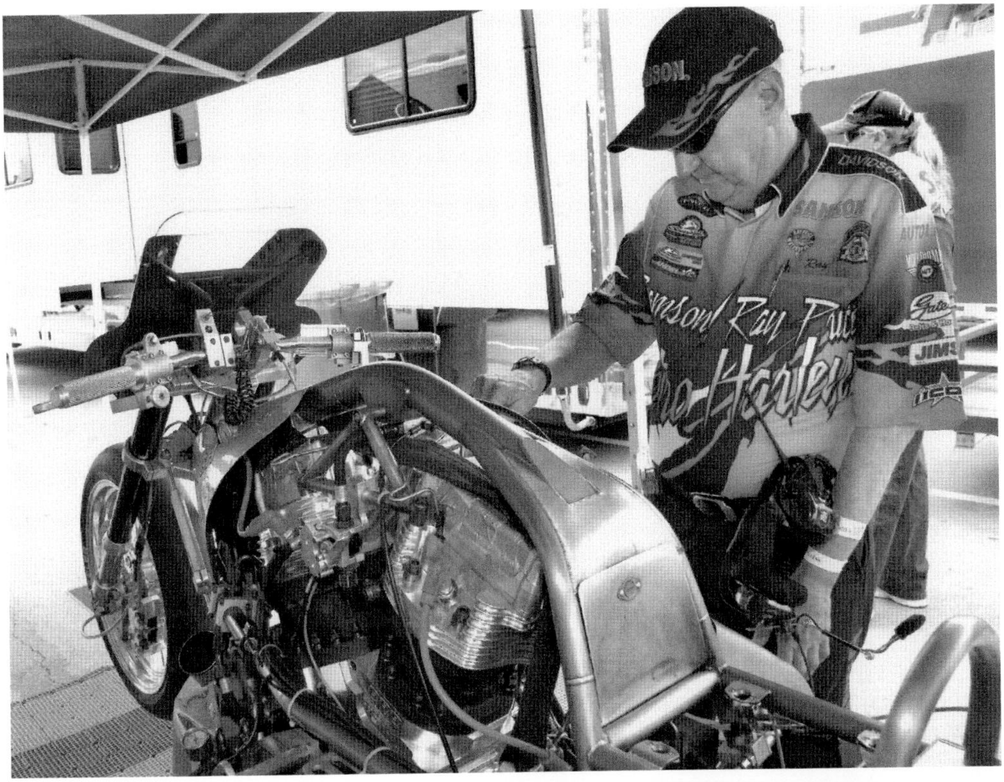

Bristol's annual Harley Davidson race, conducted by the All Harley Drag Racing Association, attracts racers and their fans from across the country. Former rider and legendary tuner Ray Price (above) works on his machine. The fastest Harley and Buell motorcycles (right) use nitromethane fuel to help make power to run in the six-second range at more than 200 miles per hour. (Courtesy *Bristol Herald Courier*; photographs by Earl Neikirk.)

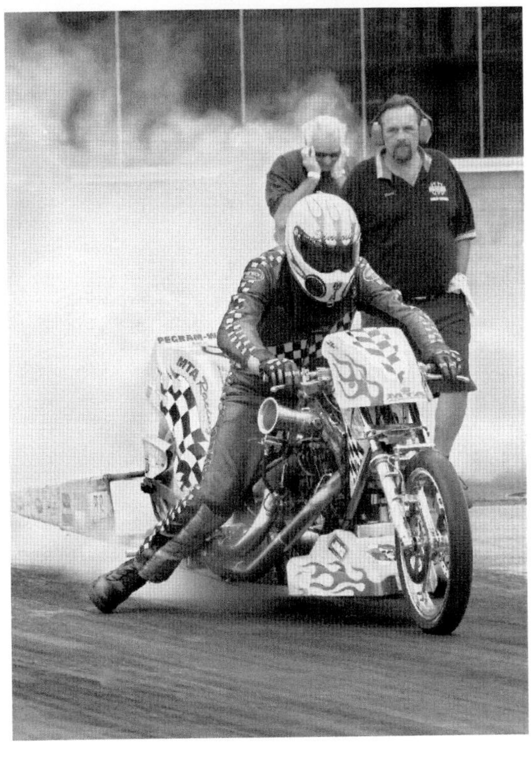

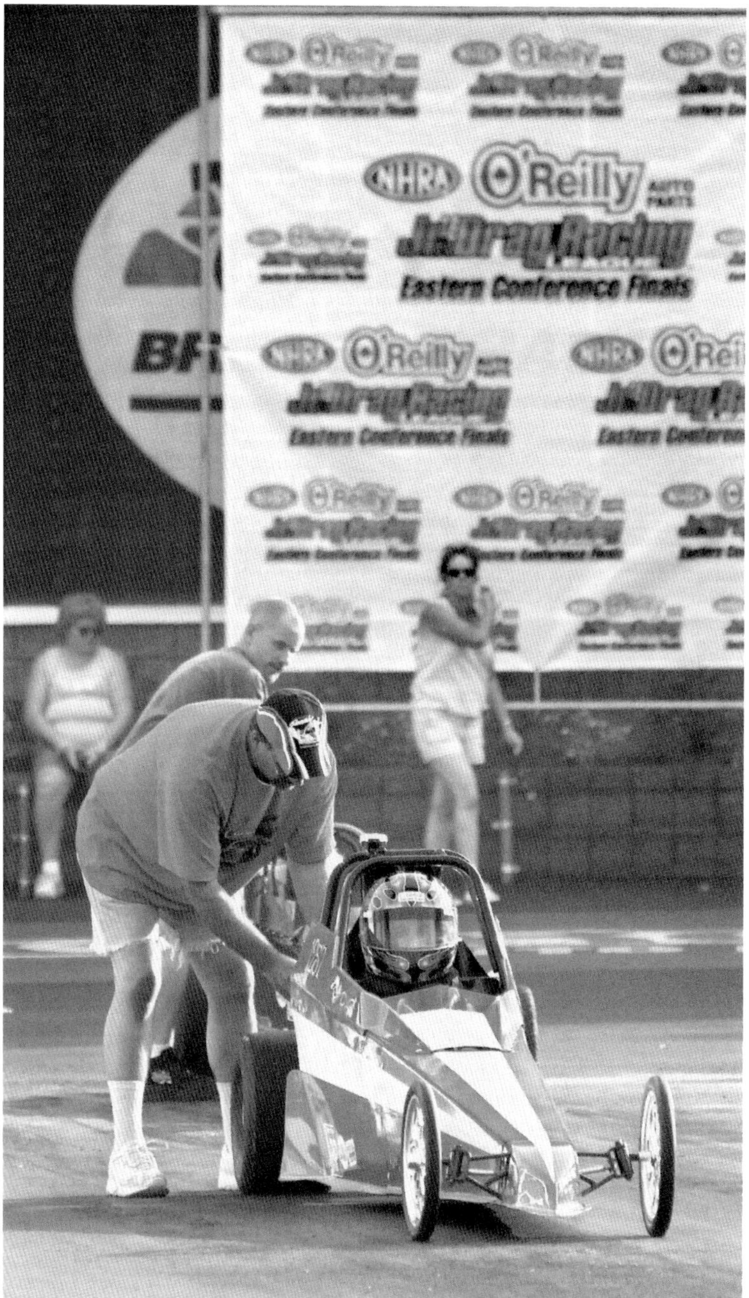

In 2004, Bristol began hosting the O'Reilly Eastern Conference Finals for Junior Dragster racers. The equivalent of a national event for racers age 8 to 17, the race annually attracts about 600 young competitors and their families from more than 20 states. Champions are crowned in eight age classes. The quickest half-scale cars can run the eighth-mile in 7.90 seconds at 85 miles per hour. The Junior Dragster class is also a part of the track's regular bracket-racing program. (Courtesy *Bristol Herald Courier*; photograph by Earl Neikirk.)

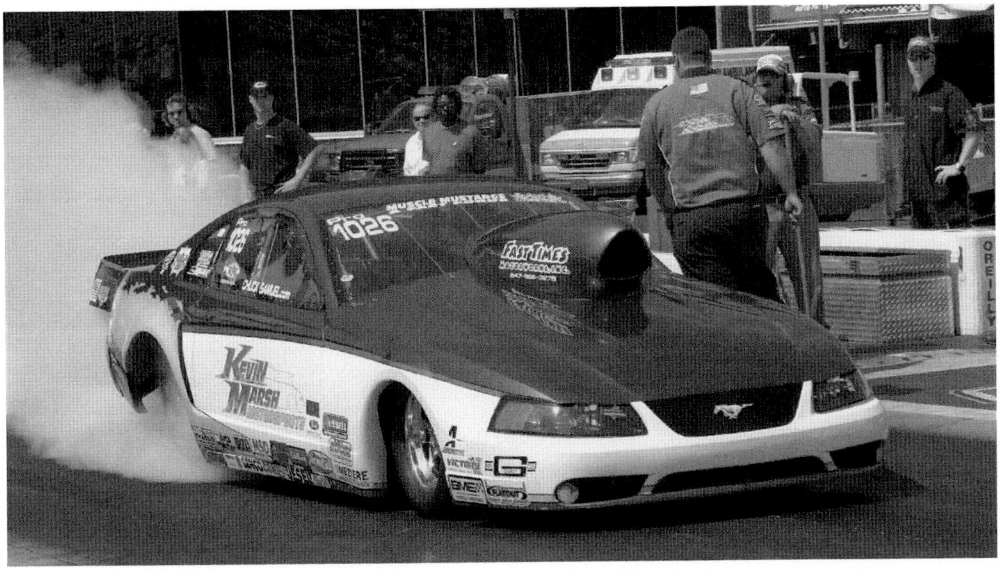

Since the mid-1990s, Bristol has hosted the annual Fun Ford Weekend, the nation's largest touring series of Ford-only racing events. Offering drag racing, a car show, and manufacturer's midway, the event is a fan favorite. Here Chuck Samuel performs a burnout with his wild, 6-second, 200-mile-per-hour Pro Mustang. (Photograph by David McGee.)

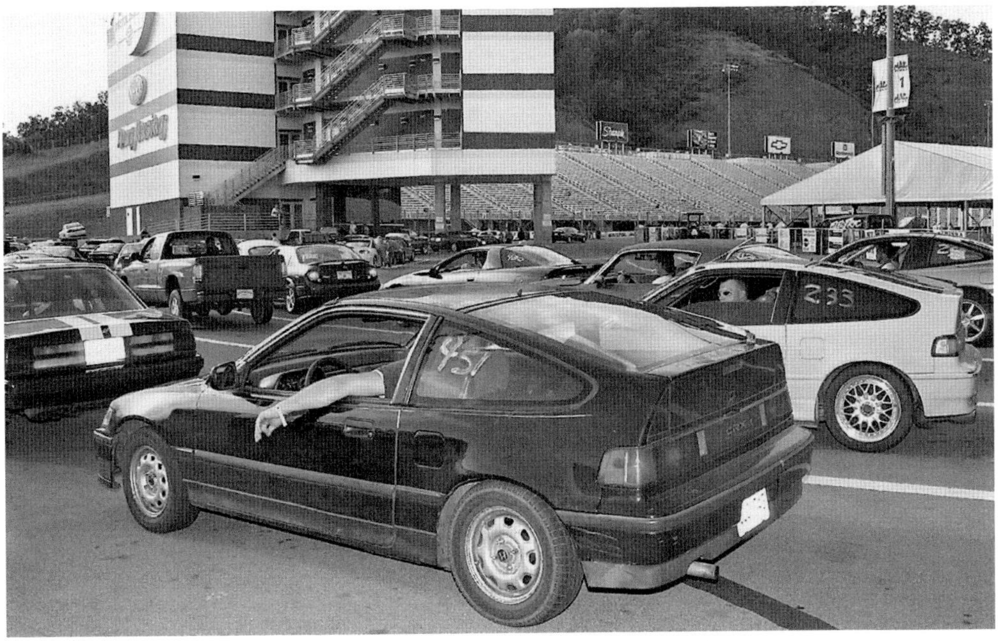

Bristol Dragway also hosts the Street Fights program, which gives local enthusiasts the chance to race their street cars for a nominal fee. Aimed primarily at young people, the program has grown exponentially and regularly attracts 200 to 300 competitors. The program provides a safe, legal place to compete, rather than on local highways—which was one of the original aims of organized drag racing. (Courtesy *Bristol Herald Courier*; photograph by Earl Neikirk.)

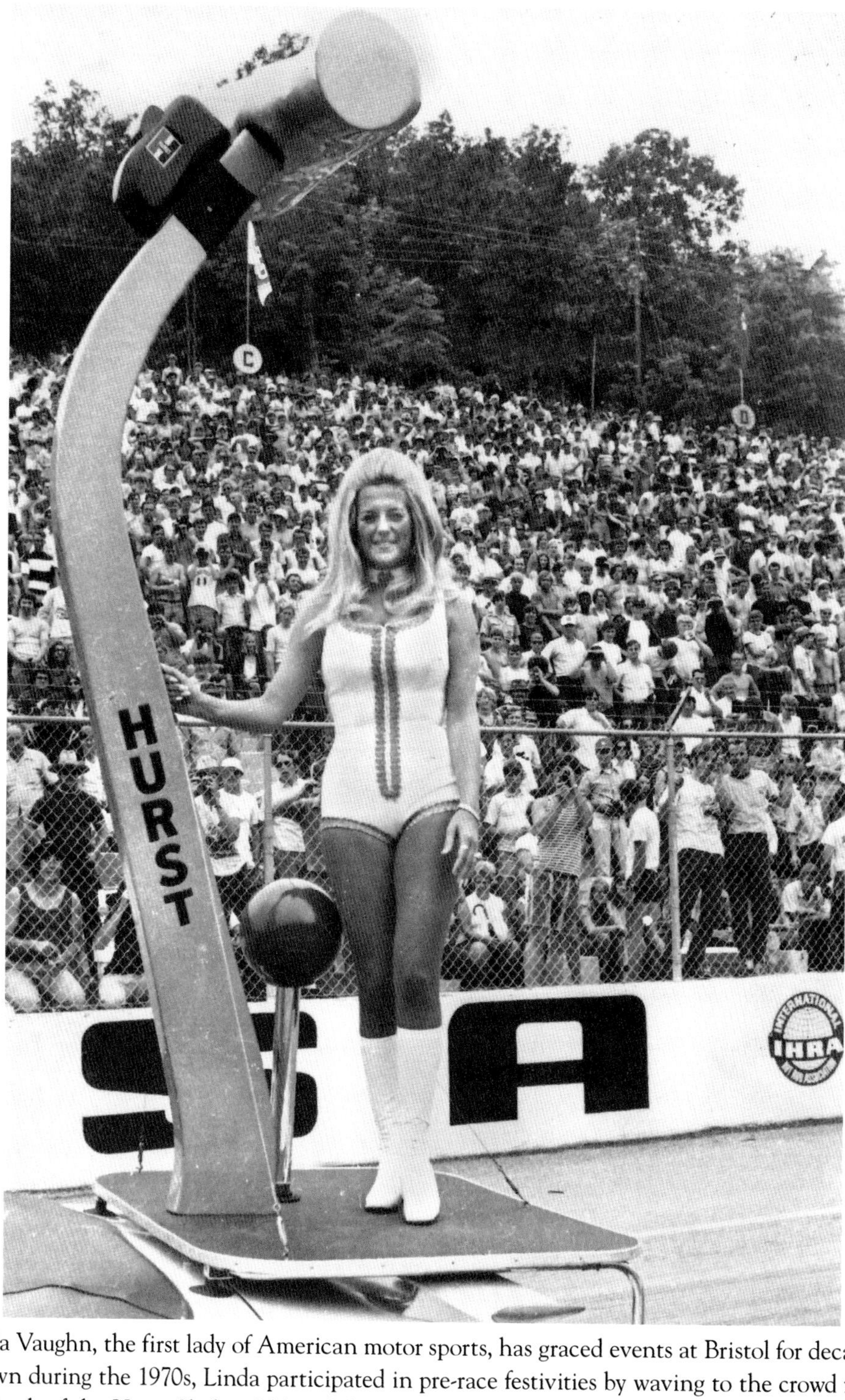

Linda Vaughn, the first lady of American motor sports, has graced events at Bristol for decades. Shown during the 1970s, Linda participated in pre-race festivities by waving to the crowd from the back of the Hurst Shifter Oldsmobile. She has continued to support Bristol events in the years since. (Photograph by John Beach.)

7

MONSTER MACHINES

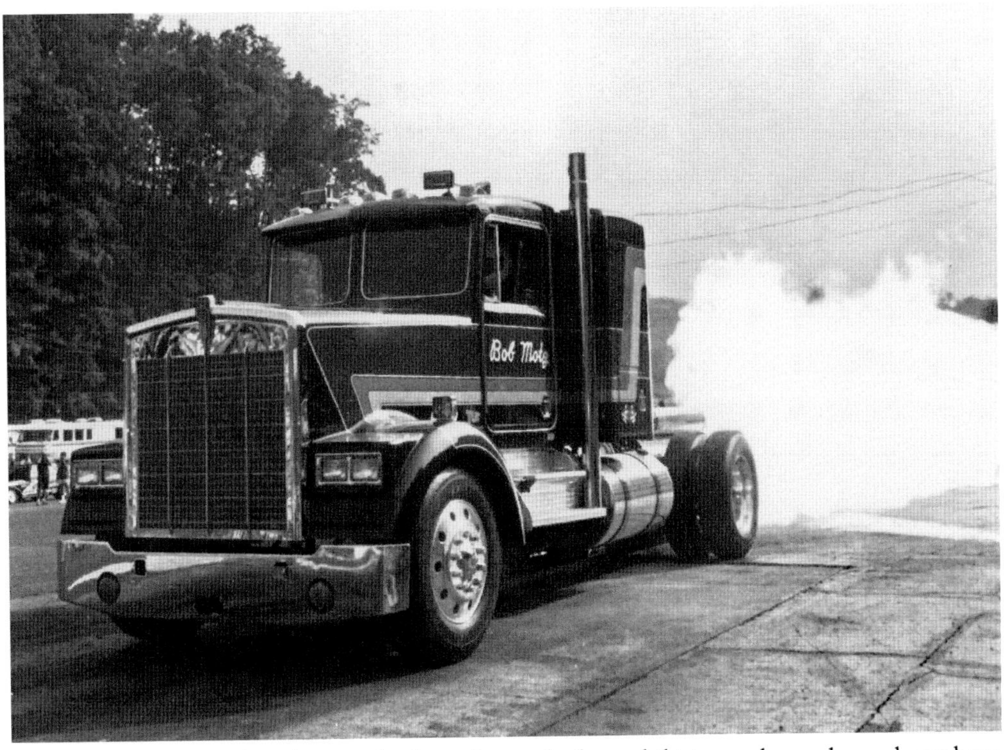

Jet and rocket-powered machines, wheelstanders and other exhibition-only cars have always been part of the show at Thunder Valley. The jet's high-pitched whine and fire show contrast with the rumble of internal combustion engines. And perhaps no jet has made a greater impression on Bristol fans than Ohioan Bob Motz and his General Electric J-79-powered Kenworth truck. From the 7,000-pound machine's first Bristol appearance at the 1980 Spring Nationals, to that year's Bracket World Finals, when thousands of fans stayed all day to witness him make one run, to the Lucas Oil Truck-A-Rama, Motz is a crowd pleaser. The truck shakes the earth, spews a 30-foot wall of fire from its afterburner and rattles windows as it runs down the quarter-mile at more than 200 mph. (Photograph by David McGee.)

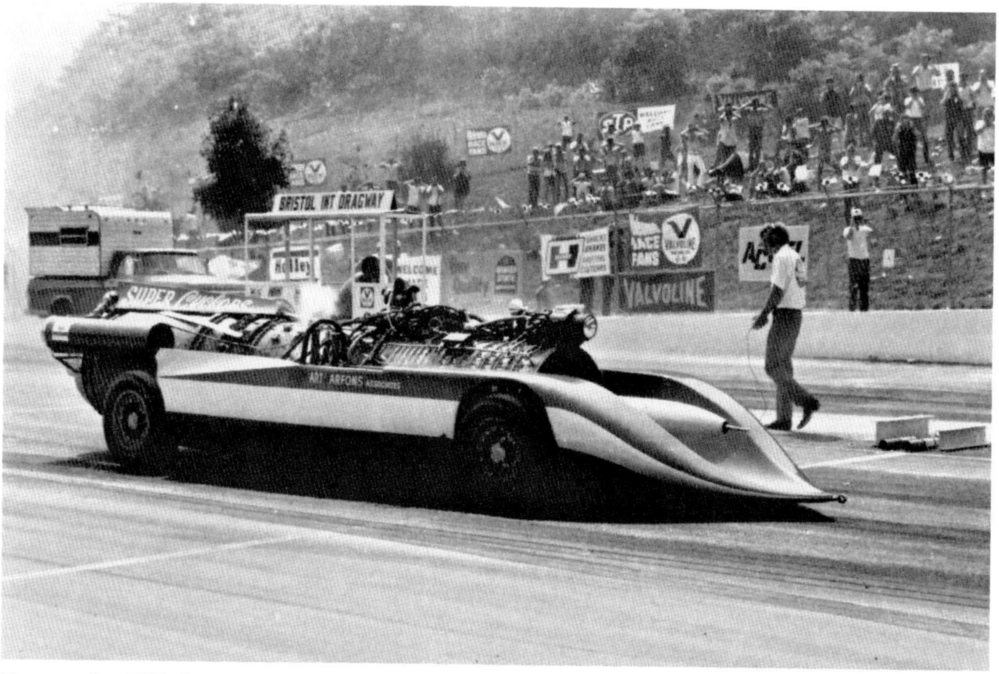

Fans at the 1971 Spring Nationals received more than expected when Art Arfons brought out his "Super Cyclops" jet dragster. On his first pass on Saturday, Arfons recorded the sport's first 5-second run at 5.96 seconds and 280 miles per hour. For an encore, the powerful J-79-powered entry returned that afternoon and blew large chunks of the asphalt starting line through the ground-floor windows of the control tower. After an extended cleanup, race officials moved the starting- and finish-line timing equipment and resumed racing. (Photographs by John Beach.)

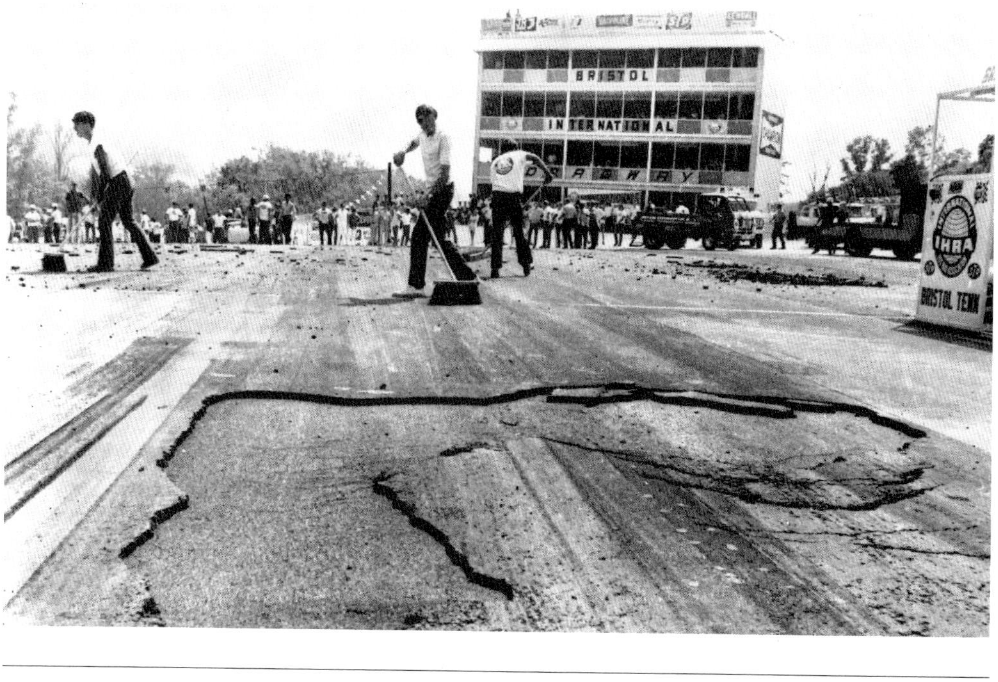

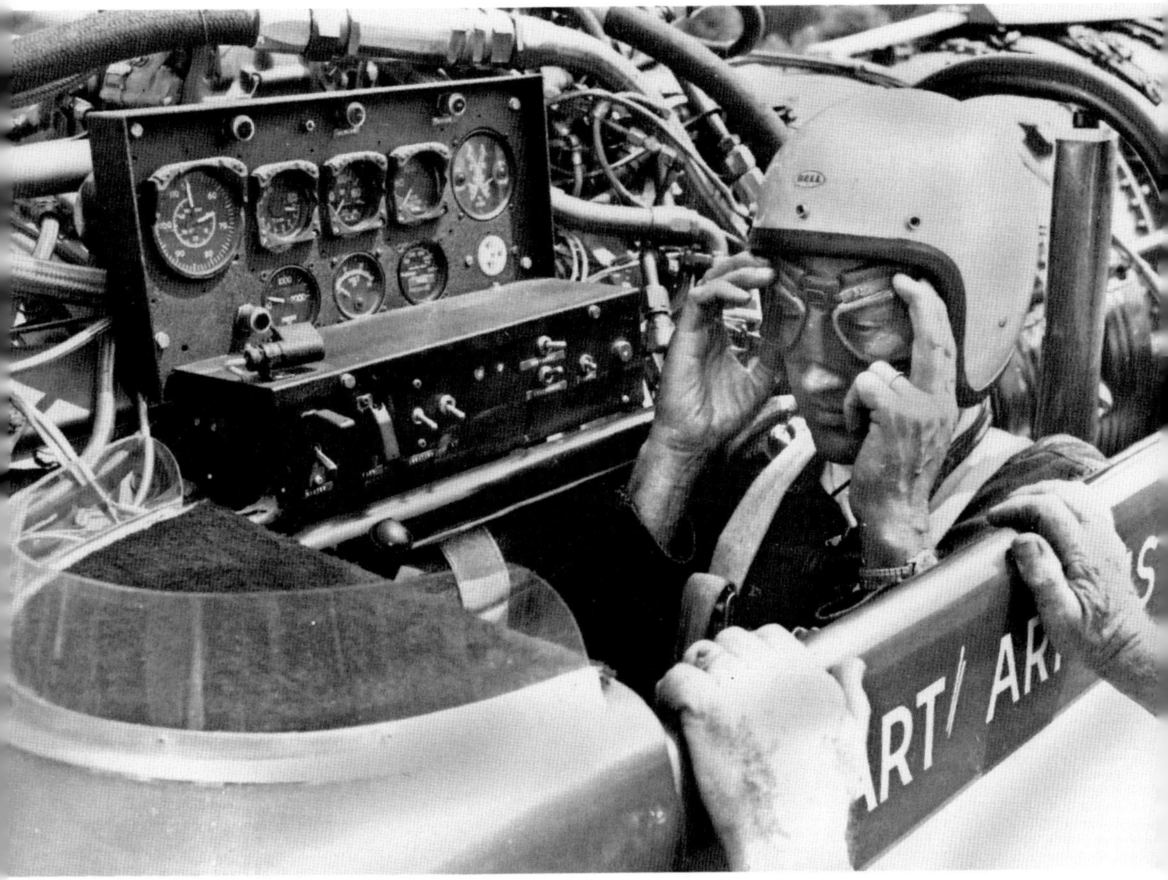

Art Arfons adjusts his goggles before making a run at Bristol in what was at that time the quickest and fastest jet-powered vehicle on the planet. After tearing up the strip at the Spring Nationals, Arfons returned to run the quarter-mile in 5.91 seconds at 284 miles per hour at the All-American Nationals. Before constructing the Cyclops machine, Arfons established three world land speed records in the 1960s, topping 576 miles per hour in Bonneville, Utah. (Photograph by John Beach.)

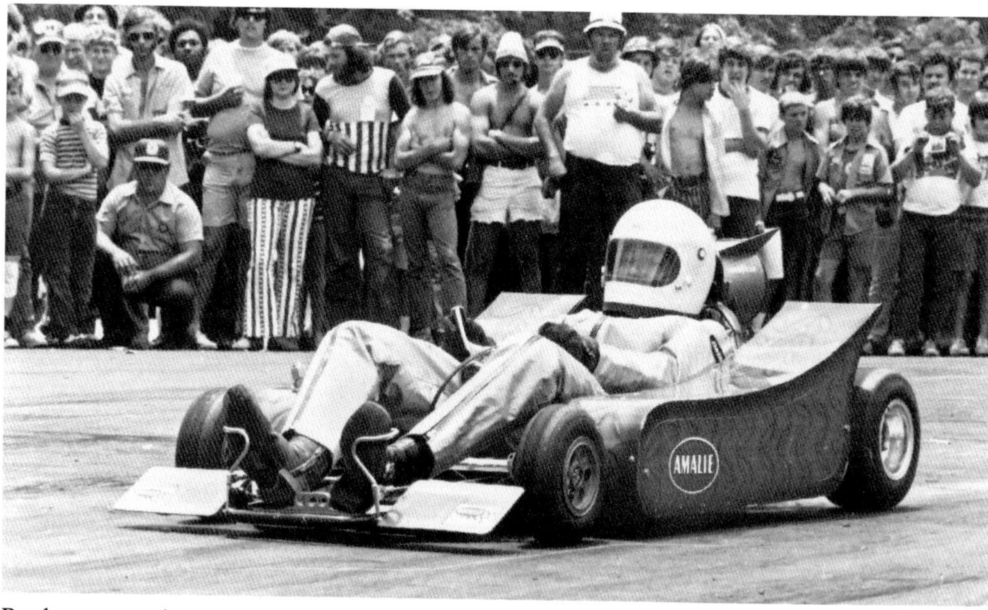

Rocket-powered cars were en vogue in the 1970s, and Bristol fans were treated to two of the wildest. Jack McClure (above) drew lots of attention from the Amalie Kart, a 200-pound machine that ran in the six-second range at 200 miles per hour. McClure, a former stunt driver, would hold the throttle of the hydrogen-peroxide rocket engine open for only two or three seconds and then use a parachute to slow down. A helmet, flame-retardant suit, and seat belts provided his only protection. At the opposite end of the spectrum, Bill Frederick's "Courage of Australia" dragster was 27 feet long and ran more than 300 miles per hour at the 1972 Spring Nationals. The car's larger hydrogen-peroxide jet engine developed 12,000 horsepower for driver John Paxton. (Photographs by John Beach.)

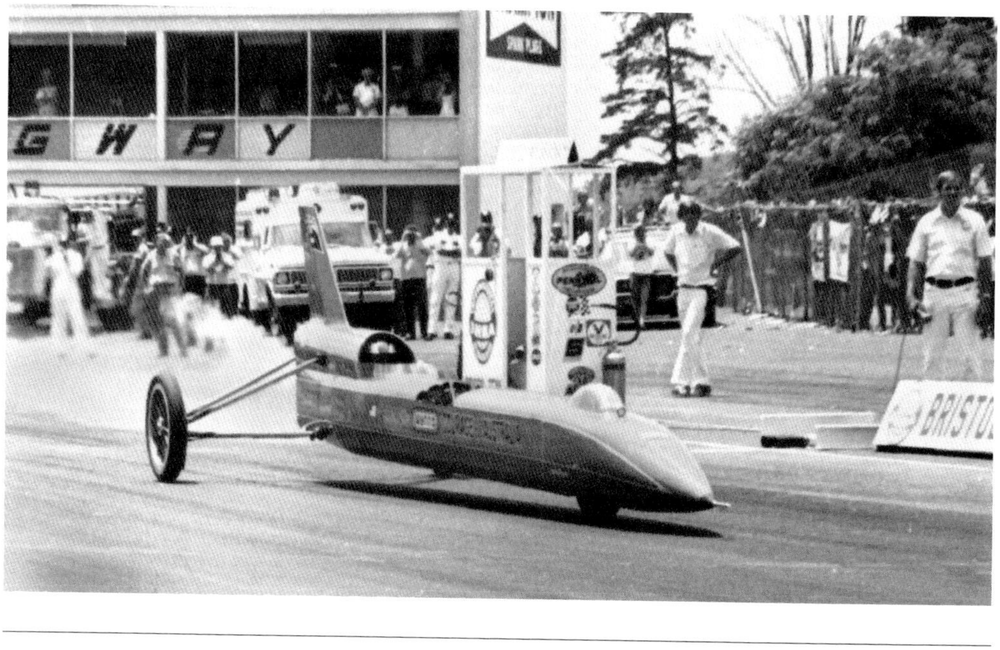

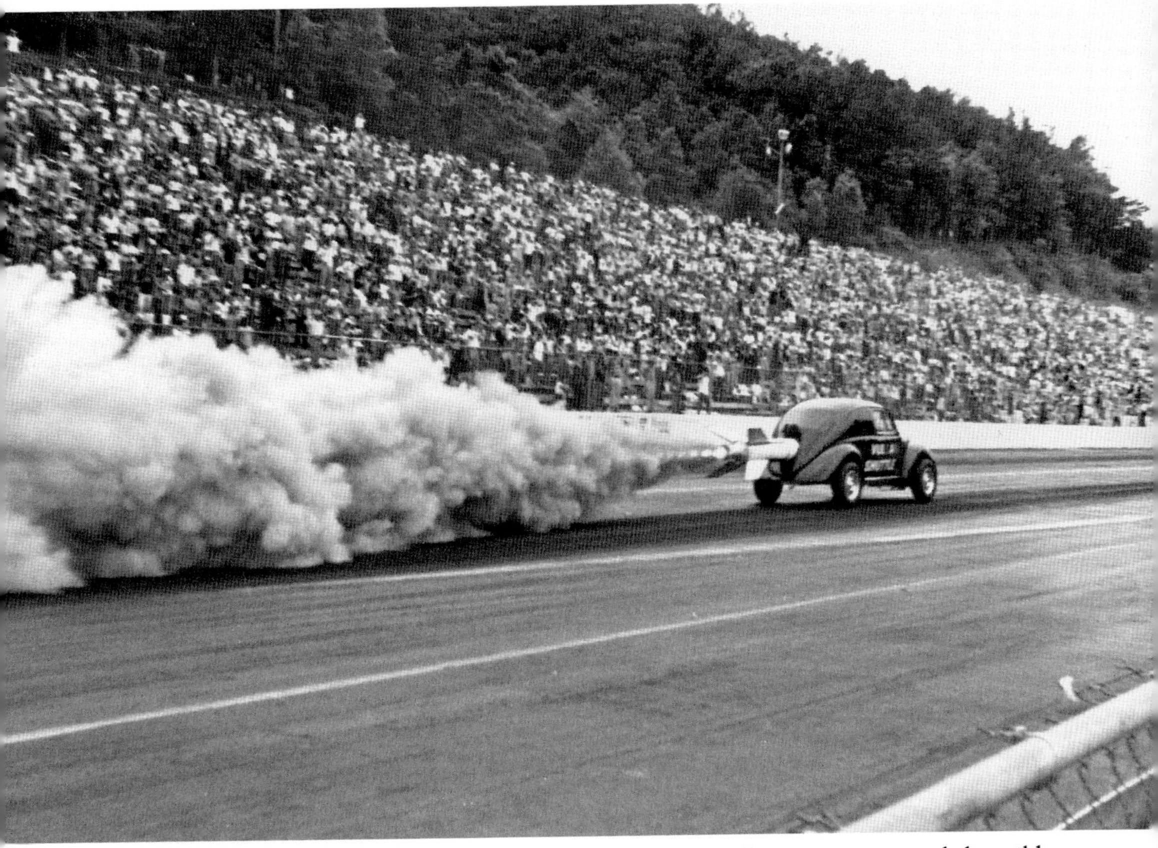

Ron Taylor's unbelievable "Vulcan Shuttle" rocket-powered Volkswagen was voted the wildest exhibition vehicle of all time by *Super Stock* magazine. One of the few times it didn't crash was the 1980 Spring Nationals, when it completed a nine-second run at 140 miles per hour. The VW was nearly stock, except for a solid-propellant rocket engine that featured no throttle control. After this run, a heavy, green fog enveloped Thunder Valley for several minutes. (Photograph by David McGee.)

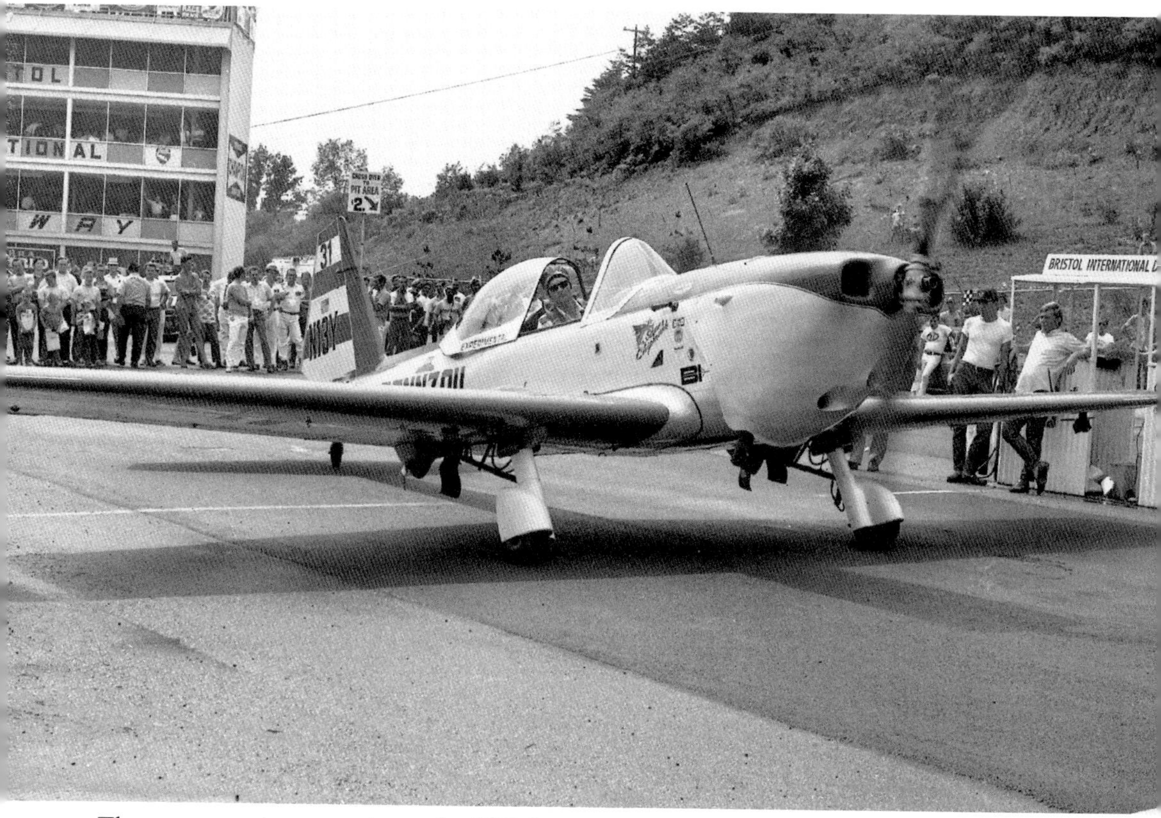

The top non-racing attraction at the 1970 Spring Nationals was legendary stunt pilot Art Sholl of Riverside, California. The "professor of flyology" took off and landed between the mountains at Thunder Valley and put on an extended aerial acrobatic display. During his closing stunt, he flew his low-wing monoplane upside down toward the control tower while waving to the fans. Sholl was later killed performing stunt work for the movie *Top Gun*. (Photograph by John Beach.)

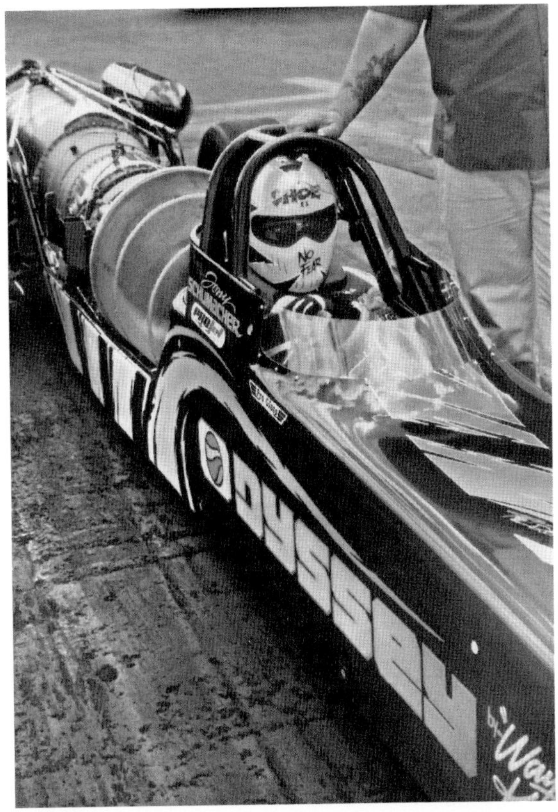

Tony Schumacher's first competitive Bristol appearance wasn't behind the wheel of his family's Top Fuel dragster. Instead, he wheeled Wayne Knuth's "Odyssey" jet-powered dragster. Schumacher turned in runs of 280 miles per hour during the 1994 Super Chevy Show event. A decade later, Schumacher won Top Fuel at the 2004 Thunder Valley Nationals in his U.S. Army dragster. (Photographs by David McGee.)

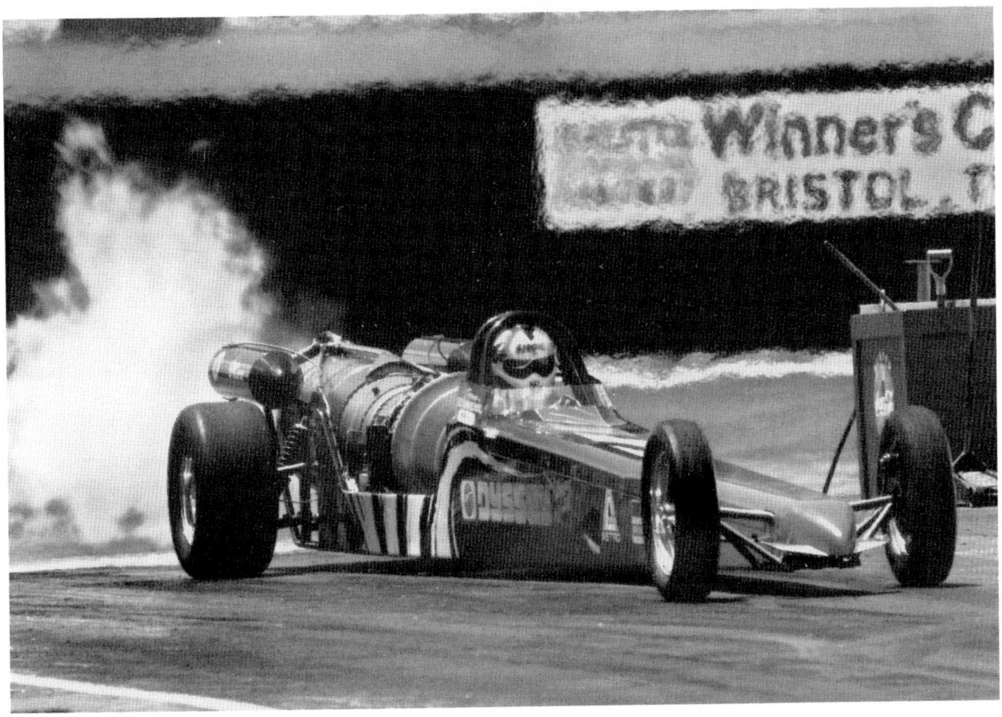

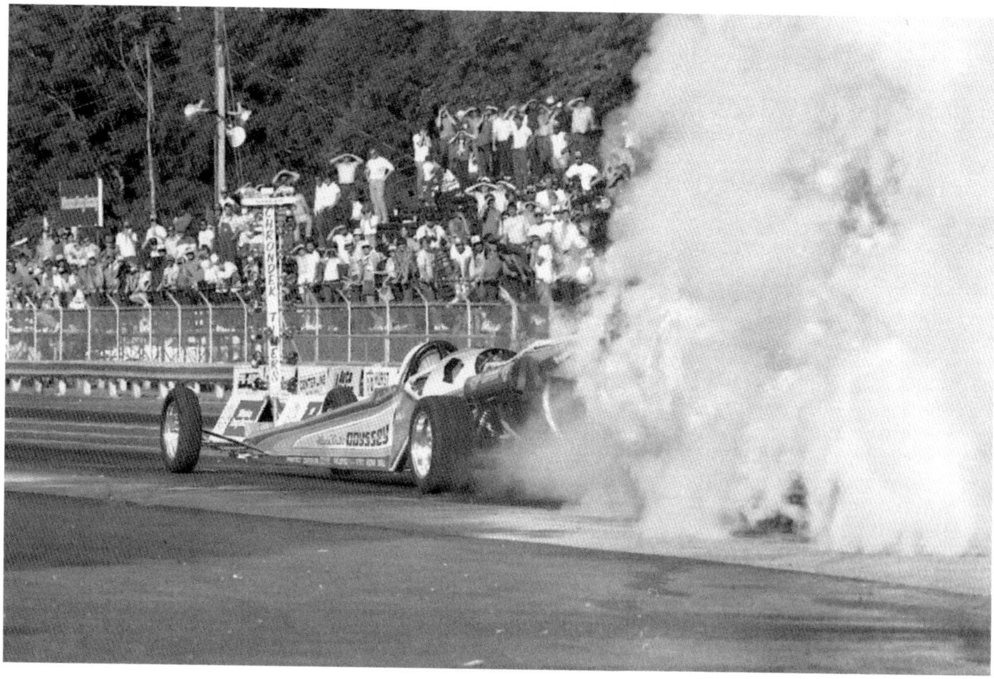

During the 1980s, Aggi Hendriks became the first female licensed to drive a jet-powered drag-racing vehicle. Aggi, a huge favorite with the fans, was a regular performer aboard a prior version of Wayne Knuth's radical "Odyssey." The lightweight entry regularly ran in the mid-5-second range at more than 280 miles per hour. (Photograph by David McGee.)

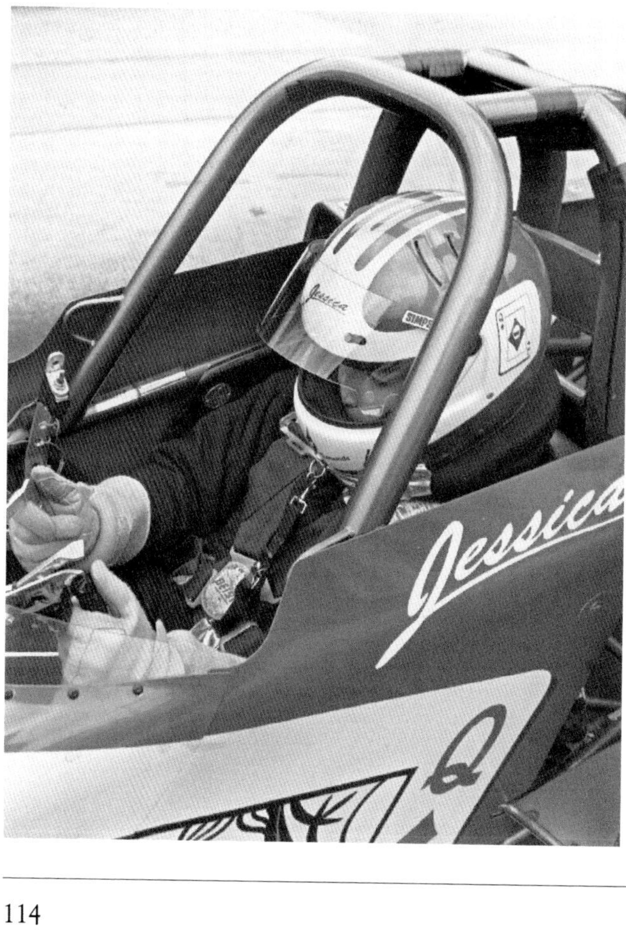

Several different women have occupied the driver's seat of the "Queen of Diamonds" jet dragster, owned by former Funny Car racer Al Hanna. At the 2001 Super Chevy Show, Jessica Willard recorded 295-mile-per-hour runs in the machine. (Photograph by David McGee.)

Fran Peppler became the first female licensed to drive a jet Funny Car in 1996. The following year, she participated in Bristol's Jet Mania event, which featured a mix of dragsters and Funny Cars. An ordained minister, Peppler returned to Bristol in 2005 with the 5-second, 280-mile-per-hour "Rock and Roll Thunder" machine powered by a J-85 jet engine. (Courtesy of *Bristol Herald Courier*; photograph by Earl Neikirk.)

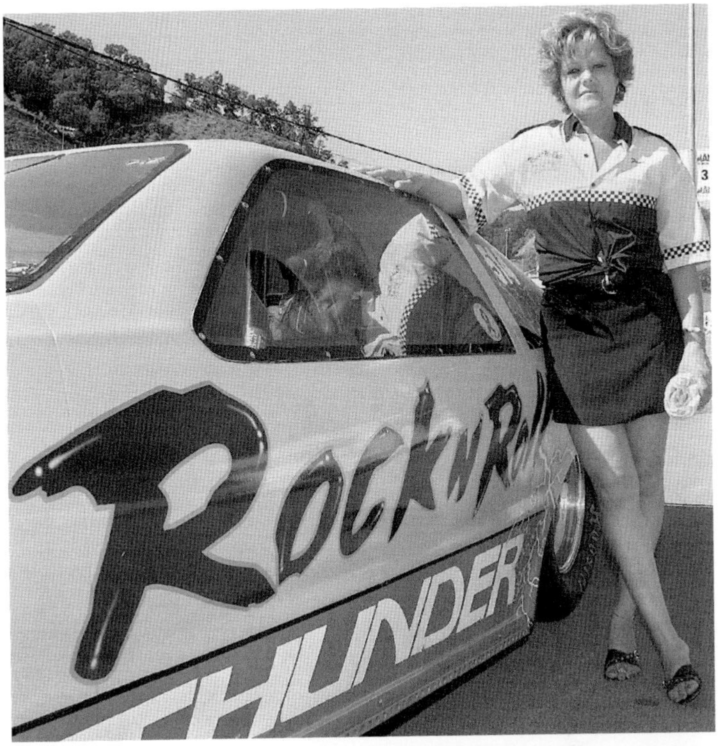

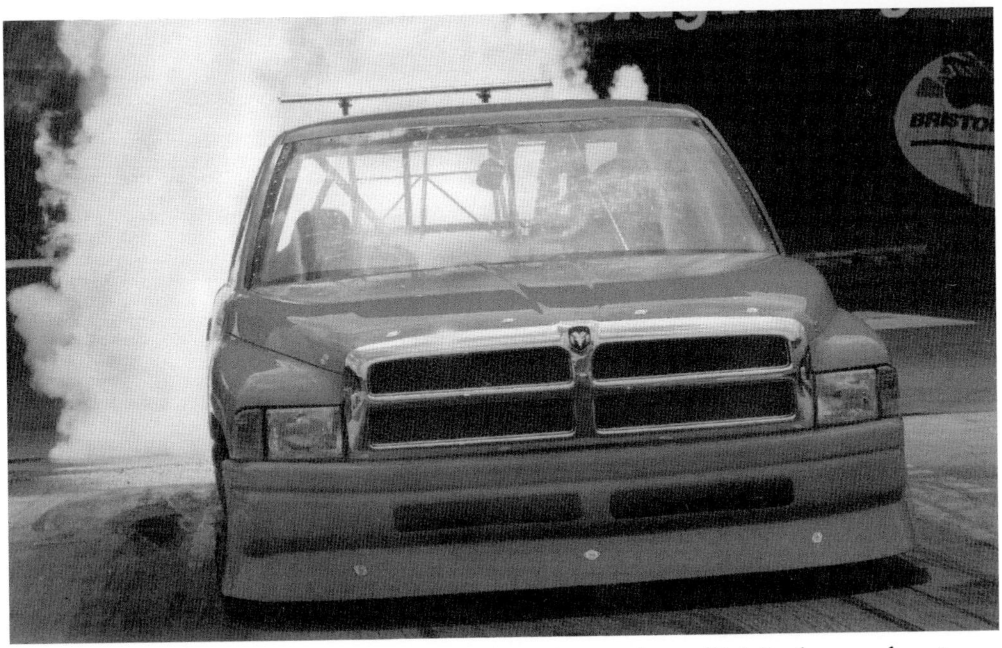

Jet-powered vehicles come in all shapes and sizes. Veteran driver Dick Rosberg made quite an impression in 2000 with the Ram-Jet, which featured a Pratt and Whitney jet engine inside a Dodge pickup truck body. The machine ran 200-mile-per-hour times and put on memorable fire shows. (Photograph by David McGee.)

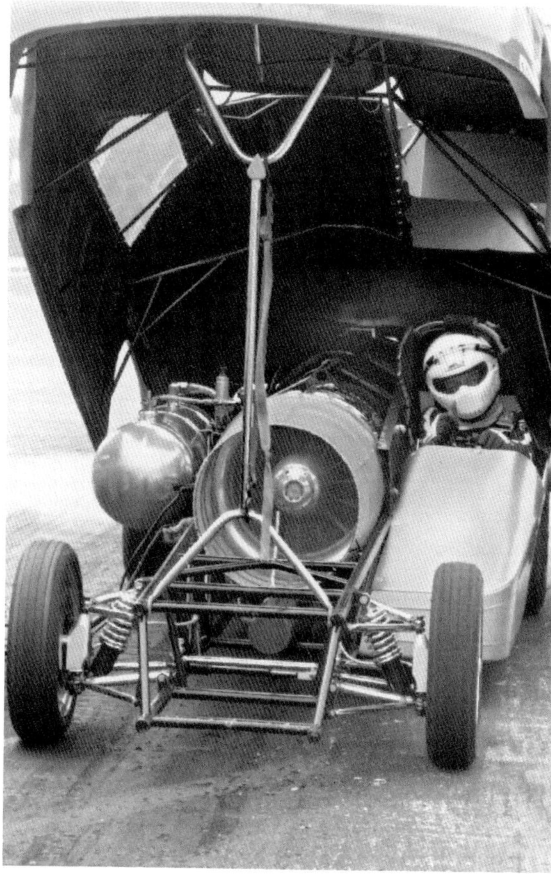

Jet Funny Car drivers like Roger Gustin must squeeze into a tiny cockpit right beside the engine, in this case a 6,000-horsepower Pratt and Whitney JT-12. The car's body can be raised to allow for driver and mechanical access. Now retired from driving, Gustin led a 1970s effort to get jets reinstated after NHRA banned them for safety concerns. (Photograph by David McGee.)

Mike Evegens blasts off the Bristol starting line during the 1994 Super Chevy Show. Evegens and teammate Jerry Gannon were regulars at the annual Chevrolet-only events, driving for jet pioneer Roger Gustin, who retired after surviving a near-fatal crash. (Photograph by David McGee.)

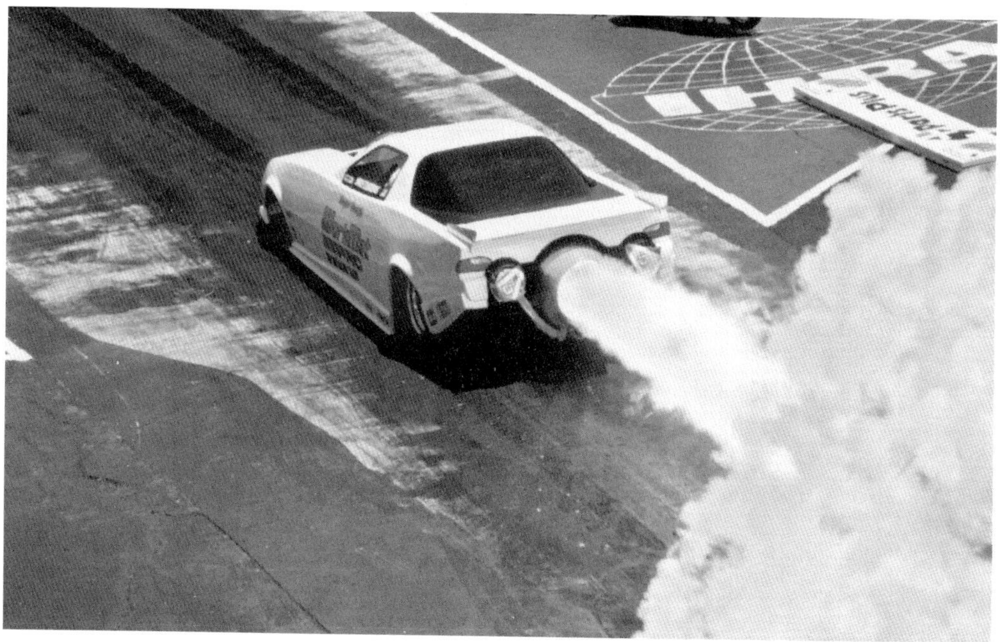

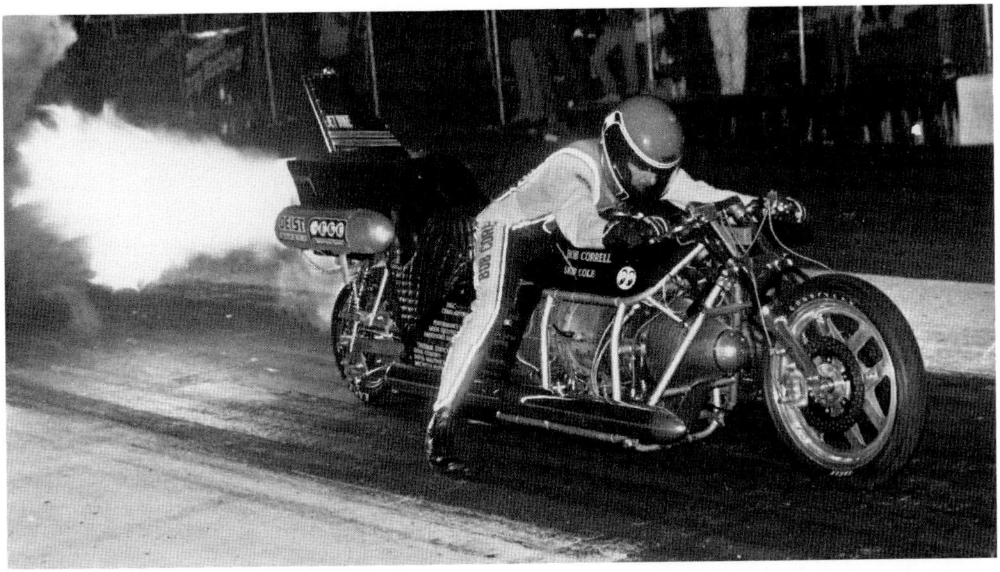

One of the wildest machines to ever run down the Bristol strip was Bob Corel's Jet Bike. In its first public appearance at the 1985 Fall Nationals, Corel made only one pass. The General Electric T58-powered machine ran 9.63 seconds at 178 miles per hour after putting on an amazing pre-run fire show. (Photograph by David McGee.)

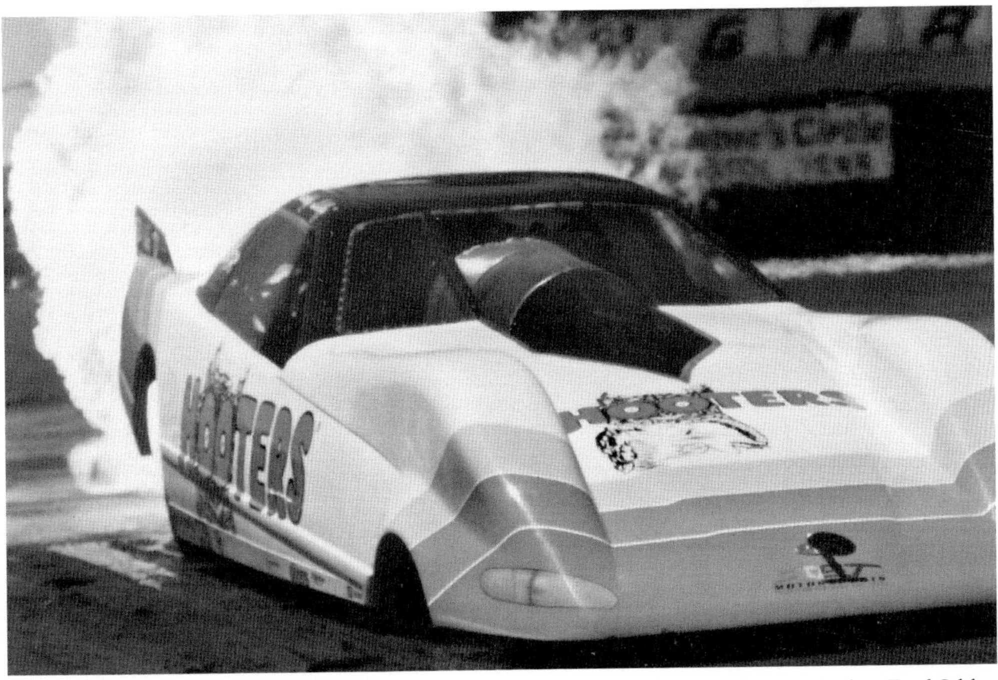

Widely regarded as one of the best showmen in the sport, second-generation jet jockey Fred Sibley Jr. made a number of Bristol appearances in his radical Ford Probe jet. The car, sponsored by Hooters Restaurants, consistently ran in the five-second zone at about 270 miles per hour. Sibley's father helped pioneer jet-powered machines in the 1960s. (Photograph by David McGee.)

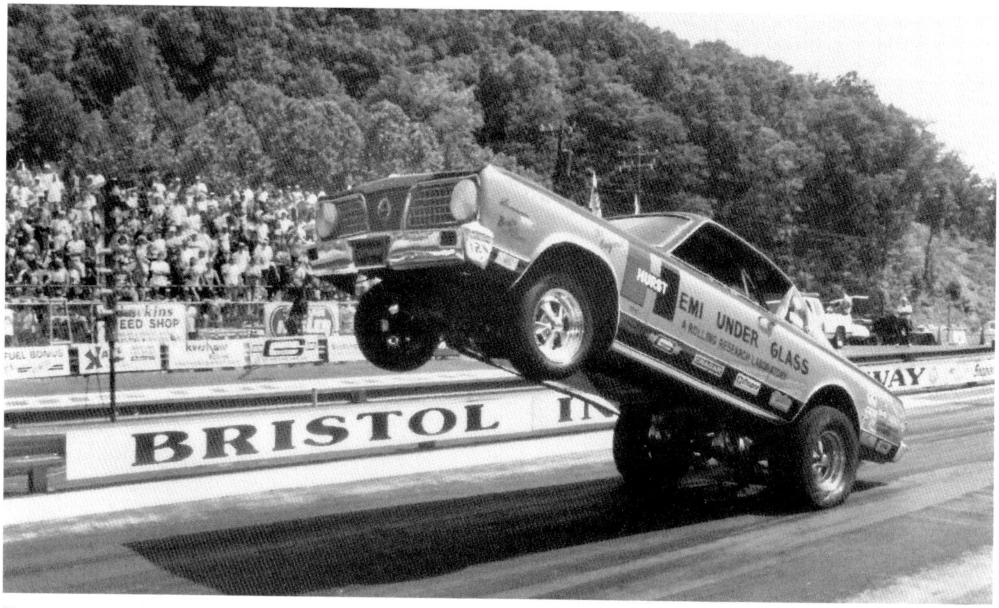

Fans got to relive some Bristol history in the 1990s when Bob Riggle made numerous appearances with the "Hemi Under Glass" Barracuda wheel-stander. Riggle was part of the team responsible for building the original car that appeared at the inaugural 1965 Spring Nationals. Like similar machines, the car travels the entire course on the rear wheels, as drivers steer using a unique braking system. (Photograph by David McGee.)

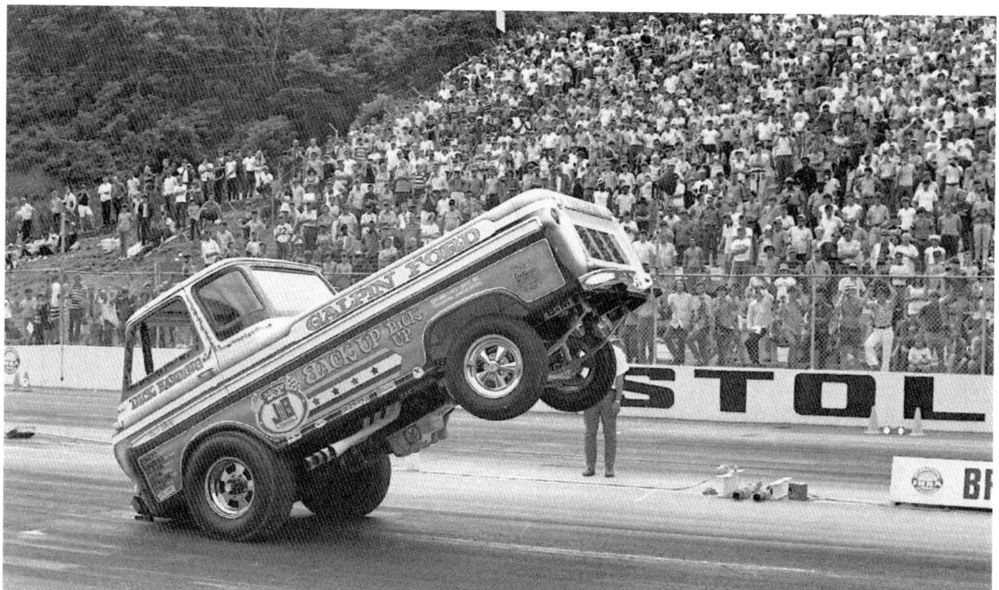

Wheel-standers were especially popular in the early 1970s and few were more unique than the "Backup Pickup." The Ford pickup-truck body was mounted backwards on the chassis, forcing the driver to steer from behind the engine and truck bed. Driver Dick Harding put on quite a show at the 1971 Spring Nationals. (Photograph by John Beach.)

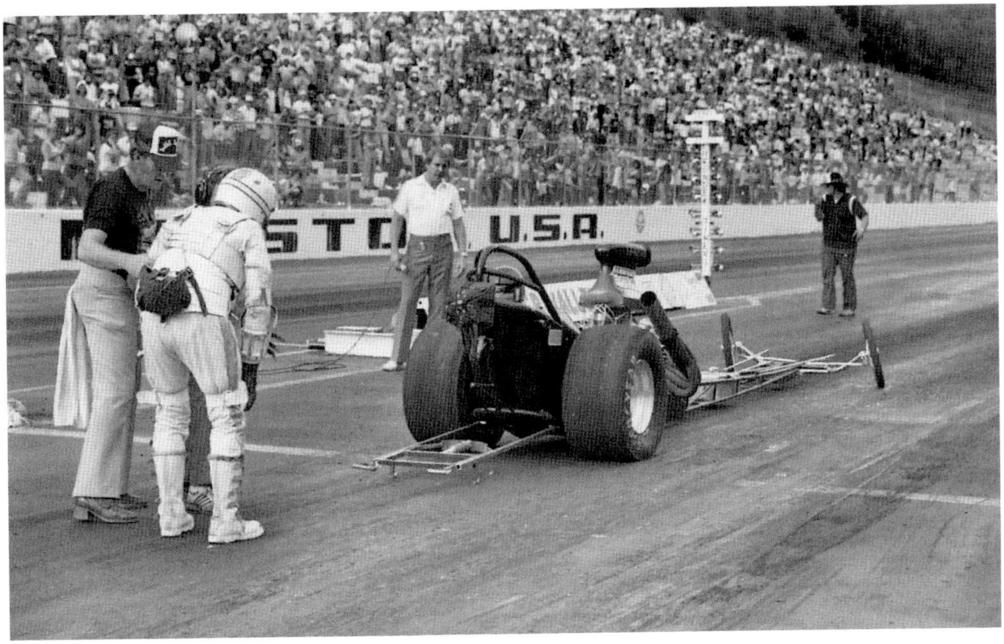

Another unforgettable sideshow attraction was stuntman Jim "Bullet" Bailey. His act consisted of putting on a jumpsuit, helmet, and protective vest and being pulled down the racetrack at more than 100 miles per hour and letting go. At Bristol, his rig was attached to Gary Heglar's sportsman dragster. (Photographs by John Beach.)

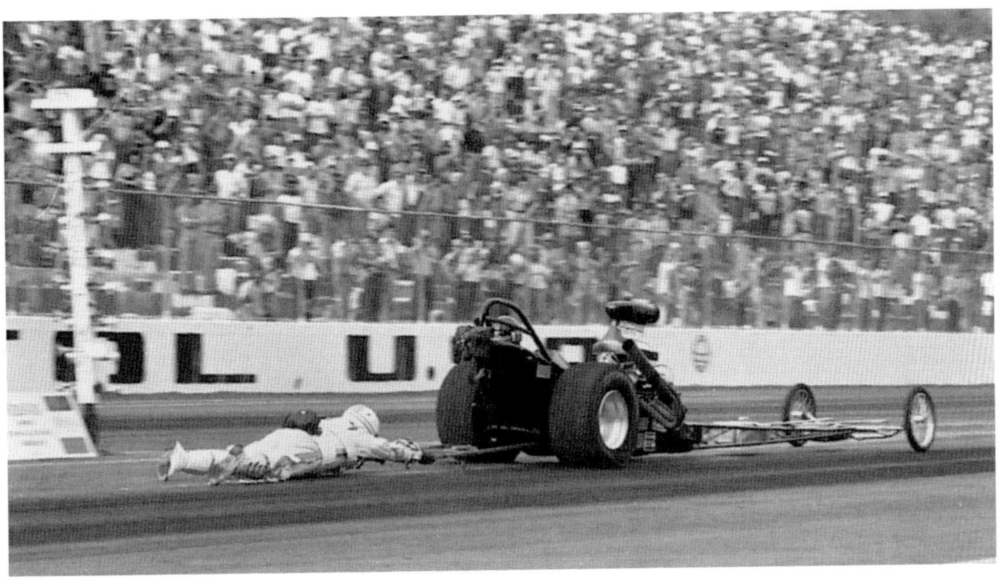

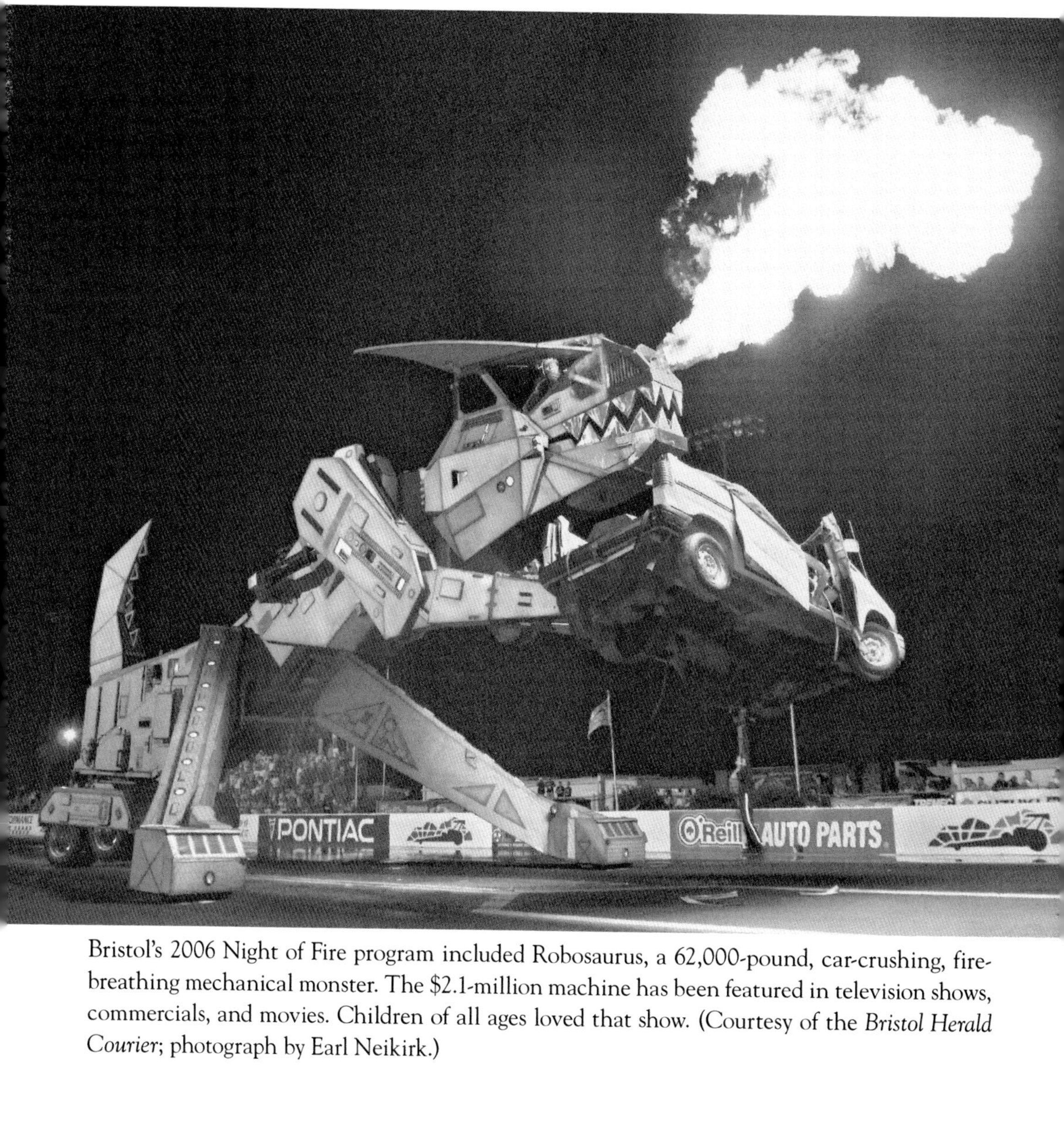

Bristol's 2006 Night of Fire program included Robosaurus, a 62,000-pound, car-crushing, fire-breathing mechanical monster. The $2.1-million machine has been featured in television shows, commercials, and movies. Children of all ages loved that show. (Courtesy of the *Bristol Herald Courier*; photograph by Earl Neikirk.)

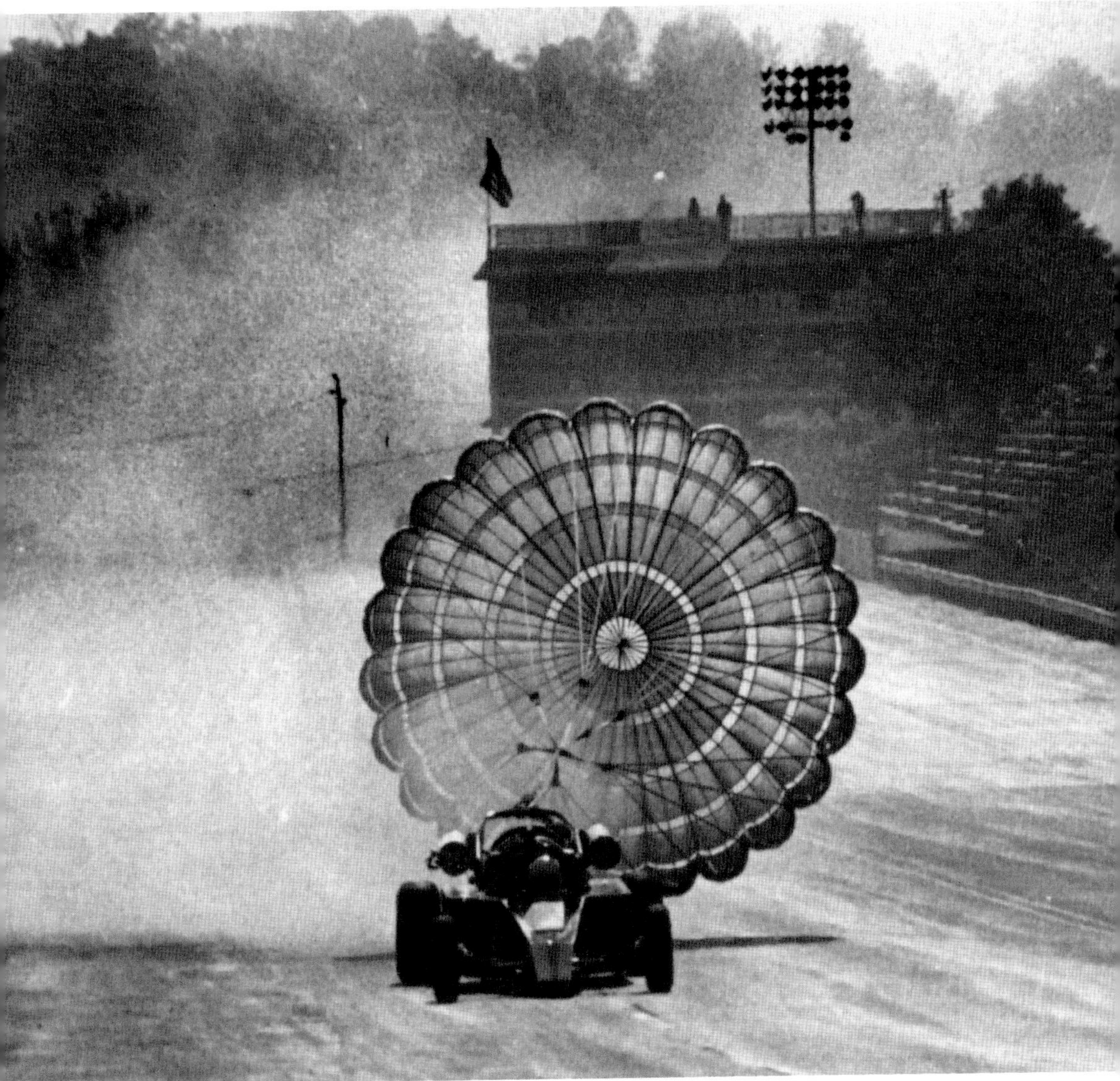

Much like their piston-driven counterparts, jet-car drivers rely on massive parachutes to aid in stopping. This classic jet dragster unfurls its ribbon-style parachute after a 200-mile-per-hour pass down the Bristol quarter-mile. (Photograph by David McGee.)

All-Time Top Fuel Winners

Year	Race Winner	Engine
1965	Maynard Rupp	Chrysler
1966	Jimmy Nix	Chrysler
1967	Don Prudhomme	Ford
1968	Chris Karamesines	Chrysler
1969	Leroy Goldstein	Chrysler
	Jim Nicoll	Chrysler
1970	Richard Tharp	Chrysler
	Pete Robinson	Ford
1971	Mike Martini	Chrysler
	Ronnie Martin	Chrysler
1972	Don Garlits	Dodge
	Pat Dakin	Chrysler
1973	Marvin Schwartz	Dodge
	Not contested	
1974	Dale Funk	Milodon
	Paul Longenecker	Chrysler
1975	Don Garlits	Milodon
	Don Garlits	Milodon
1976	Billy Graham	Milodon
	Don Garlits	Milodon
1977	Jeb Allen	Dodge
1978	Johnny Abbott	Milodon
	Not Contested	
1979	Dave Settles	K. Black
1980	Bobby Hilton	K. Black
	Richard Tharp	K. Black
1981	Jeb Allen	K. Black
	Gary Beck	K. Black
1982	Jerry Ruth	Milodon
	Connie Kalitta	K. Black
1983	Gary Beck	Milodon
	Joe Amato	K. Black
1984	Not contested	
	Not contested	
1985	Not contested	
	Not contested	
1986	Not contested	
	Not contested	
1987	Hank Endres	K. Black
	Jack Ostrander	K. Black
1988	Joe Amato	K. Black
	Eddie Hill	JP-1
1989	Jim Head	JP-1
	Earl Whiting	K. Black
1990	John Carey	JP-1
	Gene Snow	K. Black
1991	Gene Snow	K. Black
	Gene Snow	K. Black
1992	Doug Herbert	K. Black
	Bruce Larson	Dodge
1993	Doug Herbert	K. Black
	Richard Langson	K. Black
1994	Jim Bailey	K. Black
	Doug Herbert	K. Black
1995	Doug Herbert	K. Black
	Dave Bieneman	K. Black
1996	Wayne Bailey	K. Black
	Doug Herbert	K. Black
1997	Doug Herbert	K. Black
	Paul Romine	K. Black
1998	Closed	
1999	none *	
2000	Cory McClenathan*	BAE
2001	Doug Kalitta	TFX
2002	Larry Dixon	TFX
2003	Brandon Bernstein	TFX
2004	Tony Schumacher	TFX
2005	Doug Kalitta	TFX
2006	Doug Kalitta	TFX

* Top Fuel vs. Funny Car all-star race format

All-Time

Funny Car Winners

Year	Race Winner	Car
1967	Tommy Grove	Ford
1968	Bob Sullivan	Chevrolet
1969	Danny Ongais	Ford
	Terry Hedrick	Chevrolet
1970	Gene Snow	Dodge
	Gene Snow	Dodge
1971	Don Schumacher	Plymouth
	Gary Dyer	Dodge
1972	Don Schumacher	Plymouth
	Don Schumacher	Plymouth
1973	Bill Leavitt	Ford
	Dale Emery	Chevrolet
1974	Billy Meyer	Ford
	Shirl Greer	Ford
1975	Gene Snow	Chevrolet
	Shirl Greer	Ford
1976	Gary Burgin	Chevrolet
	Larry LaDue	Plymouth
1977	Dale Pulde	Pontiac
	Roy Harris	Ford
1978	Pete Williams	Ford
	Pete Williams	Ford
1979	Dale Pulde	Pontiac
1980	Billy Meyer	Chevrolet
	Paul Smith	Pontiac
1981	Billy Meyer	Chevrolet
	Raymond Beadle	Plymouth
1982	Raymond Beadle	Ford
	Dale Pulde	Pontiac
1983	Mark Oswald	Pontiac
	Mark Oswald	Pontiac
1984	Billy Meyer	Ford
	Mark Oswald	Pontiac
1985	Dale Pulde	Buick
	Dale Pulde	Buick
1986	Tim Grose	Chevrolet
	Mark Oswald	Pontiac

Year	Race Winner	Car
1987	Mike Dunn	Oldsmobile
	Paul Smith	Pontiac
1988	Mark Oswald	Ford
	Ed McCulloch	Oldsmobile
1989	Tony McCallum	Ford
	Chuck Etchells	Chevrolet
1990	D.A. Santucci	Oldsmobile
	Not contested	
1991	Not contested	
	Not contested	
1992	Del Worsham	Oldsmobile
	Not contested	
1993	Not contested	
	Not contested	
1994	Not contested	
	Not contested	
1995	Not contested	
	Not contested	
1996	Not contested	
	Not contested	
1997	Not contested	
	Not contested	
1998	closed	
1999	John Force*	Ford
2000	none *	
2001	Ron Capps	Chevrolet
2002	Whit Bazemore	Pontiac
2003	Del Worsham	Pontiac
2004	John Force	Ford
2005	Gary Scelzi	Dodge
2006	Ron Capps	Dodge

* Top Fuel vs. Funny Car all-star race format

ALL-TIME

PRO STOCK WINNERS

Year	Race Winner	Car
1969	Bill Jenkins	Chevrolet
	Gary Kimball	Chevrolet
1970	Ronnie Sox	Plymouth
	Don Nicholson	Ford
1971	Ronnie Sox	Plymouth
	Ronnie Sox	Plymouth
1972	Bill Jenkins	Chevrolet
	Don Carlton	Plymouth
1973	Don Carlton	Plymouth
	Don Nicholson	Ford
1974	Reid Whisnant	Plymouth
	Wayne Gapp	Ford
1975	Scott Shafiroff	Ford
	Wally Booth	AMC
1976	Bob Glidden	Ford
	Bob Glidden	Ford
1977	Pat Musi	Chevrolet
1978	Lee Edwards	Chevrolet
	Not contested	
1979	Warren Johnson	Chevrolet
1980	Warren Johnson	Chevrolet
	Rickie Smith	Ford
1981	Warren Johnson	Chevrolet
	Ronnie Sox	Ford
1982	Lee Shepherd	Chevrolet
	Rickie Smith	Ford
1983	Rickie Smith	Ford
	Lee Shepherd	Chevrolet
1984	Lee Shepherd	Chevrolet
	Lee Shepherd	Chevrolet
1985	Bruce Allen	Chevrolet
	Bob Glidden	Ford
1986	Darrell Alderman	Chevrolet
	Bob Glidden	Ford
1987	Rickie Smith	Ford
	Doug Kirk	Ford
1988	Warren Johnson	Oldsmobile
	Warren Johnson	Oldsmobile
1989	Warren Johnson	Oldsmobile
	Rickie Smith	Pontiac
1990	Tommy Mauney	Pontiac
	Rickie Smith	Pontiac
1991	Harold Denton	Pontiac
	Billy Ewing	Oldsmobile
1992	Rickie Smith	Pontiac
	Jerry Yeoman	Chevrolet
1993	Rickie Smith	Pontiac
	Roy Hill	Ford
1994	Robert Patrick	Ford
	Billy Huff	Oldsmobile
1995	Roy Hill	Ford
	Mike Bell	Ford
1996	Richie Stevens	Ford
	David Jenkins	Chevrolet
1997	Angelo Alesci	Chevrolet
	Tony Gillig	Oldsmobile
1998	Closed	
1999	Jeg Coughlin Jr.	Oldsmobile
2000	Troy Coughlin	Oldsmobile
2001	Greg Anderson	Pontiac
2002	Warren Johnson	Pontiac
2003	Kurt Johnson	Chevrolet
2004	Greg Anderson	Pontiac
2005	Warren Johnson	Pontiac
2006	Jason Line	Pontiac

All-Time Pro Modified Winners

Year	Winner	Car
1990	Mike Ashley	Chevrolet
	Ronnie Sox	Mercury
1991	Scotty Cannon	Willys
	Ed Hoover	Chevrolet
1992	Michael Martin	Chevrolet
	Tim McAmis	Chevrolet
1993	Scotty Cannon	Chevrolet
	Bill Kuhlmann	Chevrolet
1994	Carl Moyer	Chevrolet
	Shannon Jenkins	Chevrolet
1995	Tommy Mauney	Willys
	Scotty Cannon	Chevrolet
1996	Scotty Cannon	Chevrolet
	Shannon Jenkins	Willys
1997	Rickie Smith	Chevrolet
	Shannon Jenkins	Willys
1998	Closed	
1999	Not contested	
2000	Not contested	
2001	Quain Stott	Chevrolet
2002	Thomas Patterson	Willys
2003	Fred Hahn	Chevrolet
2004	Al Billes	Chevrolet
2005	Mike Ashley	Ford
2006	Jay Payne	Dodge

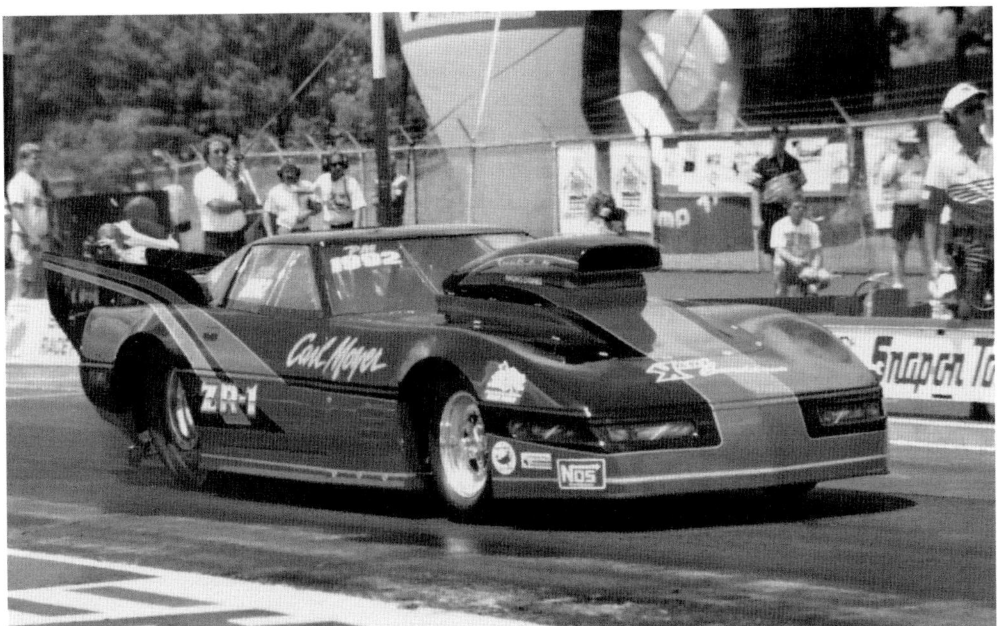

Carl Moyer, a Chevrolet dealer from Iowa, won the 1994 Spring Nationals Pro Modified crown in this wild Corvette. Moyer, a runner-up in 2003, became the eighth different Pro Mod winner in Bristol's first nine races after the class was established. (Photograph by David McGee.)

ACKNOWLEDGMENTS

The author gratefully acknowledges the support, encouragement and enthusiasm of the staff of Bristol Motor Speedway and Dragway, especially Jeff Byrd, Wayne Estes, Kevin Triplett, Lori Worley, David Rowe, Ben Trout, Christopher Perrin, Jack Cocklin, Brandon Cross and Anthony Golden. Thank you for all your efforts and belief in this project.

A very special thank you goes to Anthony Vestal of NHRA for helping me navigate the waters and to Susie Arnold and Dave Densmore.

Telling the Bristol story would have been impossible without the generous support of everyone who gave me access to invaluable photographic archives.

A special thank you goes to John Beach, my longtime friend and photographic mentor. Like the *Bristol Motor Speedway* book that preceded it, John's willingness to share his timeless photographs made the entire project an accurate and artistic success.

Another special thank you goes to Bristol Motor Speedway and Dragway and Carl and Randy Moore.

I also deeply appreciate the images of outstanding photographers Dave Bishop, Earl Neikirk, and Mike O'Dell.

Those of us lucky enough to have photographed professional drag racing comprise a tightly knit fraternity. I appreciate your friendship and encouragement, even if your images didn't make it into this project.

The little details are sometimes the most maddening. Thanks to Bobby Bennett, "Flyin' Phil" Elliott, and Bret Kepner for helping fill in the gaps.

The author's journey through drag racing would have been a lot tougher without the opportunities provided by Gene, Alberta, and Chris Barker; Larry and Shirley Carrier; Ted and Linda Jones; Jim Ruth; Chuck and Charlie Sneed; Steve Collison; and Woody Hatten.

Listing all the friends made along the way would take pages, but I will acknowledge Mike Lester and Becky White.

My thanks also to Debbie Helton for her support and encouragement despite having never attended a drag race before 2007.

This project would not have been possible without the unwavering, enthusiastic support of the entire staff of Arcadia Publishing, especially my editor Maggie Tiller Bullwinkel. She believed in the Bristol Dragway project long before the light turned green and helped keep the pedal to the floor until we crossed the finish line.

Author David McGee has been a part of the Bristol racing scene for more than 25 years, since photographing his first major event at Thunder Valley in 1980. In the years since, he has worked events there as a photographer, journalist, race official, and announcer. David currently serves as the dragway's special-events announcer and the senior announcer at Bristol Motor Speedway. A graduate of Kentucky's Morehead State University, he works as a staff writer for the *Bristol Herald Courier*. (Photograph by Earl Neikirk.)

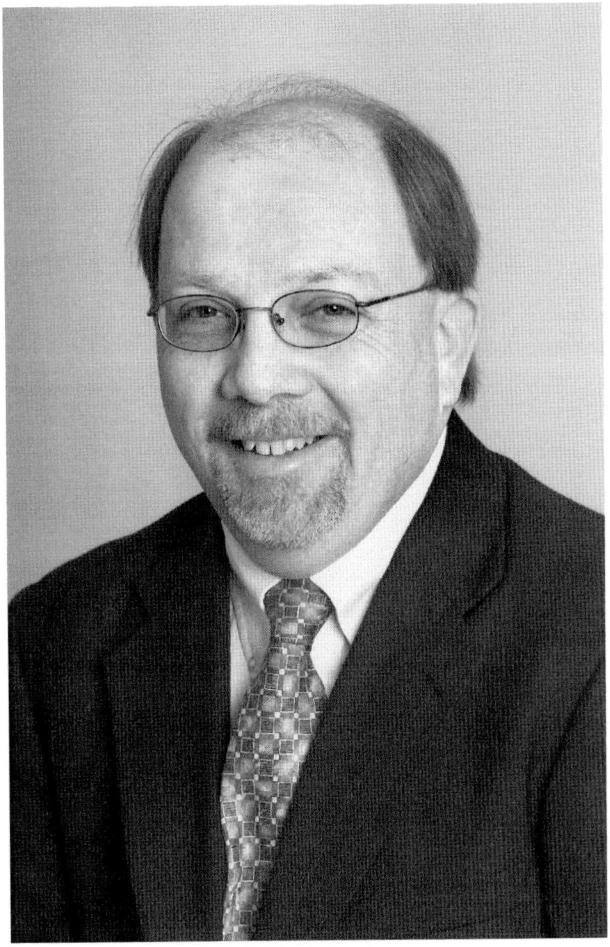

Speedway Children's Charities

As long as *Bristol Dragway* is in print, a portion of the proceeds from sales of the book will be donated to the Bristol chapter of Speedway Children's Charities. We salute this fine organization, which provides financial support to children's programs in Northeast Tennessee and Southwest Virginia, and invite others to also lend their support.

Consistent with our mission to preserve history on a local level, this book was printed in South Carolina on American-made paper and manufactured entirely in the United States. Products carrying the accredited Forest Stewardship Council (FSC) label are printed on 100 percent FSC-certified paper.

MADE IN THE USA